POETS, PATRONS, AND PROFESSORS

PUBLICATIONS OF
THE SIR THOMAS BROWNE INSTITUTE
LEIDEN

General Editor: A. G. H. BACHRACH, *D. Phil. (Oxon.)*,

Professor of English Literature in the
University of Leiden

GENERAL SERIES NO. 2

Poets, Patrons, and Professors

SIR PHILIP SIDNEY, DANIEL ROGERS,
AND THE LEIDEN HUMANISTS

J. A. VAN DORSTEN

PUBLISHED FOR THE SIR THOMAS BROWNE INSTITUTE

LEIDEN: AT THE UNIVERSITY PRESS

LONDON: OXFORD UNIVERSITY PRESS

1962

Distributed outside the Netherlands by the
Oxford University Press, Amen House, London E.C. 4

GLASGOW NEW YORK TORONTO MELBOURNE WELLINGTON
BOMBAY CALCUTTA MADRAS KARACHI LAHORE DACCA
CAPE TOWN SALISBURY NAIROBI IBADAN ACCRA
KUALA LUMPUR HONG KONG

Printed in the Netherlands

ERRATA

PREFATORY NOTE

ALTHOUGH this study was first designed as an attempt to trace a pattern in the general picture presented by the literary connexions between Elizabethan England and the Low Countries in the sixteenth century, the material itself soon suggested a focal point in the relations between Britain and the University of Leiden in the early years after its foundation. This latter relationship has been analyzed in greater detail, both, it is hoped, as a contribution to our knowledge of sixteenth-century literary traffic and for the special cultural-historical information of interest to students of the literatures concerned. In order to do justice to these themes it seemed proper to quote generous selections from some of the documents that have come to light and to supply ample reference material. As a rule no source is given for facts that can be found in the established biographical reference books.

In the course of collecting my data I have invariably met with much interest and generosity. I am deeply grateful to the Right Hon. the Marquess of Hertford for allowing repeated inspections of a manuscript of poems by Daniel Rogers in his library. Curators, Keepers, Librarians, and staff-members of the British Museum Library, the Bodleian Library, Cambridge University Library, the Public Record Office, the Leiden Town Archives, Bibliotheca Thysiana, Print Room, and Archives of the Senate and Curators, the Royal Library at The Hague, and the University Libraries of Leiden, Utrecht, and Amsterdam I wish to thank for many courtesies; and for permission to reproduce materials in their possession the directors of the Bodleian Library, the Royal Library, the Boymans Museum at Rotterdam, and the Leiden Town Archives, Lakenhal Museum, Academical Historical Museum, University Library, and Print Room.

I am much obliged to the Netherlands Organization for

the Advancement of Pure Research (Z.W.O.) and the 'Leidsch Universiteits Fonds' for their aid on some occasions when visits to English libraries and archives were requisite, and the former more particularly for subsidizing the publication of the results. I have also every reason to be grateful to the publishers and the printer of this book for their unsparing co-operation.

While acknowledging a general debt to all those who have given me the benefit of their advice, I should like to express my special gratitude to Professor A. G. H. Bachrach for so much encouragement and invaluable criticism, and for inviting me to appear in the Publications of the Institute; to Professor J. H. Waszink for very kindly correcting many of the translations; to Dr. R. B. C. Huygens for reading some of the Rogers poems with me; and to Mr. R. C. Strong of the National Portrait Gallery for his stimulating comment.

I should like to record my obligations to Mr. C. D. L. Engelbach for editorial advice. Finally, I owe a debt to my wife for much more than compiling the index.

J. A. v. D.

CONTENTS

The foundation of the University of Leiden, 1575:
Divinity School or *Academia?*—contemporary evidence
—propaganda—politics, protestantism, and the arts

PART I. DANIEL ROGERS

The first foreign tribute in verse to Leiden University—
a martyr's son—early poems—1564-66, at Paris with
Dousa—crucial contacts

Rogers and the antiquarians—lost works—Ireland—
Dousa's years of study and retirement—1572, reunion
in London

1572-74: Hadrianus Junius' English connexions—Dousa
addresses the Queen — Rogers' library — Sidney's
Grand Tour—his first entrance into the continental
world of letters

1575-77: Rogers, Buchanan, and the beginnings of
Dutch poetry—Rogers in the Low Countries—the
University of Leiden—a Leiden 'school' of poetry—
Rogers and the Sidney circle—Buchanan—Buchanan
and Van Hout—Rogers' share in Anglo-Dutch politics

PART II. SIR PHILIP SIDNEY

LIST OF ILLUSTRATIONS

INTRODUCTION

AN IDEAL *ACADEMIA*

ON 8 February 1575, some eight years after the beginning of the Dutch struggle against the tyranny of Spain and at a time so unsettled that few would have risked predicting an ultimate victory, the solemn opening ceremony of the first University of the northern Netherlands took place, little more than a month after the Prince of Orange had urged its foundation [1].

'So great is the confidence of the Gueux', the politician Hubert Languet wrote to the Duke of Saxony, 'that now they consider the foundation of a public school or Academy in the Dutch fortress of Leiden which the Spanish have besieged only a few months ago'. [2] Perhaps Leiden's loyalty in recent trials had not itself been the immediate occasion for the establishment of this Protestant University, but at least there was an obvious connexion between the University's location and the momentous year of 1574. In that year the city guard under the poet-scholar Janus Dousa (Jan van der Does), and the citizens of Leiden themselves, had successfully endured the hardships of a Spanish siege—assisted only by a handful of others, who happened to be Englishmen [3].

[1] See *Bronnen tot de geschiedenis der Leidsche Universiteit*, ed. P. C. Molhuysen, The Hague, I, 1913, pp. 1*–2*.

[2] H. Languet to August Duke of Saxony, Prague, 1 March 1575 (*Huberti Langueti epistolae secretae*, Halle, 1699, I, [ii], p. 75). See Appendix II, no. 1.

[3] Avis, 23 August 1574: 'Within the towne are noe soldiers, but the burgars (saving George Gascoyns lieutenant, named Cromvell, with 30 of his compagnye, whiche, beinge owt to discover, recoverid into the towne, as the reast of theire compagny in Valkenburgh weare invironed by the ennymye)' (*Relations politiques des Pays-Bas et de l'Angleterre*, ed. Kervyn de Lettenhove, Brussels, VII, 1888, no. MMDCCCXV). The poet-soldier Gascoigne himself had had the gates barred against him and was imprisoned by the Spanish (see G. Gascoigne, *The fruites of Warre*, in *Complete Poems*, ed. W. C. Hazlitt, London, 1869, I, pp. 147–196). A few documents relating to payments made to these

Twelve years later these same citizens were to dramatize their gruesome experience in the 'seven several shewes' with which they entertained their English Governor General, the Earl of Leicester, and his retinue on the occasion of his state entry into the University town [1]. For, then and at all times, the University has never wearied of linking its origin with those perilous months and of considering itself as having been established to commemorate the event and to further the cause of *Libertas*.

During the first few years after the great siege of 1574 the country as a whole was impoverished and badly in need of military and economic support from without [2]. With England, it is true, a close political relationship was to develop in a not so distant future. But at this stage the Dutch had little immediate hope of succour from abroad, not even from Queen Elizabeth, though Leicester, long before his actual commission—in a letter to William Davison, the Queen's ambassador in the Low Countries—shows that he is conscious of their distress in the following lines written from Norwich, 'somwhat nere you', where he could almost hear the oppressed people from the Netherlands 'crye out uppon such neghboures'. 'Well,' he added, 'God help them and us too, fearing our neede wylbe more than thers.' [3]

The 'confidence of the Gueux' seemed great indeed, but the foundation of an *Academia* must have been more than either a symbol of optimism or an irresponsible gesture of self-confidence. To at least one practical and urgent problem—the

English soldiers are preserved in the Leiden town archives (Secr. arch., nos. 1334, 1335, 1364); among them is a minute description of various goods left behind by 'Ritsard lasenbe', servant of 'Coronnel Chester'.

[1] *The Third volume of Chronicles . . . First compiled by Raphaell Holinshed . . . continued to the yeare 1586*, London, [1587], p. 1419. It is worth observing that the considerable detail with which the Earl's visit is described exceeds any Dutch account (see also p. 77, note 2).

[2] Cf. N. Bruyninck to W. Davison, Antwerp, 14 August 1578 (London, Public Record Office, SP 83/8, no. 28) on the critical condition of the Leiden and Haarlem clothtrade.

[3] R. Dudley to W. Davison, [Norwich], 18 August 1578 (P.R.O., SP 83/8, no. 36).

training of Protestant preachers—it hoped to supply the answer. Thus '*Sacra Scriptura*', seated in her chariot, led the procession of magistrates and scholars who went to hear the opening address in February 1575. She was, however, not alone, but followed by '*Justitia*', '*Medicina*', and '*Pallas*'; and in Neptune's barge, rowed down the Rapenburg canal, '*Apollo*' plucked the strings of his lute to accompany the nine Muses' singing and playing.

It may be worth our while to enquire into the background of the occasion a little further. More than once it has been shown that the guiding principle of the founders of the University of Leiden was simply to provide the Low Countries with a Protestant school of Theology. [1] That this motive remained unexpressed until Town Secretary Jan van Hout's speech in 1592 [2]—and then only to an audience of officials assembled for the opening ceremony of a 'College of Theology'—is no ground for arguing that it was not the main one, because at the time, certainly before 1581, the year of the 'Placard of Dismissal', there was ample reason to disguise so audacious an endeavour. But there is evidence in the foundation-day pageant which makes it desirable to qualify this claim.

In accordance with the tradition of the period, this pageant was a *tableau* whereby 'secret' intentions could be displayed without the stricter commitment of the written word. As a testimony, both chronologically and formally, it should surely be given priority over Van Hout's later assertion. The pageant itself was simple, crude almost compared with what Italy, France, and even Flanders would have made of it, but at least it expressed in a 'modern' idiom what the University proposed to introduce. Jan van Hout himself, Dousa's closest comrade in arms and poetry, was responsible for the devices

---

[1] See P. Dibon, *L'Enseignement Philosophique dans les Universités Néerlandaises à l'Epoque Pré-Cartesienne (1575–1650)*, Amsterdam, 1954, Ch. I, *passim*. Dibon gives a full account of other contributions to our knowledge of the subject.

[2] *Inneleydinge ende aenvang vant Collegie der theologien, 1592*, Leiden, F. Raphelengius, 1593, p. 23 [i.e. p. 15]: '. . . De voornemste bewegende oorsaecke der stichtinge deser *Universiteyt* (t'sy my geoorlooft t'geheym te openbaren) was de *Theologie*.' Cf. also *Bronnen*, I, p. 126*.

and the triumphal arches. [1] When the procession reached the University gate, '*Apollo*' and his nine Muses welcomed the four Faculties and pronounced the Latin verses which Dousa—whose motto was *Musae ante omnia dulces*—had composed for the occasion. There were thirty verses in all, including the ones painted on the arches. [2] But there is no evidence of any unusual emphasis on the Faculty of Theology —on the contrary, every figure in the pageant had his lines, except '*Sacra Scriptura*' and the four evangelists. Dousa had even added one figure, or group, to those shown on the engraving, viz. 'Artes, sive Humanitatis studia'.

When we also consider Dousa's enlightened views and remember that he held—and retained—a key-position in these formative years, we begin to realize that 'the confidence of the Gueux' had a much more general, and decidedly philosophic basis. The liberal poet-politician, who was in charge of the earliest preparations for the enterprise, was enough of a humanist to share the belief that states are ruled by knowledge, not by arms—as if to remind us, '*Plato*' also rode in the opening pageant. If a well-governed state has need of learning and virtue, the pageant seems to say, then how much more strongly must this apply to a state which is struggling to establish itself? Seen in this light, the opening ceremony symbolized not a defiant move, nor merely the foundation of a Divinity School, but the introduction of a 'new' intellectual movement into the northern Provinces.

The Frenchman Guillaume Feugueray—who had been appointed Professor of Theology—drafted in June 1575 the programme of studies in comparable terms. The opening paragraph read:

Divine Plato, whom Tully called the philosophers' god, enjoyed such a reputation for wisdom that the Thebans and Phocenses allowed him to found a city to be ruled by such laws as he deemed requisite; among other things he decided that in the perfect common-wealth all arts of mind and body should be acquired

---

[1] See R. van Luttervelt, 'De optocht ter gelegenheid van de inwijding der Leidse Universiteit', *Jaarboekje voor geschiedenis en oudheidkunde van Leiden*, 50, Leiden, 1958, pp. 87 ff.

[2] Janus Dousa, *Nova poemata*, Leiden, 1575, sig. M v-vij.

1. *Sacra Scriptura* in her chariot, attended by the four Evangelists; *Apollo* and the Muses in Neptune's barge.

From the engraving of the pageant on 8 February 1575, the foundation-day of the University of Leiden.

before the twentieth year, and the rest of a man's life devoted to the public duties of war and peace. [1]

Feugueray accordingly proposed an educational system, based on a period of fourteen years, at the end of which a doctorate in Theology, Law, or Medicine might be acquired to follow the degree of *Artium Magister* that had completed the student's schooling in the *encyclopaedia* of knowledge. Thus a School *and* a University were to be founded: that is to say, only after having been well-grounded both in Letters and in the special subject of their Faculty—Theology, Law, or Medicine—would the young graduates be fit for public office. Though Feugueray's humanistic ideal was not to be completely realized, in the statement of this professor, who had, incidentally, been recommended by the Prince of Orange [2], there is no explicit indication that the University was to be primarily a Divinity School, however patently this equality of Faculties expressed the revolutionarily scholarly approach of the time to the study of Theology. Moreover, there was a considerable number of Catholic students in the University, who suffered more from the opposition of their church authorities than at the hands of University officials, who actually protected them. [3]

Both Feugueray's programme and the foundation-day pageant express the proposed activities of the new *Academia* more clearly than the official administrative correspondence of the period. They already warrant a certain reconsideration of the popular view of the University's underlying idea. But besides, there is more evidence. To publicize the new University, which was intended to emulate Louvain and Douay, Dousa produced a volume of *Nova poemata* printed 'in nova academia nostra', for which Van Hout supplied the funds. In it, in the form of a long 'Carmen' which apparently dated

---

[1] *Bronnen*, I, no. 26. See Appendix II, no. 2.
[2] *Bronnen*, I, no. 19. To a large extent this spirit still guided the next generation, as may be seen in Constantyn Huygens's education. Cf. A. G. H. Bachrach, *Sir Constantine Huygens and Britain: a Pattern of Cultural Exchange in the Seventeenth Century*, Leiden, 1962, pp. 12–16, 44–50.
[3] For this information and that contained at p. 7, note 2, I am indebted to Dr. P. A. M. Geurts.

2

from the early weeks of 1575, he formulated his aims in eloquent and unmistakably tendentious terms. The lecturers of Louvain, he claimed, were 'rustic and unrefined', while 'the bald herd of *Baccalaurei*' at Douay suffered from a sad lack of intellectual freedom. Leiden, he promised, would bring a complete change:

The Prince himself has left Themis, the *genius* of Holy Scripture, and the art of Medicine in the hands of Minerva, saying: 'The *Lycaeum* be your concern, I gladly leave it to you because it is yours by right'.

At Leiden, he goes on to say, with us 'who favour politer Muses', the arts will be restored to their rightful place. 'Louvain must therefore give way to Leiden, and Douay must follow Louvain, and so must all other *Academiae*'—Pisa, Paris, Dôle, and even ancient Athens. 'From everywhere young men will flock to learn the *Ars Palladia* which the Greeks called *Sophia*, and the Romans *Sapientia*'. Therefore,

Ephebi from everywhere, gather where Phoebus calls and the Nine Sisters: because there Minerva presides over Dutchmen and foreigners alike. [1]

This poem anticipates both in date and content the foundation day pageant, and even Feugueray's draft for a programme of studies.

The evidence, in other words, suggests that the guiding principle in founding this Protestant University was the introduction of a complete humanistic *Academia* in which no Faculty was necessarily to be superior to another. And it can be concluded, in view of the avowed educational theories and the peculiar moment selected for putting them into practice, that the University was confidently created not in spite of, but because of the political chaos of the moment, in an attempt to let *Sapientia* establish order and harmony. The same motive is implied in the University Charter which, fearing that 'morals, science, and learning

---

[1] 'Iani Duzae Nordovicis carmen hendecasyllabis addendum, in gratiam novae ab Aurasino Principe recens constitutae Lugduni Batavorum Academiae conscriptum, Ad Cornelium Regium, & Gerardum Hoghevaenium Æmilij F. Collegas, unaque secum Decreto Publico Academiae eidem inaugurandae Curatores delegatos' (Dousa, *Poemata*, 1575, sig. P iij-Q iiij). See Appendix II, no. 3a.

would be extinguished to the lessening of the glory of God and involving great harm to the common-wealth', instructed the Senate 'freely and in public to teach Theology, Law, and Medicine, and also Philosophy and all other liberal Arts'. [1]

Explicit and final evidence is given in three *orationes* on the Academy's foundation delivered in 1591 and 1592 by Dousa's friend Bonaventura Vulcanius (De Smed) [2], the Professor of Greek who, appointed in 1578, had been lecturing at Leiden since 1581. Vulcanius, who refers to the University as 'tutissimum hoc Musis asylum', praises the Prince of Orange for making 'his *Batavia* to abound in men who not only protect it with martial courage but also stabilize the country with their insight and wisdom' [3]: at Leiden 'a new generation would grow up, educated in the best arts and sciences for the benefit of State and Church' [4]. To him the Three Faculties hold equal positions, while the study of Letters provides each with a basic discipline, and gratefully he observes that

whereas in other Universities some one art or science prospers more especially and leaves the others in a state of neglect and non-practice, here every kind of art and discipline flourishes so greatly that each seems to vie with the others. [5]

Throughout the *orationes*, Vulcanius' unbiassed testimony stresses and repeats that the founders' ideal for this *Musarum domicilium* was to cultivate *virtus* and *doctrina* [6] as a major contribution towards establishing order in church and state.

It must not be forgotten that this central aim has often

---

[1] *Bronnen*, I, no. 7.
[2] 'Oratio ... de Laudibus Academiae Leydensis, 6 July. 1592, quum Balduinus Hamaeus et Laurentius Brant doctores medicinae crearentur'; 'Oratio ... de Academiarum institutione, 4 Apr. 1591, quum Henricus Wyntgis doctor iuris crearetur'; 'Oratio ... de Academiarum institutione, 26 Sep. 1591, quum Ant. Hagenoius doctor theologiae crearetur' (all three MSS. bound up together in MS. Vulcanius 9, Leiden, Univ. libr.). See above, p. 5, note 3.
[3] f. 56^V. See Appendix II, no. 3^b.
[4] f. 63^V. See Appendix II, no. 3^c.
[5] f. 58^V. See Appendix II, no. 3^d.
[6] This phrase continues to appear in their letters: cf. J. Lipsius to J. Dousa in 1585 (see p. 118).

been modified by individual emphasis. While Van Hout in 1592 had to allude to the training of preachers, Dousa was led to favour the *bonae literae* for more or less private reasons. Both Dousa and Van Hout were concerned with the reform of Dutch poetry; and Dousa, a pupil of Dorat, acquainted with Ronsard, familiar with De Baïf, would scarcely have allowed such an ideal opportunity to pass without attempting to introduce into 'his' *nova Academia* that veneration for poetry which his Parisian period had taught him to propagate.

In fine, though there may possibly have been two 'opposite' schools of thought—one primarily interested in training for the ministry, the other more devoted to 'the politer Muses'—it seems more accurate to regard them as varying trends or interpretations within one and the same ideal *Academia*. The apparent absence, incidentally, of actual students to fill the lecture rooms in 1575 shows strikingly the idealistic nature of the experiment.

What has emerged, then, is that behind the University's foundation was a complex interaction of motives inspired by various liberal ideals within the realms of politics, religion, and the arts. This interaction was to account for the pattern of its early years, and these three aspects marked out the common ground for its first contacts with England. A growing interest in England is hinted at even in the foundation-day pageant. Dousa and Van Hout, the more deliberately because contrary to all the rules of heraldry, put a Garter —not the Golden Fleece—round the crests of the Prince and the Provinces on the festive barge. The floating pageant of the Leiden Muses displaying the Order of the Garter was not only a meaningful allegory in respect of subsequent political events, but also suggestive of the literary scene.

PART ONE

DANIEL ROGERS

———

I

EARLY EXPERIENCES

OUSA designed the University of Leiden as an enterprise which would open up new perspectives for the northern Provinces. But the publication of his *Nova poemata* implied an appeal beyond the national boundaries. Significantly, the book already included one reaction from abroad. It is the earliest specimen of a foreign literary interest in the University, a Latin poem written at Leiden on 26 April 1575, not more than three months after the foundation day.

The author, who appears to have been familiar with the town's disputed nomenclature—'Leiden' or 'Lugdunum Batavorum'—and who does not fail to comment on the 'market places tidy like your houses', undoubtedly knew what he was talking about. For he saw the opening of the University as 'a chorus of Muses entering while Mars still rages', and appropriately concluded with the crucial question:

Who would not approve of a war which moves you, Leiden, to favour the Muses and purity of religion alike? [1]

The poem is headed 'Danielis Rogerij Epigramma' and we know this writer can be identified as the English poet and diplomatist Daniel Rogers.

---

[1] Daniel Rogers, 'Ad Leidam, urbem Batavicam' (Dousa, *Poemata*, 1575, sig. Q vij—i.e. end of book). The same text is included in *Illustris. Academia Lugd-Batava*, Leiden, 1613, sig. *** iij, where it is the only foreign commendatory verse. See Appendix II, no. 4.

In order to account for the presence of this poem and to elucidate the earlier stages of Anglo-Leiden contacts, it is necessary to follow the career of this man from the beginning.

Daniel, the eldest son of John Rogers, must have been some seventeen years old when his father, then a well-known preacher, and divinity lecturer at St. Paul's, was burned at the stake in the early years of Queen Mary's reign. Once an orthodox-catholic chaplain to the Merchant Adventurers in Antwerp, John Rogers had emphasized his complete conversion to the new religion, after a brief acquaintance with William Tyndale in 1535, first by abandoning celibacy [1], and then by editing, as 'John Matthew', the great 'Matthew's Bible' which Jacob van Meteren caused to be printed in 1537, probably at Antwerp. Considering also his pronounced views after a long contact with Melanchthon at Wittenberg [2], it was almost inevitable that he should become the first Protestant martyr in Mary's reign. He showed no sign of repentance, moreover, during the series of cross-examinations of which his own reports were found in a little black book that 'his wife and one of her sonnes called Daniell', after the execution, happened to notice in his cell—'a blacke thing . . . in a blynde corner' [3]. John Day, the learned Protestant printer, remembered his cheerful equanimity in prison. He died, 'persisting in his opinion. At this conduct the greatest part of the people took such pleasure that they were not afraid to make him many exclamations to strengthen his courage. Even his [eleven] children assisted at it, comforting him in such a manner that it seemed as if he had been led to a wedding.' [4]

With all the terror of this almost baroque martyrdom still

---

[1] Daniel Rogers' mother was one Adrienne (van) der Weede of Antwerp. See Figure 1.

[2] After his return to England in 1548 John Rogers lived in the house of Edward Whitchurch who printed in the same year: *A Waying and Considering of the Interim, by . . . Melanchton, translated into Englyshe by John Rogers.* On the significance of 'a Wittenberg background', cf. Marlowe, *Doctor Faustus*, ed. A. G. H. Bachrach and tr. D. Verspoor, The Hague, 1960, commentary, pp. 194-195.

[3] J. Foxe, *Ecclesiasticall History*, London, 1576, II, p. 1419.

[4] Thus the French ambassador in London, Count Noailles, in a letter quoted without full reference in the *D.N.B.*, 49, p. 129.

vividly before him, Daniel revisited his place of birth, Wittenberg, where it was intended that, as a student under Melanchthon, he should become one of that host of preachers
whose training had been his father's last instruction to John
Day. He subscribed to the 'new discipline', perhaps at
Frankfort where Anthony à Wood reports him to have
been, on 21 December 1557. [1] He may have been wanting
in vocation, or perhaps his continental travel, alone and
away from his theological acquaintances at home, had made
him a devotee of renaissance letters. At any rate the Marian
exile abandoned his earlier course, and having returned to
England on Queen Elizabeth's accession, took an Arts degree
at Oxford in August 1561, and found ways to be introduced
at Court by the Queen's French secretary, an old Flemish
friend of his father's, who more than a quarter of a century
later was to become his own father-in-law [2]. Many sixteenth-
century scholars sought preferment in the more exciting and
hazardous world of the Court. Rogers' continental humanism,
his staunch adherence to England's Protestant cause, and his
probably thorough knowledge of a variety of modern languages made him a suitable candidate for such preferment.

Like a true humanist Rogers had begun to test his poetic
abilities with great enthusiasm. From 1562 [3], or possibly
earlier, he wrote a prodigious amount of Latin verse, much of
which has survived in manuscript. But with that modesty
affected by the courtier-poets he permitted himself only one
independent publication, an early work singing the praises
of Antwerp. In it the descriptions of which he was so fond
make delightful reading, as, for example, when he gives an
account of the opening hours of the Antwerp Exchange where

... you will see the people, of all origins under the sun, flocking
towards it in dense array, the happy throng of Englishmen taking
their places (they alone occupy the spaces in the middle), Italians
on the right and Spaniards adjoining, stalking warily through

[1] C. H. Garret, *The Marian Exiles*, Cambridge, 1938, [Census] 351.

[2] D. Rogers to C. Clusius, Rostock, 19 August 1588: '... Ego ante
annum uxorem duxi, [Susannam] Nicasii Yetsweirtii filiam, qui
Serenissimae Reginae, in Gallicis secretarius fuit: ...' (Leiden, University Library, MS. Vulc. 101).

[3] D. Rogers, 'Ad Petrum Torrium ode', dated 9 November 1562 (Paris,
Bibliothèque Nationale, MS. Dupuy 951, f. 24).

the front halls; the offspring of France walks on the left, and one may even discern Dutchmen . . .: you hear a discordant noise, the very place is filled with various languages and various costumes.

O choice delight to the eye, and wonder to us all!
The greater orb has come to life in a tiny circle. [1]

And he merrily recalls how 'sweetly he drank his wine, and bought his books' in the middle of the river Schelde when it had frozen over that winter. [2]

When he reached Paris in or about 1565 he was therefore not altogether inexperienced as a poet. There he was to become a member of the household of the English ambassador, Sir Henry Norris, for whom he was frequently employed in travel, and who describes him as 'one Rogers very well learnid in the Greke and latin, whose father was burnt for the Relligion; this man being stewarde of my howse, and allso instructer to my children' [3]. In that setting where he gradually met the interesting people, writers, politicians, and the like, to whom his verses pay tribute [4], he found more and more scope to indulge his delight in recording innumerable events and encounters in poetry. Hardly any name of renown is absent from his manuscripts. Many of his dedicatees were

---

[1] D. Rogers, *De laudibus Antverpiae oda sapphica . . . etiam alii eiusdem versiculi quidam*, Antwerp, Plantin, 1565, sig. B3ᵛ–4. See Appendix II, no. 5.
That same year a commendatory verse of his was printed in Georgius Schroegelius, *Elegia ἐγκωμιαστικὴ in urbem Handoverpiam*, Antwerp, 1565, sig. B4ᵛ.

[2] Rogers, *De laudibus*, sig. B5. See Appendix II, no. 6.

[3] The passage continues, characteristically:
'. . . he was captured the other day, but they had nothing to obiect ageinst him, but that he is of the Relligion. wherwithe they have not to do being myne. for that I wold not kepe him if he were otherwise'. H. Norris to W. Cecil, Jenville, 11 February 1569 (P. R. O., SP 70/105, f. 97).

[4] Hundreds of them have survived, mainly in two MSS. The Paris MS. Dupuy 951 (to which Dr. H. van Crombruggen has kindly referred me) is the earlier, and most miscellaneous in character; it comprises 334 ff. The other is now in the possession of the Marquess of Hertford (Ragley Hall, Alcester). Its 583 ff. have obviously been selected and arranged by Rogers himself for publication; parts have been indexed in the *Report* of the H. M. C., Hertford. Hereafter references will be made to 'Dupuy MS.' or 'Hertford MS.'.

gentlemen of similar poetic tastes and offered their verses in return.

From among the lasting friends he made in Paris, one at least should be brought to the fore. He is the same Janus Dousa whom we have already met, and who, at the time, was a student at Paris. In this young Dutchman's Album Rogers wrote five epigrams [1], thus starting a close literary friendship which was to cover three decades.

Dousa, who had not yet visited England, arrived in Paris early in 1564, fresh from study at Louvain and Douai, not quite twenty years old and still a Roman Catholic. His years with Rogers coincided with the prelude to the Dutch Eighty Years War. There is, it seems, reason to believe that his future renown as one of Holland's most liberal, yet most faithful champions of Protestantism, and his never-ceasing concern for the *bonae literae* were directly inspired by his early days in France (during this period when the alliance between the Guise and the exponents of a *politique* religious policy was at its height [2]) and by the wealth of literary experiences which he there shared with the martyr's son, 'whose rare faithfulness could for ever dispel all future doubts as to the permanence of his friendship: whose good will was only to be expected, if not because of his learning, prudence, and virtuousness, then at least because he was so very dear to Valens (Germanus Valens Pimpontius), Buchanan(us), Auratus (Dorat), Baïf(ius), Florens (Florent Chrestien), Altarius (Des Autels), Thorius (Thore), and indeed to all men.' [3]

The way in which Englishmen and Dutchmen first became acquainted with the poetry of French scholars and courtiers, that poetry's early impact on some British visitors, their private and imitative experiments, in short all the questions which arise during the uncertain years before a *Countesse of Pembrokes Arcadia* could be written, literary scholarship

---

[1] Leiden, Univ. Libr., MS. BPL 1406, ff. 20–20ᵛ.

[2] For an outline of Anglo-Dutch political connexions in these years, see H. Brugmans, *Engeland en de Nederlanden in de eerste jaren van Elizabeth's Regeering (1558–1567)*, diss. Groningen, 1892.

[3] J. Dousa to D. Rogers, Leiden, 1575 (Dousa, *Novorum poematum secunda Lugdunensis editio*, Leiden, 1576, sig. Q vᵛ). See Appendix II, no. 9.

has left largely unanswered. [1] The proper significance and antecedents of 'the new poetry' have hardly been defined. Although this term, which is generally applied as from *The Shepheardes Calender* of 1579, must remain vague as long as no serious attention is paid to the actual genesis of the new movement in English poesy, a student of Anglo-Continental history cannot altogether overlook more than twenty years of Anglo-French literary contacts, that preceded, let us say, the writing and the implications of Sidney's *Apologie for poetrie*.

On the whole, these exchanges at Court and in the Universities seem to have been conducted in Latin and Greek, and much less frequently in a modern language. [2] This, incidentally, resembles the practice of the French themselves who maintained that a good French poet should be in the first place a good humanist. [3] The inspiration which English poets were then receiving from France appears, generally, to have been exerted on three levels: the academic, the courtly, and the religious. The first, in which De Baïf's Academy must have played its part, is responsible for what may be the earliest and strongest fields of contact and has left more traces in the correspondence of its humanist participants than the second, which (apart from a number of dedications, some Pléiade echoes in Elizabethan writings, and evidence in the form of printed sources) remained so informal as to become obscure to later generations. The third led English writers to apply the poetic accomplishments of the other two to religious themes. Combining all that was 'sweet and profitable', and adding new significance to *vates* as a poet's title, the religious element introduced a French-inspired literary movement in the enlightened Protestant circles of England [4]

---

[1] See A. H. Upham, *The French influence in English literature*, New York, 1908; and S. Lee, *The French Renaissance in England*, Oxford, 1910; both works restrict themselves to noticing similarities, borrowings, and translations in sixteenth-century English literature. See also I. Silver, 'Ronsard in European literature', *Bibl. d'Hum. et Ren.*, XVI, 1954, pp. 241-254; and P. Laumonier, 'Ronsard et l'Ecosse', *Rev. de lit. comp.*, IV, 1924, pp. 408-428.

[2] Cf. Sidney's own case, pp. 101-103.

[3] See P. de Nolhac, *Ronsard et l'humanisme*, Paris, 1921, p. 141.

[4] It was continued, through Sidney, in the circle of Mary, Countess of Pembroke.

and the Low Countries [1]. Thereafter, in a milieu determined by politics and scholarship, a cultured poetry both Latin and vernacular was to emerge and to prove 'new' indeed in prosody, sentiments, subject-matter, and not least in the purposes for which it was used. The odes, sonnets, elegies, epigrams, and the like, written by these poets, whether in Latin, Greek, English, French, or Dutch, display all the 'generalized emotion', devotional exhortation, political message, and polite compliment which they were expected self-consciously but non-professionally to phrase in classical metaphor and witty conceits of the early-renaissance kind. The French origin of some late sixteenth-century courtly verse in Britain and the Low Countries is known. But the earlier stages of this interest in French letters, which included the introductory work of neo-Latin poets, are obscure. [2] Many a reference in the following chapters will be seen to suggest that the key to much of the literary history of England and the Netherlands in the sixteenth century must be found in Paris, 'in illo hominum eruditorum velut microcosmo' [3], during the 1550s and 1560s.

A considerable amount of evidence could be adduced to show that great numbers of English, Scottish, Dutch, and German scholars and politicians were very familiar with the literary activities of the Parisian writers—De Baïf, Ronsard, Du Bellay, Dorat, and many others—with whom they were often personally acquainted. Moreover, the foreign visitors (among whom we find various young men who were to become prominent poets in their own countries) were no passive audience; for they themselves became contributors to the

[1] See W. A. P. Smit, *De Dichter Revius*, Amsterdam, 1928, pp. 21-31; and see below, p. 36, note 1.

[2] Cf. C. Maddison, *Apollo and the Nine*, London, 1960, p. 288, where it says: 'Since the ode enters English literary history in this later period [*viz. after 1584*] it comes under the auspices of the French. However, once the English began emulating the Pléiade and writing odes, their classical education . . . caused them to go from the French to the ancient and neolatin poets for their models'; but no proper evidence is given for this statement.

[3] F. Foppens, *Bibliotheca Belgica*, Brussels, 1739, I, p. 165, biography of C. Utenhove (see below, p. 16, note 2), of whom Foppens writes: 'Praeter vernaculam ac graecam, calluit linguas gallicam, anglicam atque Italicam'.

Parisian literary scene of the 1560s. [1] The hundreds of poems, letters, and dedications in which the evidence is contained indicate that a careful study of guests and hosts at their poetic *rendez-vous*—which certainly includes the 'sacra Musarum aedes' of Morellus (Jean de Morel) and his accomplished daughters—would reveal important details about much foreign apprenticeship. [2] With special, though not exclusive,

---

[1] See De Nolhac, *Ronsard et l'humanisme*, Pt. II; and *Un poète rhénan ami de la Pléiade, Paul Melissus*, Bibl. lit. de la ren., n.s. XI, Paris, 1923.

[2] An excellent example of one such guest-apprentice is the multilingual Ghent poet Carolus Utenhovius (Utenhove: see fig. 1), who was a good friend of Buchanan, Rogers, Dousa, Paulus Melissus and many others, and almost a member of the Pléiade. It was Utenhove who admonished Ronsard to apply himself to divine poetry; and Buchanan, while calling Utenhove 'censor meorum carminum', granted him in 1564 the rare privilege of publishing his works. Utenhove had been tutor to Morellus' daughters before coming to England—where lived his uncle Jan, one of the founders of the London Dutch church—in November 1562 as a companion and secretary of Paul de Foix, the French ambassador. In the next few years he found a patron in Cecil, wrote poems to numerous English personages, including nineteen to the Queen (some in French, others in Latin, Greek, and Hebrew—one of which latter poems Camille Morel rendered in Latin), and taught Cecil's accomplished wife Greek. He left this hospitable country in 1565, the year of the Bayonne Conference and of Ronsard's dedicating his *Elegies* to Queen Elizabeth (below, p. 18, note 3), a copy of which was given to her, through De Foix, by Cecil—who was being kept informed about 'the archpoet of France' by Sir Thomas Smith, English ambassador in Paris (see P. Champion, *Ronsard et son temps*, Paris, 1925, pp. 217-225). Three years later Utenhove published at Basle Buchanan's *Franciscanus* and further works, adding much poetry by Du Bellay and others, and his own *Xenia* which was dedicated to Elizabeth. This remarkable book contains poems by most Pléiade writers and has, among Utenhove's own poems, verses addressed to a variety of notables, including De Heere, Leicester, William of Orange, and Hubert Languet. In 1560 he had already published his *Epitaphium* on Henry II, in twelve languages (the English and Scottish translations being by one H. Keir), with epitaphs on Du Bellay. In 1568 he hoped to dedicate a 'history of the Spanish Inquisition' to the Queen (see *Cal. S. P. for. 1569-1571*, no. 47). In 1570 Dorat wrote the epithalamium on his marriage. He was to have no children, but later adopted Janus Gruterus (see fig. 1 and cf. pp. 109-110). See De Nolhac, *Ronsard et l'humanisme*, pp. 172, 348, 349; W. Janssen, *Charles Utenhove, sa vie et son oeuvre (1536-1600)*, diss. Nijmegen, 1939; *George Buchanan Glasgow quatercentenary studies 1906*, Glasgow, 1907, pp. 403, 432-434.
Dousa's Album contains inscriptions by Morellus (f. 27ᵛ) and his

reference to England two other meeting places appear to be of interest: the English embassy at Paris and the French embassy in London [1], where poetry followed and supported the trend of politics—a phenomenon that was to recur in later years [2].

In this light Dousa and Rogers are typical representatives of the humanists who visited Paris in these years. They were both destined for a life of action in their respective countries' service, and derived an essential part of their intellectual make-up from early literary experiences in Paris. In one and the same city they saw the great politico-religious movements of the day, heard renowned lecturers in every branch of modern scholarship, and listened to the brilliant products of the most advanced school of poetry: as poets they learned— as Dousa was subsequently to recall [3]—that letters are as serviceable to the common-wealth as politics. It is difficult to overestimate the effect of these stimulating experiences on the two young men. Personal contacts and friendships with men of letters they sought and enjoyed. In the following twenty years we shall again and again find allusions to these

daughters (f. 28). The Hertford MS. ends with a number of poems (f. 366 ff.) addressed to Rogers by various Pléiade writers, and includes verses by him to C. Utenhove (f. 54ᵛ), Dorat (f. 62ᵛ), De Baïf (ff. 87ᵛ, 291), Buchanan (f. 88), and Ronsard (ff. 294, 348); the Dupuy MS. has many more, also some connected with Morellus.

[1] Not surprisingly, numerous courtly writers of the Tudor age seem connected with France through these embassies, often enjoying the patronage or friendship of the literary-minded ambassadors themselves.

[2] See below, Pt. I, ch. v, and Pt. II, ch.i-v. There is reason to believe that some contacts were facilitated besides by kinship as much as by friendship, as for example in the case of French and Flemish refugees (cf. fig. 1), who, after all, often acted as active and not seldom accomplished supporters of the English Protestant Court. Finally, some Flemish poets (such as Jan van der Noot, Lucas de Heere, or Carolus Utenhove), who were less slow in following the French, may be found to have had more influence in the northern Netherlands and even in England than has so far been realized.

[3] J. Dousa to J. van Hout, Leiden, 1576: 'Dabimus ansam reprehensionis ijs, qui nesciunt, maximum ad virtutem incitamentum esse Poeticam, atque (ut rectissime ab Horatio scriptum est) mares animos in Martia bella versibus exacui: nec cogitant, non minus in libris & literis, quam in curia & foro Rempub. tractari posse, . . .' (Dousa, *Poemata*, 1576, sig. S iij).

events in letters and poems written long after they had left that accomplished society of French courtiers and scholars. [1] Dousa appears to have been a pupil of Dorat, and to have met most other *literati* of the Parisian world, including—it has been argued [2]—Ronsard. Rogers, too, knew them and collected their verses, including one addressed to himself by the same Jean-Antoine de Baïf [3] who had shared the first few pages of Dousa's Album with Jean Dorat [4]. The precise details of their Parisian sojourn—and indeed of visits by numerous others like them—are as yet unknown and really lie outside the scope of the present enquiry. It should suffice to stress the obvious, general significance of the circumstances under which two young scholars from England and Holland first met.

When Dousa departed in 1566 to travel north through the disintegrating Low Countries, he took with him that intellectual keenness which seems to have ruled and inspired his whole ambitious generation. As a promising poet he imported its ideas into the northern Provinces. Rogers could do the same a little later. But Dousa was to have the greater opportunity for introducing his 'Parisian' views when nine years later he gave shape to 'his own' *Academia*—a singular privilege for a humanist.

---

[1] See for examples Appendix II.

[2] See P. van Tieghem, *La littérature latine de la renaissance*, Paris, 1944, p. 84; and De Nolhac, *Ronsard et l'humanisme*, pp. 211 ff., 224, 346.

[3] A. de Baïf, 'D. Rogerio, Anglo' (Dupuy MS., f. 116ᵛ). Cf. also p. 100. It may be worth noting that the only acknowledged English translation of a work by Ronsard (an honoured guest in England, who had dedicated to Queen Elizabeth his *Elegies, Mascarades et Bergeries*, 1565, which included eulogis of Leicester and Burghley) was Rogers' friend Thomas Jeney's *A Discours of the Present Troobles*, Antwerp, 1568, dedicated to Norris.
Another of Rogers' Parisian friends was Sir Thomas Hoby, translator of the *Cortegiano*, English ambassador in Paris during the last few months of his life (1566). The Hertford MS. (ff. 171–176) contains a separate collection of commemorative poems addressed to Hoby's widow, in MS., entitled: *Tumulus ... Thomae Hobbij ... Elaborata omnia Danielis Rogerii, partim industria, partim eius studio a doctissimis amicis conquisita et in libelli formam coniecta.*

[4] Leiden, Univ. libr., MS. BPL 1406, ff. 4–5.

II

YEARS OF STUDY

ROGERS meanwhile remained in France, occasionally travelling to England. His employer, Sir Henry Norris, was replaced by Francis Walsingham—like Rogers a former 'Marian exile'—whose instructions were even more strictly concerned with Huguenot policy. Undoubtedly Rogers was having the best of diplomatic schooling under his 'especial frende and patrone' [1] and learned from him the many abilities which he could soon practise in more independent positions. Foreign activities were increasingly concentrated on all the movements that preceded the catastrophe of St. Bartholomew, and Rogers, too, remained fully occupied with French affairs. At this time his connexions with Dutchmen were not entirely suspended—witness for instance his inscription in the poet-painter Lucas de Heere's Album [2]—but the initial promise of strong ties with Dousa and his circle was not to be fulfilled until later. Nor did this mean a temporary banishment from the world of letters generally. On the contrary, these years were among his most active in at least one field of 'modern learning', factual history. He collected historical manuscripts [3], compared traditional authors, travelled, and made extensive notes of all coins and ancient tablets he could lay hands on. His kinship with Abraham Ortelius [4], by one and all accounted the greatest geographer of his time, and consequent familiarity with the antiquarian world of historians and map-makers was an obvious source of inspiration in this field.

[1] As he would frequently call him: e.g. in the endorsement of a letter to Walsingham, 6 January 1585 (o.s.) (P.R.O., SP 12/186, no. 9).

[2] 'In Phylophylacium Lucae Dherjj, pictoris celeberrimi', London, 15 November 1569 (Hertfort MS., f. 322^V); Rogers saw De Heere primarily as a painter.

[3] Such a collection made for him in 1569 and containing his own notes is B.M. MS. Add. 21, 088.

[4] See fig. 1.

In 1572 he sent Ortelius a summary of his antiquarian occupations. [1] He had completed a work called 'De Moribus Veterum Britannorum' which he had still been working on in 1570 [2], at a time when Ortelius' *Theatrum* had recorded that 'de veterum Britannorum moribus et legibus scripsit Commentarium Daniel Rogerius cognatus noster, sed nondum edidit' [3]. Later editions omitted the 'nondum edidit', but not, apparently, because the book had been published: Camden's *Britannia*, twenty years later, still hopefully advertised

quid vero Britanni primis temporibus gesserint, quam Reipublicae formam habuerint, quibus institutis vixerint, vir optimus & eruditione ornatissimus D. Daniel Rogersius optime de me meritus suis scriptis nos docebit [4];

and was afterwards obliged to substitute 'nos docebit' by

nos docere promisit, sed cum morte immatura praereptus nihil praestiterit, de antiquis ipsorum moribus haec paucula ipsis antiquorum verbis habeto [5].

A treatise on Roman Britain, he had added in his letter of 1572 to Ortelius, was causing him more trouble because there was no other information except inscriptions and old coins—for which, incidentally, he requested the help of Hubertus Goltzius the engraver [6]—to assist him in fighting traditional errors in even the most recent historians. His findings (probably the 'Antiquae Britanniae observationes' which have survived in manuscript [7]) were circulated without the intention of immediate publication, since five years later, to show

---

[1] D. Rogers to A. Ortelius, the Court at Windsor, 20 October 1572 (*Ecclesiae Londino-Batavae Archivum*, ed. J. H. Hessels, I, Cambridge, 1887, no. 42).

[2] D. Rogers to A. Ortelius, 15 February 1570 (B.M., MS. Harl. 6990, f. 96; cf. B.M., MS. Cotton Titus B VI, no. 37).

[3] f. 6.

[4] W. Camden, *Britannia*, 1590, p. 29.

[5] E.g. ed. 1659, p. 13.

[6] C. van Mander, *Het Schilder-Boeck*, Haarlem, 1604, quotes in Dutch an epigram by Rogers on Moro's portrait of Goltzius (ed. Wereldbibliotheek, Amsterdam, 1936, p. 328).

[7] 'Danielis Rogersij Angli Antiquae Britanniae observationes manu propria' (B.M., MS. Cotton Titus F.X.).

2. Drawing and inscription in the Album of Emanuel van Meteren (f. 3) by his kinsman Daniel Rogers, 1578.

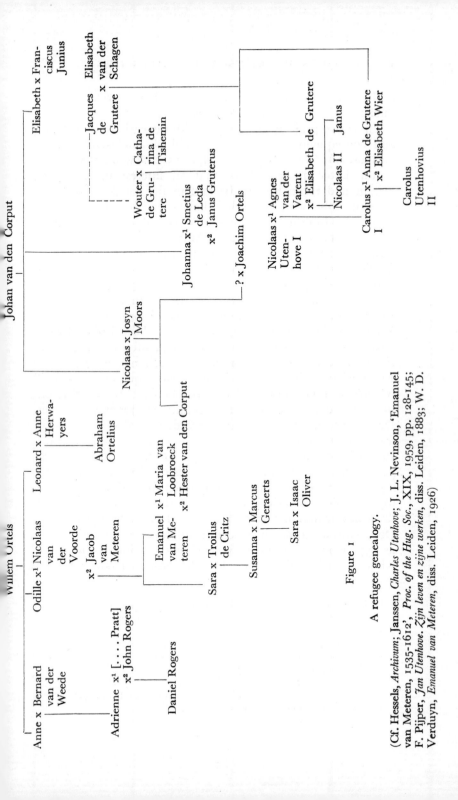

Figure 1

A refugee genealogy.

(Cf. Hessels, *Archivum*; Janssen, *Charles Utenhove*; J. L. Nevinson, 'Emanuel van Meteren, 1535–1612', *Proc. of the Hug. Soc.*, XIX, 1959, pp. 128–145; F. Pijper, *Jan Utenhove. Zijn leven en zijne werken*, diss. Leiden, 1883; W. D. Verduyn, *Emanuel van Meteren*, diss. Leiden, 1926)

he had written on Roman Britain, he had to refer George Buchanan [1] to Ortelius' *Theatrum*.

These two projects link Rogers with the early antiquarians, and consequently with another field of Anglo-Dutch connexions. After some foreign travel, in 1572 he wrote to Ortelius in the letter quoted above that an interest in surveying Britain had taken him to Ireland in the company of some German noblemen. He added that he had bought a manuscript of Giraldus Cambrensis' *Topographia Hybernica* and sent it to his learned friend in Antwerp to have it printed. Strangely enough, neither Ortelius who would quote from Giraldus in his *Theatrum*, nor John Hooker in Holinshed's *Chronicles*, Stanyhurst in *De rebus in Hibernia gestis*, or Camden in his *Anglica*, who were all concerned with Giraldus Cambrensis, ever made mention of Rogers' proposed edition. Whatever these editorial intentions may have been, Rogers wrote his own book on Ireland and frequently commented on its existence. The London-Dutch merchant and historian Emanuel van Meteren [2], a kinsman, had requested on behalf of Ortelius notes connected with this book. Three years later, in 1575, Rogers told Hadrianus Junius (De Jonghe), another Dutch historian with English antecedents [3], that some of his friends had urged him to turn the notes into a publication. [4] Junius immediately added his plea for preserving the Topography with 'the pictures of Irish costumes'. [5] There is, it seems, a probable connexion between Rogers' book and the topographical description and fine set of British costume drawings by his good friend Lucas de Heere [6]. Two years later Dousa was asked to supply commendatory verses; and as late as 1578 Rogers mentioned Wechel as the printer of his book while renewing his request for 'the promised ode expected

---

[1] D. Rogers to G. Buchanan, Westminster, 28 February 1572 (i.e. 1577) (G. Buchanan, *Opera omnia*, Edinburgh, 1715, I, p. xx).

[2] Cf. Plate 2.

[3] See below, Pt. I, ch. iii.

[4] D. Rogers to H. Junius, Antwerp, 4 February 1575 (*Hadr. Junij epistolae*, Dordrecht, 1[6]52, p. 628).

[5] H. Junius to D. Rogers, n.p., n.d., (ibid., p. 499).

[6] See *Beschrijving der Britsche eilanden door Lucas de Heere*, ed. Th. M. Chotzen and A. M. E. Draak, Antwerp, 1937.

by my Hibernia' [1]. Perhaps the undertaking was suddenly abandoned. The only survival of Rogers' Irish studies is a long 'Elegia, quae Hiberniae descriptionem . . . continet', dedicated to Thomas Rehdiger during an early visit to Ireland. [2]

Regardless of the quality of his antiquarian studies, familiarity with Roman remains in Ireland—a subject of considerable interest to his contemporaries—must have eased his introduction to the professional experts in classical antiquity of the Universities of the Low Countries where his diplomatic missions were then beginning to take him. It also made him one of the very first in a distinguished group of writers, such as Campion and Stanyhurst, Edmund Spenser and his major informant Buchanan [3], who all studied the mysterious history of that island of which Sir Henry Sidney was three times Lord-Deputy. Rogers' active interest in the past of Ireland brings him into the company of this group of scholars, and also of the Sidneys. The first English work dedicated to Philip Sidney was a poem entitled 'The image of Ireland', by one John Derricke, dating from about the same years; Philip Sidney's own literary *début* was *A discourse on Irish affairs*. [4]

Unlike his industrious friend Rogers, Dousa had spent the post-Parisian years at Noordwijk in aristocratic retirement, detached from all political tangle, with his newly-wed Elisabeth van Zuylen: 'illud tempus', as he rather bluntly put it, 'quo primum in patriam ex Galliis reverso liberorum quaerundorum gratia uxor credo obiecta est mihi' [5]. There

---

[1] D. Rogers to J. Dousa, Dordrecht, 3 May 1577; D. Rogers to J. Dousa, Antwerp, 16 January 1578 (B.M., MS. Burney 370, ff. 11, 12).

[2] Dublin, 16 August 1572 (Hertford MS., ff. 6–17^v; the first poem of this collection). Ortelius referred to this Elegy in his *Theatrum*, ed. 1580, f. 12. Rehdiger (1540–1576) was a much-travelled German scholar and a great collector of books, manuscripts, and coins.

[3] E. Spenser, *View of the Present State of Ireland* (wr. 1596); G. Buchanan, *Rerum Scoticarum Historia*, Edinburgh, 1582, from which Spenser is said to have drawn heavily.

[4] J. Derricke, *The image of Irelande* . . . *1578*, London, 1581; Sidney, *A discourse*, [1577] (*The complete works*, ed. A. Feuillerat, III, Cambridge, 1923, pp. 46–50).

[5] J. Dousa to D. Rogers, Leiden, 1575 (J. Dousa, *Poemata*, 1576, sig. Qv^v).

he remained, still a Catholic, and seemed to care for little
else but study and poetic exercise. He was visited by Victor
Giselinus (Ghyselinck), at one time a proof-reader in Plantin's
Office [1], a lover of poetry who was soon obliged to 'add the
study of medicine to the study of letters, applying himself to
it out of care for his family rather than out of his own free
will' [2]. Giselinus spent two months at Noordwijk in 1568 [3],
and returned in April 1570 to introduce another Flemish
humanist, whom Dousa had unfortunately missed when
they were both in Paris: Janus Lernutius [4]. The intimate
circle of these three enterprising poets—all of them well-
acquainted with the new French poesy and with Rogers—
widened when the two southerners, having gone to Louvain,
had the good fortune to find a kindred spirit in Justus Lipsius.
Dousa was immediately urged to come and join them, and
there in May 1571 [5] the four began a long and fruitful friendship: on shared poetic interests they built their future renown
which in another ten years was to make Dousa and Professor
Lipsius perhaps the two most famous of the Leiden *literati*.

Meanwhile, and in spite of solemn pledges, Rogers had failed
to keep in touch with Dousa after Paris. 'Then you said to
me', Dousa publicly complained after three years of silence,
'that you would not come to me with verses only, but with
whole volumes: but why should I, like a fool, complain that
you have never sent me a word, you who have obviously
never given me anything but words?' [6]
Soon, however, they were able to make up for years of
separation, and letters were superfluous. For having moved
to Leiden in 1570, Dousa at long last decided to join the
Dutch revolt. He gave up his secluded life and sailed to England on diplomatic business, less than two months after the

---

[1] In 1564: see M. Rooses, *Christophe Plantin*, Antwerp, 1882, p. 108.
[2] P. Hofman Peerlkamp, *Liber de vita Nederlandorum qui carmina Latina
composuerunt*, Haarlem, 1838, p. 162.
[3] Cf. J. Dousa, *Poemata*, 1576, sig. Ff viij; and Dousa's Album, f. 28ᵛ.
[4] See H. van Crombruggen, *Janus Lernutius*, Brussels, 1955.
[5] Cf. Lipsius' inscription of 8 May 1571 in Dousa's Album, f. 16ᵛ.
[6] J. Dousa, *Epigrammatum lib. II*, Antwerp, W. Silvius, 1569 (2nd ed. 1570)
pp. 20–21. See Appendix II, no. 7.

massacre of St. Bartholomew, in 1572—the year of Gascoigne's Dutch adventures, of Duplessis Mornay's escape from France, of Sidney's first continental tour—carrying a letter of introduction to William Cecil written by Hadrianus Junius [1].

[1] H. Junius to W. Cecil, Haarlem, 17 October 1572: 'S.P. Batavicae reipub. nomine ad vos profecturi legationemque obituri Ianus Douza, et Theodorus Neopyrgus [*i.e. Nieuburg*], rogatum me voluere, ut in peregrina sibi, mihi vero notissima olim regione, portum aliquem notitiae ipsis aperirem: quod officij genus quum denegare claris amicisque capitibus non possem, in magna amicorum, quos vel mors vel calamitas mihi ademit, inopia, unus ornatiss. Cecilli occurristi reliquus, cui illos tribus verbis commendarem, quem humanitatis comitatisque omnis laudibus cumulatissimum et compereram et expertus olim fueram, ac tanto quidem studiosus, quod per alium neminem quam per te, quo velut fidissimo Nestore potentissimi regni res feliciter innituntur, accessus ad R. Maiestatem interiusve concilium proclivior paratiorque patefieret. Ex his Douza ut antiqua nobilitate, ita ingenij et lepidi poëmatis gloria clarus existit: alter patritia familia et iurisperitiae laude non postremus. Dabit itaque illustris tua et nota omnibus humanitas, aures, uti solet, faciles istis atque adapertas, testimonijque mei fidem non elevabit. Pluribus vigiles tuas et sacras curas interpellare nolo, precorque Deum Op. Max. ut quam diutissime incolumis salutarem reipub. Christianae opem praestare queas'. (P.R.O., SP 70/125, f. 324).

III

YEARS OF INTRODUCTION

WHERE Dousa still had to make his way into English circles, Junius was eminently suited to arrange an introduction. 'Literatissimus Hadrianus Junius' [1] had last visited the country in 1568 to present his *Eunapius Sardinianus* to Queen Elizabeth, and his life-long interest in England had been undisturbed by the changing tides of the Tudors. This scholar had been thirty-three when Bishop Bonner had induced him to come to England. He had quickly attracted the attention of the poet Henry Howard, Earl of Surrey, while practising as a physician in his father's household. [2] He had then become tutor to Surrey's children, and there will have met at least one other contributor to Tottel's *Miscellany*, Thomas Churchyard, professional soldier and for half a century devotee to the Dutch cause. [3] In 1553, after the untimely death of his patron and three years in the Netherlands, Junius attempted to present his *Philippeis* on her marriage with Philip II to Queen Mary [4], and in 1558 renewed the effort by dedicating his *Commentarius de Anno & Mensibus* to her. Lastly, in 1568, he offered Queen Elizabeth his *Eunapius*, which was afterwards to be translated into English [5]. Her gracious reception seems doubtful when seven

---

[1] The phrase is William Camden's when quoting Junius' verses on Ireland in *Magna Britanniae regna*, ed. Amsterdam, 1659, [II], p. 32.

[2] See W. de Hoog, *Studiën over de Nederlandsche en Engelsche Taal en Letterkunde*, Dordrecht, 1853, II, p. 29.

[3] Witness his share in *A lamentable description of the Wofull Warres in Flaunders*, London, 1578, and in *A true discourse of the Civill warres Translated and collected by Thomas Churchyard Esquire, and Ric[hard] Ro[binson] out of the Reverend E. [van] M[eteren]*, London, 1602.

[4] See D. J. Gordon, "Veritas filia temporis' Hadrianus Junius and Geoffrey Whitney', *Journal of the Warburg and Courtauld Institutes*, III, 1939–40, pp. 228 ff.

[5] *The Lyves of Philosophers and Orators*, London, 1579. His *Nomenclator* was also translated (by John Higgins): *The nomenclator or remembrancer of Adrianus Junius*, London, 1585.

years later one finds Rogers suggesting that Junius should dedicate another work to her Majesty and give him a copy of the *Eunapius* to take along. [1] From all this, and from his published correspondence, Hadrianus Junius appears to have been one of the earliest intellectual links between Holland and England, and had he not 'changed this life for death, in the year of Christ 1575, at the age of 63, on the 16th day of the month of his name' [2], shortly after his appointment among the first professors of Leiden, Junius would have probably been a main figure in the present enquiry. He did find his way into English literature (after his death) when from his famous *Emblemata*—one of which had been 'Ad Vict. Giselinum' [3]—twenty blocks and much inspiration were taken by Geoffrey Whitney for his *Choice of emblemes* as published at Leiden in 1586.[4]

It is not surprising, therefore, that Janus Dousa, one day Junius' successor as official historiographer to the States, should have called upon the one Dutchman who was widely known in England and of similar scholarly tastes to give him introductions for his first visit to the country with which he was to become so familiar.

The official status of this small embassy ('legatiuncula') —'my own destiny, which was more fortunate than that of the commonwealth' [5]—is hard to define. Not wishing to depend entirely on the effect of Junius' letter, Dousa made sure of the reception of his dispatch by expressing it in two Latin odes, one addressed to Mr. Secretary Cecil [6] as a 'covering letter' for the other and more important one to the Queen. In the second he followed, perhaps unknowingly, the example of the great Huguenot Philippe Duplessis Mornay who, having just escaped from the Massacre, had arrived

---

[1] D. Rogers to H. Junius, Antwerp, 4 February 1575 (*Hadr. Junij epistolae*, p. 628). Rogers and Junius had not yet met in 1572: see p. 34, note 2.

[2] *Illustris Academia Lugd-Batava*, Leiden, 1613, sig. B ij[v]. See Appendix II, no. 8.

[3] Junius, *Emblemata*, ed. Leiden, 1585, no. 43.

[4] See Pt. II, ch. iv.

[5] See p. 23, note 5, and Appendix II, no. 9.

[6] J. Dousa, *Poemata*, 1575, sig. G iiij[v].

with a poem in which he pleaded on behalf of the Protestant cause [1].

Dousa deliberately addressed Elizabeth as

> Queen, issue of great kings,
> Yourself taught by the hand of the Muses,
> Second to none among the Graces . . .

The Queen was warned of the approaching end to 'religious liberty'—not 'Protestantism'—'as though she knew it not from former dangers of her own', and Dousa concluded by begging

God and the Queen of a wealthy island to make us see our country in its former condition, ruled by one God, and restituted to Him. Then we shall sing your praise with a worthier sound of our Zither, and the future will not belie our words [2].

Rogers, whose idea it was, perhaps, to win a learned Queen by poetic force, hurried to Kingston to meet his long-neglected friend [3]. Their reunion after eight years was moving: 'who could ever have thought that I should, in the middle of England, in London, find Paris?' [4] The Englishman simply buried his friend in books and manuscripts by himself 'and other learned friends' whom they 'had shared in France' [5], and Dousa spent those months in London eagerly copying great quantities of modern literature from the apparently well-furnished library which Rogers had collected in eight years of travel between the courts of Britain and France. After Dousa left England [6] and her Queen whose '*doctrina, eloquium, forma et pietas*', he had in another poem asserted, 'never could nor would in future times be paralleled' [7], Rogers' liberal distribution of reading matter did not cease. 'The dearest things to my mind', Dousa wrote, 'are those

---

[1] See *Mémoires et Correspondance de Duplessis-Mornay*, Paris, 1824, I, pp. 36–37.

[2] J. Dousa, *Poemata*, 1575, sig. G j^v–ij^v. See Appendix II, no. 10.

[3] See p. 23, note 5.

[4] Dousa, *Poemata*, 1575, sig. N iij. See Appendix II, no. 11.

[5] See p. 23, note 5, and Appendix II, no. 12.

[6] He was still in London on 20 January 1573 when Jacobus à Miggrod (cf. p. 44) wrote in his Album (f. 81). A meeting with Emanuel van Meteren is implied in the latter's inscription of 1584 'cum iam secondo illi se in Anglia obtulissent' (Album, f. 64).

[7] J. Dousa, *Poemata*, 1576, sig. I i. See Appendix II, no. 13.

letters which you sent me some time after my departure
[1573?] to accompany copies of Ronsard's *Franciade* [1572],
Belleau's *Bergeries* [1565]' [1], and other works.

It is curious that so stimulating an infusion of contemporary
French literature should have reached the receptive mind of
Janus Dousa through the library of his English friend. He
was to have ample chance to read these books during the
great siege of the following year, and their impact may have
contributed to the beginnings in the near future of a new
Dutch poetry.

In the middle of the same year, 1572, eighteen year-old
Philip Sidney had gone 'out of England into parts beyond
the seas, with three servants and four horses... for his
attaining the knowledge of foreign languages' [2]. Naturally
this educational tour would bring so promising a young
gentleman into contact with precisely the same people with
whom Dousa and Rogers were acquainted. Though there is
little documentation to ascertain exactly which of the illustrious
poets, patrons, and professors whom he could have met
in Paris, Strassburg, Heidelberg, and Vienna were in fact
introduced to him, some such contacts have been proved
beyond question. At Paris, in Walsingham's house, he was
able to feel the atmosphere so familiar to Dousa and especially
Rogers, even though Sidney's personal acquaintance with
the poets of the 'Pléiade' is uncertain. Driven out of Paris
by the Massacre [3], Sidney travelled for about a year through
Germany and Austria, spending some time at Johannes
Sturm(ius)'s famous school in Strassburg [4] where he renewed

---

[1] See p. 23, note 5, and cf. Rogers' poem to Dousa dated 'Londino.
Idib. Martijs M. D. LXXIII' (J. Dousa, *Poemata*, 1576, sig. Gg iii^V).
See Appendix II, no. 12.

[2] Licence to pass beyond the seas (A. Collins, *Sidney Papers*, London,
1784, I, 98).

[3] 24 August 1572. Rogers happened to be in Ireland (see Pt. I, ch. ii), but
showed his deep concern in a number of poems, e.g. two 'In indignissi-
mum Petri Rami fatum' (Hertford MS., ff. 65 and 85^V).

[4] See A. Koszul, 'Les Sidney et Strasbourg', *Bulletin de la Faculté des Lettres
de Strasbourg*, XVII, 2, 1938, p. 37 ff. Various poems in the Hertford
MS. testify to Rogers' interest in Sturmius; cf. also below, p. 73, note 2.

his recent contact with the great printer Henricus Stephanus (Henri Estienne). This renowned humanist had followed Sidney from Heidelberg to Strassburg in order to see him and present a small autograph manuscript of Greek maxims, in anticipation of later dedications of scholarly productions from his own press. [1] It was on this tour that Sidney began his famous friendship with Rogers' 'old Burgundian friend' [2] Hubert Languet. They first met either at Frankfort in the house of the printer Andreas Wechel [3]—a scholars' *rendez-vous*—or, more likely, in Vienna where Sidney spent part of the summer with him [4] and other ex-pupils of Melanchthon like Carolus Clusius (Charles de L'Escluse), a future Leiden Professor of Botany [5].

---

[1] *Novum Testamentum Graece*, Paris, 1576; *Herodiani Historiae Libri VIII*, Geneva, 1581. See M. Poirier, *Sir Philip Sidney le chevalier poète Eliza-béthain*, Lille, 1948, p. 259.

[2] Hertford MS., f. 369.

[3] Wechel printed Th. Banosius, *Petri Rami Commentariorum*, Frankfort, 1577, and W. Temple, *Petri Rami Dialecticae Libri II*, Frankfort, 1584, both dedicated to Sidney. See B. Siebeck, *Das Bild Sir Philip Sidneys in der Englischen Renaissance*, Weimar, 1939, pp. 182–183.

[4] See R. W. Zandvoort, 'Sidney in Austria', *Wiener Beiträge zur englischen Philologie*, LXVI, 1957, pp. 227–243. Vienna does seem the more likely place, for cf. H. Languet to August Duke of Saxony, Frankfort, 8 June 1577: 'Regina Angliae ante aliquot menses misit ad Imperatorem Legatum adolescentem summo loco inter Anglos natum, & ea animi indole, ut de nullius hominis virtute maiorem spem unquam conceperim.Ante quattuor annos cum proficiscens in Italiam iter faceret Vienna, ex paucorum dierum consuetudine me eo amore est complexus, ut ex Italia reversus sit Viennam, quo posset mecum aliquandiu vivere. Viximus itaque una per aliquot menses, viditque eum aliquando mecum Dominus Damianus a Sebottendorff. Discedens nuper ex aula Caesarea venit Heidelbergam. Habebat enim a Regina Angliae quaedam mandata ad Electorem Palatinum. Heidelberga unum ex suis Ministris ad me huc misit, & a me petiit, ut ad se irem, quod pro mea erga ipsum observantia ipsi denegare non potui. Inde profectus est ad Illustrissimum Ducem Ioannem Casimirum, qui nullum genus humanitatis erga ipsum praetermisit. Discedens ab eo recta contendit Coloniam, & inde Antverpiam, ubi reperit literas suae Reginae, quibus iubebatur ire ad Principem Orangium, quam ob causam non audivi: Nullas enim literas ab eo tempore ad me dedit. Comitatus sum eum Coloniam usque, cum id a me valde petiisset: . . .' (*Huberti Langueti epistolae secretae*, Halle, 1699, I, [ii], pp. 291–292). Cf. Appendix I, no. 4.

[5] The only letter by Sidney to Clusius which had survived was one dated

The untiring devotion of Languet, whose vast experience in matters of religion, diplomacy, and education remained at Sidney's disposal until his death in 1581, is too well-known to require any comment. In 1573 he wrote to Robert Beale, who was to be a travelling companion of his old refugee-friend Rogers and of Sidney, as follows:

We have with us an extraordinary young man, whom I greatly admire for his charming manners, his witty mind, and really a wisdom that generally exceeds what his age would lead one to expect. In one word, I think he is full-sail persuing virtue, and I tell you, happy the parents who gave birth to a son of such exceptional talents. [1]

These words can be paralleled by numerous similar statements —if not quite so parental as Languet's—from other learned gentlemen who with delighted astonishment were quick to appreciate Sidney's 'exceptional talents'. The good-will engendered by his educational tour, was a benefit to all, both for the present and in the future: thus, for instance, he was 'whithe Counte Lodovik the prince of Oronges seconde brother, whose honorable usage was', says Sidney to Leicester, 'suche towardes me, and suche good will he seemes to beare unto your Lordeshippe, that for wante of furdre habilitie, I can but wishe him, a prosperouse success' [2]. Sidney clearly attained far more than 'the knowledge of foreign languages' on this first tour abroad. He was appreciated by and became interested in the great yet intimate world of continental humanism, that of the diplomats who influenced his Protestant views, and the writers who initiated him in continental scholarship and poetry. The humanists saw in him the promise of realizing the ideal derived from their renaissance doctrine —and, more particularly, a Protestant, north-European doc-

22 April 1576. It used to rest in the library of the De Vos van Steenwijk family. The library was bombed in 1945, so Baron A. N. de Vos van Steenwijk informs me; and the letter was never transcribed or calendared.

[1] H. Languet to R. Beale, Vienna, 7 September 1573 (B. M., MS. Egerton 1693, f. 11v). See Appendix II, no. 14. Beale shares with Dousa the honour of having an exceptionally great number of poems addressed to him in the Hertford MS. of Rogers' poems.

[2] P. Sidney to R. Dudley, Frankfort, 23 March 1572 (o.s.) (*Works*, III, no. 6).

trine—though it should be remembered that they enabled him to see this ideal.

In the summer of 1574 Sidney was in Italy, Rogers at Court, and Dousa besieged in Leiden. In October, when Leiden was liberated, Sidney returned to Austria for the remaining months of his Grand Tour [1], while Daniel Rogers went with Sir William Winter to Antwerp on his first mission to the Netherlands.

[1] Leiden was liberated on 3 October 1574; Sidney wrote from Vienna on 27 November (*Works*, III, no. 20).

IV

A GATHERING OF DUTCH *VATES*

DANIEL ROGERS' many movements during the following few years make him an eye-witness of nearly every Anglo-Dutch happening within the political developments of that period. A diary survives of only some few months [1]; but his scattered correspondence and dozens of his verses record the details of countless visits to the Low Countries, as an independent ambassador, or travelling with Sir William Winter, Thomas Wilson, Philip Sidney, or Robert Beale.

Continuous friction between the Merchant Adventurers and the 'sea beggars' gave him an early opportunity to display his diplomatic talents, while the Prince of Orange's small confidence in an English alliance kept Rogers far from unemployed. The entourage of the Prince, the *'Pater Patriae*, for so they commonly call and accompt him' [2], was that group of Protestant diplomats whose future manoeuvring was to determine the early stages of the establishment of the Dutch Republic. The group included Philip Marnix of St. Aldegonde who 'feareth God, and is therefore greatelie hated in Bryssels and of al men' [3]. Marnix was to visit England for an early offering of sovereignty to Queen Elizabeth in 1576 [4] with that unfortunate Anglophile Paulus Buys, who one day was to be the prisoner of his champion the Earl of Leicester.

It should be unnecessary to repeat that busy employment by no means excluded these literary politicians from non-

---

[1] January-July 1576 (Lettenhove, VIII, nos. MMMXXXVIII–MMMCLXXI).

[2] W. Davison to F. Walsingham, Brussels, 28 September 1577 (Lettenhove, IX, no. MMMDLXXIX).

[3] T. Wilson to R. Dudley, Brussels, 27 December 1576 (Lettenhove, IX, no. MMMCCLXXVII).

[4] For an introduction to Marnix, see A. A. van Schelven, *Marnix van Sint Aldegonde*, Utrecht, 1939.

political activities. One can imagine that during their frequent spells of seclusion on the small islands of Zeeland, Dousa and Rogers with men like Marnix and Adriaan van der Myle [1] would concern themselves with literary matters. Rogers used his first few months to become acquainted with Hadrianus Junius [2] who had written to him after receiving some of his verses from Dousa [3]. There was an exchange of poems—just before Junius' death [4]—which, much to Dousa's delight, consolidated their friendship [5]. Nor is it surprising, therefore, that the English diplomat also availed himself of the first opportunity to pay a visit to Leiden soon after the foundation of the University, the spirit of whose inauguration, as discussed above, must have been particularly congenial to him.

By now it must seem a matter of course that Rogers should have celebrated the foundation in verse—his lines 'In Lugdunum novam Batavorum Academiam' quoted before. At about the same time he wrote a few more poems in honour of Dousa, the first of which contained the following compliment:

A quarrel about you, Dousa, arose among the gods, when Mars called you his, and Phoebus called you his also. Phoebus said, 'to us he has been devoted from the very cradle'; 'in our service he is', Mars said, 'because he has chosen a military profession'. Jupiter feared a sad discord between the two gods, and therefore said, to settle the dispute: 'He will serve Phoebus in peace, but Mars in turmoil of war. Dousa, o Mars, is yours, and, Apollo, he is yours also'.

---

[1] This poet-politician had only just returned from literary studies at Padua and Venice.

[2] D. Rogers to H. Junius, Antwerp, 4 February 1575: '. . . who I am, ask Charles Boisot and our friend Dousa . . .' (Hadr. Junij epistolae, p. 628). See Appendix II, no. 15.

[3] H. Junius to D. Rogers, Middelburg, 23 January [1575] (ibid., p. 476). See Appendix II, no. 16.

[4] Two poems by Rogers before Junius' death, 'Ad Junium (Middelburg, 8 May 1575) and 'Elegia ad Junium' (n.d.), and two of later date, 'Tumulus Junii' (Middelburg, 1 August 1575) and 'In Obitum Junii Elegia' (Dordrecht, 15 August 1575), survive in Hertford MS. (ff. 169, 29, 217, 31); the last one also in Dousa, Poemata, 1576, sig. Cc vij, which adds a 'Danielis Rogerii Elegia Funebris' on sig. Cc viii.

[5] See J. Dousa to H. Junius, [1575] (Hadr. Junij epistolae, p. 644).

You fulfil the words of Jupiter as they were decreed, Dousa, and serve both Mars and the learned Gods in times of war. For Mars is sweet to you, but 'dulces ante omnia Musae' [*i.e.* *Dousa's device*]; one hand draws the sword, the other stretches out for a book. Since both admired the vigour of your genius, Mars gave you a sword, Apollo gave you a lyre. [1]

This flattery—which called forth Dousa's protest 'I am not whom you think, not that Apollo about whom Rogers, that poet of yours, has recently been telling you lies' [2]—is hardly unusual. But it is curious that this verse should in its conceit repeat Rogers' poem on the University: Mars-Apollo or Mars-the Muses, and not the obvious image for the University of Mars and Minerva. This shows that Rogers was celebrating not a great Seat of Learning, but a recently liberated town where, within the youngest University of Europe, the Muses had found a refuge.

What he found were the tentative beginnings of Dutch renaissance 'poesy' and even of a 'Leiden school', so to speak, which in the following ten years was to include such names as Lips(ius), Dominicus Baudius (Baude), Georgius Benedicti (Werteloo), Janus Gruter(us), and Jacob Walraven, well before Daniel Heinsius made Leiden a European centre of literary scholarship [3]. Rogers witnessed the obscure early days from which, apart from Junius, who did not live to see the sequel, only two figures stand out clearly: Janus Dousa and Jan van Hout.

Leiden has had the unique fortune of bringing forth Dousa and Van Hout, two *vates*, one of Latin, one of Dutch verse. Both are called Janus: should a third Janus, the god, be with them, then all barriers will open up to their wit. Seeing that, o Leiden, he will call you happy in them both, he will wish your Keys [4] for himself. And Rome, which used to honour him, will have enough of Janus, will desert him, and will wish, o Leiden, your Januses for itself. [5]

In these two Januses, whom Benedicti justly describes as 'key-figures' in the history of Dutch writing, we find the juxta-

---

[1] Dousa, *Poemata*, 1576, sig.* v. See Appendix II, no. 17.
[2] Ibid., sig. M ij^v. See Appendix II, no. 18.
[3] Heinsius' influence on English poetic theory is to be treated by P. R. Sellin for the Sir Thomas Browne Institute Publications.
[4] The arms of Leiden show two crossed keys (cf. Plate 1).
[5] *Delitiae poetarum belgicorum*, 1614, I, p. 527. See Appendix II, no. 19.

position of various elements that were ultimately to create a new literature. Dousa was an aristocratic scholar whose first-hand acquaintance with the best writers of his age had already qualified him for most humanistic modes of expression with Latin as a solid means of international communication. Van Hout on the other hand was no nobleman but a non-academic Town Clerk, lover of vernacular writing, critical supporter of the old Chambers of Rhetoric, a man of small Latin but great energy. [1] At a time when vernacular verse was rarely published because those few readers who would be interested could always obtain a manuscript copy, their Dutch poetry had little chance of survival. Consequently very few of Van Hout's poems have come down to us, and those few are obscured by masses of printed Latin by his humanist fellow-writers. Van Hout was probably representative of the other poets in having also a personal hesitancy towards publication: 'I have never been much concerned with such honourable-seeming vanity in my youth, wherefore should I now?' he wrote in his testament bequeathing his poems to a friend (who subsequently lost the manuscript). But it did not mean that they had not, privately, been playing seriously with their 'ink-wasting toys'. From what one can gather about their first joint attempts, Dousa inspired Van Hout with a deep concern for the *bonae literae*—with some emphasis, probably, on what was being done in France; while Van Hout in his turn tried to influence Dousa to write in his own language. The result was, though on a smaller scale, the same kind of literary reform which Ronsard, De Baïf, and their friends had, some years before, advocated in Paris, and which, some years afterwards, Sidney, Spenser, and their group were to bring about in England.

The date when Dousa and Van Hout began to take an interest in each other's work is uncertain. A reference to Van Hout in a manuscript verse on the visit of Giselinus and

---

[1] Many data concerning Van Hout and the early Leiden poets may be found in J. Prinsen, *De Nederlandsche renaissancedichter Jan van Hout*, Amsterdam, 1907; J. Prinsen, 'Het 'gezelschap' van Jan van Hout', *Album opgedragen aan Prof. Dr. J. Vercoullie*, Brussels, 1927, II, pp. 217 ff.; and J. C. H. de Pater, *Jan van Hout*, The Hague, 1946.

3. Janus Dousa (left) shaking hands with Jan van Hout after the siege of Leiden. Painted by Van Hout in Dousa's Album(f. 102ᵛ), and accompanied by Dutch verses.

Lernutius to Holland in 1570 [1] suggests an earlier date than 1574, the one generally assumed. What does stand out quite clearly, at any rate, is that their proposed reform was really becoming articulate by 1575, soon after the siege of Leiden. Then a lasting friendship between the two prominent defenders, captain Dousa and secretary Van Hout, was initiated in quantities of verse—not unlike Sidney writing his *Arcadia* in banishment. Van Hout, who 'first ventured to touch the strings of the Dutch lyre' was the more important in that it was he, chiefly, who attempted to overcome the greatest and most characteristic obstacle of the time, that of finding a new poetic diction in the vernacular. In spite of his contempt for popular opinion and his admiration for classical and neo-Latin poetry he wrote in the vulgar tongue, Dutch. The great hesitation of Leiden scholars to follow him is a measure of the radical nature of his task. Sometimes, as in the case of Lipsius, they were quite unwilling to lay themselves open to such perils: 'what should I be but the laughing-stock of sailors and inn-keepers? Like Icarus who fell in his flight because he rose on deceptive wings' [2]. Indeed, Van Hout's efforts must have met with much more resistance in an academic world than they would have done in the metropolitan and courtly setting of Paris or London. And whatever we may think of the quality of these first odes and sonnets in the literature of the northern Netherlands, he alone had inspired that literature's growth. 'Will you hear the truth from me, my friend?', one critic, less confident of his successors, prophesied, 'I will tell you: while you live, Batavian wits shall live, and when you die, they shall die' [3].

One cannot fully appreciate the literary developments which took place in Leiden during this unsettled time without taking two more aspects into account. One is that Dousa by his correspondence and meetings with friends in Flanders and by the useful experience of his days in Rogers' library,

---

[1] Dousa's holograph in the Leiden University Library copy of his *Epigrammata*, 1569, press-mark 765. F. 17, p. 55.

[2] J. Lipsius, 'Ad I. Hautenum, Non esse aptum se Belgicae Musae' (*Delitiae poetarum belgicorum*, 1614, III, p. 305). See Appendix II, no. 20.

[3] Lipsius 'Ad I. Hautenum. De versione eius Plauti' (ibid., p. 328). See Appendix II, no. 21.

had been kept abreast of contemporary literature. The other is the vast amount of poetry (in addition to the few verses still extant) which Van Hout, like Dousa, is known to have produced before they began to formulate their views: divine poetry, psalms, odes, sonnets, epitaphs, epigrams, love poems, [1] at the same time as or followed by translations from Des Portes, Buchanan, Petrarch, Horace, Janus Secundus [2], and Plautus [3].

By itself this impressive list of literary exercises—enough, incidentally, to suggest that the 'new school' had started well before 1574—gives the outlines of Van Hout's intentions almost as eloquently as his intriguing address 'To the gathering and assembly of those within the new University of Leiden who are exercising themselves in Latin or Dutch poetry, and of all other lovers of the Dutch language' [4]. The address amounts to an Apology for Dutch Poetry, which Van Hout composed to introduce his (lost) translation into Dutch alexandrines of George Buchanan's *Franciscanus* [5]. It should be read together with two of Dousa's letters from the same year [6]. The modest sum is a light-hearted plea for poetry as a useful thing, tracing its ancient descent through inspired poets like Moses, David, Orpheus, and Homer, and for its practice as 'poesy' rather than rhetoric with a proper regard for 'new subjects' and a 'modern appearance': somewhat less than the English *Apologie for Poetrie*, but, except for its moral bias, the similarity is evident.

The struggle with a vernacular which scarcely seemed to

---

[1] These seven catagories are referred to in his own 'Tot het gezelschap . . .' (see below, note 4).

[2] According to Janus Dousa the Younger, *Poemata*, 1607, p. 130. Some of the Secundus translations survive (see J. Secundus, *Het boeck der kuskens*, ed. A. A. M. Stols, Maastricht, 1930).

[3] Plautus, see above, p. 37, note 3.

[4] 'Tot het gezelschap ende de vergaderinge der gener, die hem inde nieuwe universiteyt der stad Leyden ouffenende zijn inde Latynsche of nederduytsche poëziën ende allen anderen liefhebberen der Nederlandsche sprake'. Printed by J. Prinsen in *Tijdschrift voor Nederlandsche taal- en letterkunde*, XXII, 1903, pp. 219–224.

[5] *Franciscanus*, [Paris?], 1566.

[6] J. Dousa to J. van Hout, Leiden, 1576 (Dousa, *Poemata*, 1576, sig. S iij) ; J. Dousa to P. Melissus, Leiden, 1576 (ibid., sig. V ijv).

allow either the eloquence or the prosody of classical verse
—a continuous source of trouble and delight—need not now
be treated from the Dutch point of view. In this subject they
were to have a common meeting-ground with English writers.
But one even stronger link with England already existed in
the person of Daniel Rogers, that least alien of foreign visitors
to Leiden. For Rogers, whose interest in the martial Muses
of Leiden had appeared at such an early date, was by this
time finding his way into the very court circles which would
produce—or, more likely, were beginning to produce—the
Protestant group of courtly writers which has long been
mistakenly referred to as the 'Areopagus', namely the Sidney
circle.

He may first have become personally acquainted with
Sidney as a scholar, or as a faithful supporter of Walsingham's
Protestant policy, or as a lover of Ireland: when exactly they
first met seems difficult to decide, but again perhaps much
earlier than can be proved. His first demonstrable connexion
is, significantly, in verse. Written in 1575, shortly after the
young nobleman's return to England, it is the earliest poem
ever addressed to Philip Sidney.

To Philip Sidney, a most promising and talented young man

Now that you have roamed through the country of Italy, now
that you have met the people of France and have with wandering
steps explored the states of Bohemia after seeing the towns of
Germany, was it Ireland that was left for you to inspect, that land
beyond the western bays? I am inclined to think that Fate has
moved you to travel towards such coasts, to the distant plains
of Ireland.

You will not come to find yourself a visitor in these regions,
like most people who live as strangers in these parts, but rather
to teach them whatever you may have learned in all the other
places, and so to cultivate those barbarians. Thus, Philip, you
will show yourself worthy of your father whom Ireland claims
for its own father. Who knows whether fate will not leave you
to rule this country, a viceroy to keep the viceroy (his father)
company? For the house of Sidney was destined for the land of
Ireland, a house that is worthy indeed to prescribe the law to
a state.

Therefore, young man, prepare yourself for the rule of Ireland,
for you are the son of a viceroy, and born for command. [1]

---

[1] Hertford MS., f. 221. See Appendix I, 1.

Of course, this one poem—in which the prophecy gives an unexpected clue to Sidney's days of idleness before the 1577 embassy—is not enough to associate Rogers with Sidney's literary milieu. But many a reference in the five years following, particularly the long and relevant Elegy of 1579 [1], will demonstrate his close acquaintance not only with Sidney, but also with Fulke Greville and Edward Dyer. This again implies connexions with Gabriel Harvey and Edmund Spenser, borne out by one of Harvey's well-known *Familiar Letters*:

> You [*i.e. Spenser*] may communicate as much, or as little, as you list, of these Patcheries, and fragments, with the two Gentlemen [*Sidney and Dyer*]: but there a straw, and you love me: not with any else, friend or foe, one, or other: unlesse haply you have a special desire to imparte some parte hereof, to my good friend *M. Daniel Rogers:* whose curtesies are also registred in my Marble booke. You know my meaning.
>
> *Nosti manum et stylum.* G. [2]

If one fails to 'know his meaning', at least Rogers is seen to emerge in the 'Immerito' correspondence as one who shared with Sidney and Dyer the Anglo-Latin prosodic experiments of Harvey and Spenser. Rogers will appear again and again as one who is uniquely familiar with the progress of writing on both sides of the North Sea. But one thing makes his exact place difficult to determine: not a single line of his English poetry appears to survive. This puts us in almost the same position as Anthony à Wood who was obliged to

---

[1] See Appendix I, 4, and pp. 62–67.

[2] *Three proper and wittie familiar letters lately passed betwene two Universitie men*, London, 1580, conclusion. Rogers' Dutch kinsman Emanuel van Meteren was also to become acquainted with Harvey, as the first letter, signed by Christopher Bird, in *Foure letters touching R. Greene*, London, 1592, shows: 'To ... my very good frend M. Emmanuell Demetrius, at his house by the Church in Lime-streete in London. Master Demetrius, I earnestly commend this bearer, M. Doctor *Harvey*, my good frend, unto you: being a very excellent generall Scholler. Who is desirous of your acquaintance and friendship, especially for the sight of your antiquities & monuments: and also for some comference touching the state of forraine countries: ...' (*The works of Gabriel Harvey*, ed. A. B. Grosart, London, 1884, I, p. 159). In *Pierces Supererogation* Harvey gives a list of his 'worthy favorers' which includes in a prominent position 'M. Daniel Rogers of the Court' (*Works*, II, p. 83).

state that Rogers 'hath also published . . . *Poems* in *English* mentioned by other Persons with great commendation, but these I have not yet seen' [1].

While it would be somewhat premature to expect a conscious affinity between the two 'new schools' of writing at a date when the Sidney circle had not yet undertaken anything seriously, it may be worth noting, if only in anticipation, that both sides were already developing one similar trait through their admiration for the kind of divine poetry they found in George Buchanan's works. This, of course, is hardly surprising when one considers their common idea of poets as *vates*, of which 'the chiefe, both in antiquitie and excellencie, were they that did imitate the inconceiveable excellencies of God' [2]. Moreover, it must be remembered that the new poetry in both countries originated in groups which, though not to an equal extent, derived their characteristics from being determined chiefly by a politico-religious cause. In the case of England this became particularly clear when in these same years the Leicester-Sidney circle took the side of Walsingham against the anti-Puritan policy of Burghley. With their philosophical conception of 'divine poetry' and their obvious desire to assimilate the 'new' religion and 'new' poetics, Duplessis Mornay, Guillaume du Bartas, and 'so piercing wits as George Buchanan'—to use Sidney's own phrase—naturally excercised a lasting influence on their admirers' poetic ambitions. It has even recently been argued that Buchanan was a member '*in absentia*' of the Sidney circle[3], loved, admired, and emulated.

At the time when Dousa and Van Hout were first experimenting, and before their vernacular theories became fully articulate, George Buchanan, the leading neo-Latin divine poet, could not fail to be a source of inspiration. These writers were more concerned with themes and ideas such as were to be found in Buchanan than with the minor points of 'rhyming and versing' which have received such emphasis in modern times. Thus one is not surprised to discover that Buchanan's

---

[1] A. à Wood, *Athenae Oxonienses*, ed. London, 1721, I, p. 246.
[2] Sidney, *Apologie for Poetrie* (*Works*, III, p. 9).
[3] J. E. Phillips, 'George Buchanan and the Sidney Circle', *Huntington Library Quarterly*, XII, 1948, p. 23 ff.

work was known even before it officially appeared in print. How Anglo-Leiden contacts made this possible may be illustrated by the following example.

Rogers, whom Languet was to describe to Buchanan as 'communis noster Amicus, qui te unice colit'[1], had been among Buchanan's correspondents for many years, probably long before 1571 when he was thanked for his French news 'de statu Religionis et Literarum'[2]. It has been shown[3] that after Thomas Randolph, the English ambassador in Scotland, he was Buchanan's closest English friend. Subsequent to the publication of some of Buchanan's works in the late seventies through the interest of the Sidney circle, Rogers personally supervised the 1580 edition of the Divine Poems in consultation with Buchanan and many friends, some of whom are actually named[4]. Sturmius, Hottomannus (Hotman), and Dousa are among them. Dousa was a familiar name to Buchanan, thanks to Rogers: 'I introduced Dousa to you when you were staying in Paris, and am now with the author's consent sending you a recent edition of his poems', he wrote in 1576[5]. For Rogers was pleased to describe in this same letter that he had found in the Low Countries 'plurimos, duos imprimis tui Nominis studiosissimos, *Janum Douzam*, & *Philippum Marnixium*'—'whom you have known in Paris'—'Ingenio, Genio, et Genere nobilissimos'. Ten years later the poet Paulus Melissus Schedius (Schede) was to put Buchanan, Rogers, and Dousa side by side in his 'Ad Elisabetham . . . Epos primum' as representatives of three different nations, a fine compliment to Rogers and Dousa.[6]

---

[1] H. Languet to G. Buchanan, Delft, 20 February 1581 (*Georgii Buchanani epistolae*, London, 1711, p. 83).

[2] G. Buchanan to D. Rogers, Lethae, 29 July 1571 (ibid., p. 13).

[3] See p. 41, note 3.

[4] D. Rogers to G. Buchanan, n.p., 7 November 1579 (ibid., p. 50). Cf. below, p. 71, note 3.

[5] D. Rogers to G. Buchanan, London, 30 August 1571 (ibid., pp. 26–27). See Appendix II, no. 22.

[6]   O mihi si Musae tantas in carmine vires
        Annuerunt, quantis ad sidera tollere par est
        Praestantesque viros & Diis genitos heróas:
        Splendida virtutum memorans quam facta tuarum,
        Bella per & paces ex autlatum laborem
        Sublimi insererem thyrso! sed Scotica quo se

This personal contact is probably another reason why Buchanan's *oeuvre* found its way into Dutch literature on a larger scale than incidental borrowings, on a larger scale even than the derived work *Rerum caelestium liber primus* (1591) which Dousa's son Janus wrote after the first publication of Buchanan's completed *Sphera* in 1586 [1]. And indeed through these contacts some of Buchanan's poetry entered Dutch literature at a very early date. For at Leiden Jan van Hout had access to his works and produced translations of some of his poems. He translated not only *Franciscanus* [2]—interesting because it fits in with other anti-catholic satires like Marnix's *Beehive* [3]—and an epigram which survives in Van Hout's *Dienstbouc* (1602), but also the *Sphera*, as we know from references in poems of the Dousas [4].

It is interesting that Van Hout was able to translate the *Sphera* as early as 1574–76 (the assumed date), many years before its first edition and at a time when several scholars in vain requested Buchanan to send them a copy of his composition [5]. Part of the answer may lie in a postscript to the earliest edition (of only 310 lines of Book I), which appeared in 1584: 'The rest is *desideratum*', it read, 'in Mr. Daniel Rogers' apograph. Meanwhile the reader should use, and benefit by

> Terra, Caledoniis latê notissima silvis,
> Vate (nec immerito) jactat, Buchananus, abunde
> Qui latices plenos bibit Aoniae Aganippes,
> Hoc melius faciet. Facies hoc docte Rogersi,
> Cuius primitias sibi vindicat Anglia, quemque
> Fausta Albimontis genitura agnoscit alumnum.
>   Hoc & idem Batavus Rheni flaventis ad undas
> Sponte suâ facturus (ut est studia ad sacra natus)
> Non sine felici Musarum Dousa calore
> Aggredietur opus, priscique imitabitur aevi
> Nomina, perpetuâ semper dignissima vitâ.

(P. Melissus, *Schediasmata poetica*, Paris, 1586, II, p. 8).

[1] See J. R. Naiden, *The Sphera of George Buchanan*, Univ. of Washington, 1952, p. 16.

[2] See p. 38.

[3] See p. 58.

[4] See J. van der Valk, 'Jan van Hout', *Tijdschrift voor Nederlandsche taal- en letterkunde*, XXV, 1906, pp. 75–77.

[5] See J. R. Naiden, *The Sphera*, p. 26.

this fragment'.[1] It would be tempting to connect this edition from 'an apograph of Rogers', printed perhaps in Geneva, with Rogers' request in 1576 'that you would send us a copy of your books of the Spheres, for which I have asked you again and again' [2]. But this would rule out the possibility of Van Hout's using a Rogers manuscript in the preceding years.

The history of the circulation of this manuscript prior to publication is more satisfactorily explained in that letter to Rogers in which Dousa had recalled his first visit to England, his *legatiuncula* of 1572 [3]. For there we find: 'do you think that I could forget that kindness with which . . . you then communicated these works to me? Among others the work of the Sphere by that great Buchanan, of which—I have reason to recall the event—I received a copy from Miggrod [4] who had with his own hand most accurately transcribed it, in my honour, and with your permission'. At what date Rogers possessed a manuscript of the poem is therefore not such a 'profound mystery' as has been thought. [5] In 1572–73 he must have owned an early and incomplete version which could in his transcript circulate in Europe until one derived manuscript was printed in 1584. His request of 1576 referred of course to the later completed version, printed in 1586, which Buchanan was so reluctant to part with. The early version was the one Dousa brought to Leiden in 1573, a valued piece of 'divine poetry' which Van Hout could read and translate in the earliest days of his literary experiments. This is but one instance of the way such treasures might impart their message to scholars in Holland even before any proper literary traffic could be established.

Such an interest in the poetry which he himself had helped to transmit and the signs of promising developments in literature account for the delight which Daniel Rogers showed

---

[1] 'Reliqua in Clariss. viri Danielis Rogertis apographo desiderantur. tu hoc fragmento interea utere, fruere'.

[2] D. Rogers to G. Buchanan, London, 30 August 1576 (*Buchanani epistolae*, p. 26).

[3] See p. 27, note 5, and Appendix II, no. 12.

[4] Cf. p. 28, note 6.

[5] See p. 43, note 1.

in the poem celebrating his first visit to the University of Leiden in 1575. He immediately made his own contribution, again largely practical, and it was received with deep gratitude. 'I speak', Dousa was to write, 'of that wonderful collection of very select books which were sent to me from the most distant parts of France and had to be transported again from London to Holland'. [1] With due thankfulness Dousa dedicated the 'libri adoptivi et selectiora carmina' in his important collected poems of 1576 to his considerate friend, meanwhile blaming him, as usual, for being an irregular correspondent: 'be careful', he writes, 'you are dealing with a Dutchman, and, what is more, with one who is beginning to acquire a taste for the *genius* of this adolescent Academy; you know, of course, what arrogant pedants they are who suffer from a poetic calm; you must abandon the severer Muses and drive all politics from your mind until some other time'. [2]

Rogers did his best and wrote numerous verses that autumn. Besides poems to Thomas Wilson, to Burghley, and some to Dousa, he wrote one on the death of Charles Boisot, the Sea-Beggar commander who fell in a skirmish off one of the isles of Zeeland—where Rogers happened, as usual, to be present—and yet another on the death of Lodewijk Boisot, the liberator of Leiden. [3] He could, on the other hand, scarcely afford to

---

[1] J. Dousa to D. Rogers, Leiden, 1576 (Dousa, *Poemata*, 1576, sig. Kk iiij). See Appendix II, no. 23.

[2] See p. 23, note 5. See Appendix II, no. 12.

[3] For instance in the Hertford MS.: 'Elegia VIIIIᵃ Ad Clariss. virum. Thomam Wilsonum ...' dated 'Brila Idus Novembreij 1575' (ff. 33–36); 'Ad ... Thomam Wilsonum ...' dated 'Roterodami 14 Octobr. 1575' (f. 185); 'Clarissimi ac nob. Viri D. Caroli Boisotti ... Tumulus' subscribed 'Occidit ... incomparabili amicorum dolore III Kalend. Octobris 1575. ad orientalem Duvelandiae insulae aggerem' (f. 182ᵛ; printed in Dousa, *Poemata*, 1609, p. 483); 'Tumulus Ludovici Boisotti freto Mattiaco, dum Scaldianae Insulae hostilem aggerem oppugnavit, defiscente navi suo mersi, VI Kalend. Iunii. 1576' (f. 189ᵛ). An Elegy to William Cecil, written in Brill one day before the above elegy to Wilson, may be found in a letter by D. Rogers to [A.] van der Myle, Brill, 12 November 1575 (*Illustrium & clarorum Virorum epistolae*, Leiden, 1617, II, xxxi): '... Mitto his adiunctam Elegiam, quam ad Nestorem Britannicum, dum hic commoror, exaravi: ex qua & meum erga Rempublicam vestram studium cognosces ...'

let his thoughts drift from politics to poesy too often, for these were busy years. The Merchant Adventurers at Antwerp had elected him secretary in July 1575 [1]—his father had been their chaplain thirty years before—but Rogers does not appear to have taken his appointment very seriously. Perhaps he was too busy negotiating in respect of far greater Anglo-Dutch interests: 'I cannot express how much I have (these two years) tried to make the Queen take an interest in the Prince's cause' [2], he confided to Buchanan. For more than a year he followed the Prince of Orange from town to town and sent the results of his conversations and dealings in a regular series of reports to England. Few of them give such a lively picture of his informal meetings as an entry in his 1576 journal which records a piece of after-dinner conversation at Vere (in the presence of Robert Beale, and probably also Marnix and Paulus Buys). The Prince tells

how that he had bene in Englande about the year 1556, at which tyme he understood that the Quene which now is, at the coronation of Quene Marie, should have carryed her trayne: at which tyme Quene Marie had at dinner with her divers embassadors, wher likewyse the Quene did sitt, but after the ambassadors. The French Ambassador after dinner came to the Quene, which now reyneth, and declared unto her how that daye Her Majestie had carryed the Queens traine and satt at dynner; that he doubted not but Her Majestie should wer the crowne and that the other should carry her trayne. [3]

Further details would only mean a repetative list of the activities, literary and political, of Rogers in those months. There is, for example, the description of his unsuccessful search for Dousa at Bruges in December 1576 [4], the more unfortunate because Dousa had just left there after a whole week together with Hubert Goltzius, Lernutius, and Giselinus. [5] He often had meetings with Lipsius (in Louvain),

---

[1] See Merchant Adventurers (signed Thomas Heton, Governor) to D. Rogers, Antwerp, 3 July 1575 (*Cal. S. P. for. 1575–77*, no. 204).

[2] D. Rogers to G. Buchanan, London, 30 August 1576 (*Buchanani epistolae*, pp. 25–26). See Appendix II, no. 24.

[3] 'Journal de Daniel Rogers', 18 May 1576 (Lettenhove, VIII, no. MMMCXLVII).

[4] See D. Rogers to J. Dousa, Leiden, 25 April [1577] (B.M., MS. Burney 370, f. 10).

[5] See H. van Crombruggen, *Janus Lernutius*, Brussels, 1955.

who in the same year had written to Dousa of his love for 'your sweet Rogers' who 'in ipsa paene mensa extorsit epistolam istam' [1]. Besides, this must have been a decisive year mainly for the political career of Rogers. He was a successful diplomat who had gained the esteem of his immediate superior, Sir Thomas Wilson, the English ambassador. On New Year's Eve 1576 the latter went so far as to write this postscript to Leicester:

> Your Honour maye not forgett poor Mr Rogers, when any bysshoppes are choysen. Suerlie it is greate pitie to see learnynge and honestie joyned together to go a beggynge. He hath wel deserved a bysshoppes lyvinge, not onelie a pension of 50li. [2]

Rogers never became an Anglican bishop—perhaps his affinities with the Puritan party were too evident. Yet the idea did not seem too preposterous for Wilson. Rogers was now an enlightened diplomatist with a strong interest in Anglo-Dutch affairs; his familiarity with continental Protestant circles and his extraordinarily wide contacts in France, Germany, and the Low Countries marked him out as a most eligible ambassador for these countries. It seems reasonable to assume, therefore, that he might have claimed to have done a vast amount of work with regard to Anglo-Dutch dealings in preparation for the following period of eight years which preceded the arrival of Leicester.

He went back to England in February 1577 with letters for Walsingham, only to return to Flanders in the early days of March in the company of Philip Sidney, her Majesty's new envoy.

---

[1] J. Lipsius to J. Dousa, Louvain, 3 April 1576 (B.M., MS. Burney 370, f. 36).

[2] T. Wilson to R. Dudley, Brussels, 30 December 1576 (Lettenhove, IX, no. MMMCCXCIII).

V

ROGERS AND SIDNEY

EVEN to sixteenth-century politicians an ambassador of twenty-two must have contrasted with so grave a mission. Sidney's ostensible reason for visiting the new Emperor was to convey the Queen's condolences on the death of his father, but there is little doubt that the real motive of his first embassy was to investigate 'the ways by which a league between the English and the Protestant Germans may be arranged to protect the safety of our religion'[1]. Sidney's manners were so charming that Don John of Austria, in spite of his 'Spanish haughture', 'found himself so stricken with this extraordinary Planet, that the beholders wondered to see what ingenuous tribute that brave, and high minded Prince paid to his worth; giving more honour and respect to this hopefull young Gentleman, than to the Embassadors of mighty Princes'[2]. Even the Emperor, though 'few of wordes, sullein of disposition, very secrete and resolute'[3], was not wholly averse to an ambassador whom Languet could still introduce as 'adhuc quidem adolescens, sed excellente ingenio'[4]. It is true, also, that Sidney knew the Courts of Germany, and that the late 'Emperor had sent for him and had received him most kindly'[5]. But it would have been most unlike the cautious

[1] D. Rogers to G. Buchanan, Westminster, 28 February 157[7] (*Georgii Buchanani opera omnia*, Edinburgh, 1715, I, p. xx). See Appendix II, no. 25. Rogers' formal description of Sidney as 'Proregis Hibernici filius illustrissimae virtutis juvenis' would suggest that no personal acquaintance had been established yet between Buchanan and Sidney.

[2] F. Greville, *The Life of the Renowned Sir Philip Sidney*, 1652, ed. N. Smith, 1907, p. 32.

[3] P. Sidney to F. Walsingham, Heidelberg, 3 May 1577 (*Works*, III, no. XXIX).

[4] H. Languet to August Duke of Saxony, Frankfort, 'die Resurrectionis Dominicae 1577' (*Huberti Langueti epistolae secretae*, Halle, 1699, I, [ii], p. 290).

[5] H. Languet to August Duke of Saxony, Prague, 1 March 1575 (*Langueti epistolae secretae*, I, [ii], p. 75). See Appendix II, no. 26.

Queen and her shrewd councillors to have sent a young man as envoy solely on the strength of his virtuous manners and continental education. In this same year Sidney was almost invariably called 'the son of the Viceroy of Ireland'. This curious epithet, which made Sidney strictly speaking a 'Prince' and even a potential 'Prorex', was more than just a matter of decorum. For by this title he, the only 'Prince' in England, was able to deal directly with foreign Princes on terms of equality. Sidney was young, but he alone was qualified for such a series of Court visits. Thus he travelled round in 1577, as the Prince and promotor of a Protestant league; as such he would be remembered when returning to the northern Provinces for a second and last time in 1585.

His diplomatic business [1] does not now concern us, except that it involved a decisive re-union with scholars of the continent, not as a boy and a student this time, but as an illustrious courtier. During his first week in Flanders he was accompanied by Rogers. This included the embassy to Don John at Louvain and a short stay in Brussels from where Thomas Wilson, the ambassador, had written: 'I have provyded lodginge, and doe make my selfe readie to wayte upon hym, as he cummeth in, and I mynde to conferre with hym, and to give unto hym the best advise that I can' [2]. It must be remembered that Sidney's first host in the Low Countries was a typical example of the literary-minded man whom he was wont to meet. This same Wilson was author of a famous literary treatise [3], and considered by Harvey to be among his 'honourable favourers' [4]; he was also very familiar with the Low Countries, and a friend of Ortelius, in whose Album[5],

---

[1] See J. N. Bakhuizen van den Brink, 'Het Convent te Frankfort, 27–28 September 1577', *Nederlandsch Archief voor Kerkgeschiedenis*, XXXII, 1941, pp. 235 ff.

[2] T. Wilson to F. Walsingham, Brussels, 1 March 1577 (P.R.O., SP 70/144, f. 5^V).

[3] *Arte of Rhetorique*, 1553.

[4] Thus Harvey in the third letter of *Foure letters touching Robert Greene*, London, 1592.

[5] A. Ortelius, 'Album Amicorum' (Cambridge, Pembroke College Library, MS. LC.2.113), f. 19. Wilson signed the Album on 30 September 1578.

carried by Rogers, he was in the following year 'to have his symbol painted' [1].

One of the many literary friendships which Sidney made on this diplomatic journey was with the late Emperor's poet laureate, the German Pléiadist Paulus Melissus [2], and, what is clear from Rogers' epigram to Dousa of the previous year on Melissus' first edition of *Schediasmata* [3], one of the most accomplished friends of the Leiden poets. With more than average warmth Melissus recalls his early days with Sidney:

O, Sidney, renowned for your study of the Muses, son of the Viceroy of Ireland, again you will sail down the Rhine to return to your native country along the wide waves of the vast Ocean. The illustrious Queen of your *Britannia* is eager to learn what you will have to report from the Imperial Court on your return as her Ambassador. O, if Nereus and the Nereids themselves were to see me as your travelling companion to share your conversation and plough the long seas in a wind-driven barge: then I should not fear the black waves, nor the monsters of the deep, nor the turmoil of Eurus when borne on the impetuous wings of Boreas or Notus; because your virtuousness, O Philip, would warrant our safety; and that voice which, by its serenity, could hold the Emperor's eyes and speech spell-bound, that same voice would stay the raging gods of the sea and the tempests of the unhappy brethren who speed across the turbulence of the resounding waters. Although the savage force of Africus might drive us to the sea of the remote Orkneys: unhurt we should beat the salt stream with victorious oars, we could set our sails in the opposite direction and merrily arrive at the intended port.

But I can only make my way now, like Myrtilus, along the hard rocks of the Alps, and the dreadful chasms of its precipices. Wherever we may go, the gods be with us both and favour us; London will soon receive you—splendid ornament for cities— in its parental embrace; I, on the other hand, led by Vaquerius, shall be welcomed by the seven hills of Rome. [4]

Melissus, like many continental poets after him, addressed his lines to 'one renowned for his study of the Muses'. This is

---

[1] D. Rogers to A. Ortelius, Norwich, 19 August 1578 (Hessels, I, no. 76). See Appendix II, no. 27.

[2] The very title of an early work of Melissus explains his obvious affinities with Sidney and the Leiden poets: *Di psalmen Davids In Teutische gesangreymen, nach Französischer melodeien unt sylben art*, [Heidelberg], 1572. For Melissus, see De Nolhac, *Un poète rhénan ami de la Pléiade*.

[3] 'Ad Ianum Douzam Epigramma de Paulo Melisso' (Dousa, *Poemata*, 1576, sig. Gg v^v). The *Schediasmata* first appeared in 1574–5.

[4] See Appendix I, no. 2.

actually not only the first foreign tribute but also the earliest reference anywhere to Sidney as a poet. [1]

During some weeks with Languet—'the shepherd best swift Ister knew'—he was back again among his old friends from Vienna. Clusius was absent but gratefully acknowledged a letter which Fulke Greville, Sidney's travelling companion, had apparently brought him on a sightseeing tour in Vienna. [2] Another future Leiden Professor, the theologian Lambertus Danaeus (Daneau) whose works were already being translated into English [3], joined their circle by dedicating his *Geographiae Poeticae* to Sidney—'cui Pater est Prorex' [4].

When this mission, 'the first prize which did enfranchise this Master Spirit into the mysteries, and affairs of State' [5], had been completed, Sidney moved from Cologne to Antwerp, from there to Brussels, where a letter from the Queen was given to him in which he was commanded 'to visit the Prince of Orange and attend the baptism of his daughter in her name'. [6] Languet's letter is at this point incorrect, for

[1] Melissus does not, surely, refer to 'Sidney's reputation as a patron' (J. Buxton, *Sir Philip Sidney and the English renaissance*, London, 1954, p. 91).

[2] F. W. T. Hunger, *Charles de l'Escluse*, II, The Hague, 1943, p. 69, assumes that Clusius had not yet met Sidney, but the letter (pp. 340–341) itself implies the opposite: '. . . ad nos venit Generosus Adolescens Dominus Fulko Grivel, Illustris Legati Anglici Domini Philippi Sidnei consanguineus, urbis videndae causa, qui per dispositos equos, ut venerat, Pragam revertitur. Ei literas tradidi. Gratulor tibi plurimum qui et Domini Legati, et Domini Huberti [Langueti] rursus consuetudine sis familiariter usus. Utinam res ita me tulissent [ut] ipsum convenire potuissem. Sed quod licuit, literis amicis me salutavit per hunc suum consanguineum. Ei sane plurimum debeo ob tam benigne conservatam nostri memoriam'. (C. Clusius to J. Camerarius, Vienna, 12 April 1577). In 1582 Clusius dedicated the *Simplicium Medicamentorum ex Novo Orbe Delatorum Historiae Liber Tertius*, translated from the Spanish of N. Monardes, to Sidney and Dyer (Hunger, *Charles de l'Escluse*, The Hague, 1927, p. 154).

[3] See L. D. Petit, *Bibliographische lijst der werken van de Leidsche hoogleeraren*, Leiden, 1894.

[4] *Geographiae Poeticae . . . Lamberti Danaei opus . . . Lugduni, Apud Ludovicum Cloquemin. M.D. LXXX*, sig. ❡ 3. The same edition exists with a different imprint: *Apud Iacobum Stoer, M.D. LXXXIX*.

[5] Greville, *Life of Sidney*, p. 45.

[6] H. Languet to J. Camerarius J. F., Frankfort, 17 June 1577 (*Huberti Langueti ad Camerarium Epistolae*, Groningen, 1646, pp. 234–235). See Appendix II, no. 28.

Sidney was to stand godfather on behalf of Leicester who had just written to the Prince of Orange:

J'ay entendu par le sieur de Melville que vous avez envoyé pardeçà, le grand honneur qu'il vous a pleu me faire, me daignant choisir, entre tant d'autres princes et grands seigneurs de vos bons amys, pour le parain de vostre jeune fille, honneur que j'estime vrayement d'aultant plus grand qu'en cela je voye une démonstration singulière de la bonne affection que Votre Excellence me porte, pour laquelle je vous en suis grandement redevable, vous asseurant, Monsieur, combien que vous avez peu choisir auquel la chose eust esté plus agréable, ny que vous en demourera pour icelle et pour beaucoup d'aultres faveurs plus fidelle et dévotieux amy at serviteur, comme Monsieur Dyer, présent porteur, gentilhomme de bien et mon fort amy, vous dira plus particulièrement de ma part: par lequel j'ay escript à mon nepveu, messire Ph. Sydney (lequel, estant en chemin de retour de la Cour de l'Empereur, viendra, comme il m'a escript de Heidelberg, descendre par le Rhin de Zéelande baiser les mains de Votre Excellence), qu'il debvra suppléer à mon absence pour ladite baptesme; mais, où il n'arrivera pas en bonne heure et que Votre Excellence ne vouldra plus long-temps différer, j'ay baillé la charge à ce dit gentilhomme, auquel je vous supplie d'adjouster foy en ce qu'il vous dira de ma part et de l'excuser, s'il vous semble un peu fascheux pour n'avoir autre langage que latin et italien. [1]

Sidney arrived in time, however, and there was no need for poor Mr. Dyer to feel the embarrassment of his slight linguistic talents. In the last days of May 1577 he met the Dutch leader in Geertruidenberg and accompanied him to Dordrecht. To the bystanders—Greville, Dyer, Dousa, and Marnix among them—it must have been a rare occasion to see 'one of the ripest, and greatest Counsellors of Estate' [2] with the one man who might have rightfully reserved that title for himself, the legendary William the Silent. 'I love that Prince', Sidney in his turn wrote to Languet, 'and have in some way perhaps done him a greater service than he himself will have realized'. [3] That service and 'the prophesy concerning Orange which Languet had spoken of in Vienna' remain a mystery: but there is no doubt about Sidney's

---

[1] R. Dudley to William of Orange, Greenwich, 8 May 1577 (Letten-hove, IX, no. MMMCCCCXVIII).

[2] Greville, *Life of Sidney*, p. 27.

[3] P. Sidney to H. Languet, The Court, 10 October 1577 (*Works*, III, no. XXXI). See Appendix II, no. 29.

entry into the 'Orangist party', and the sudden, but apparently abandoned suggestion of Sidney marrying one of the Prince's sisters and thereby becoming Lord of Holland and Zeeland. [1] Whether this whole confrontation was a clever move on the part of Orange to play up to the Englishman's politico-religious and social ambitions, the result remains the same: after his first appearance in the northern Provinces Sidney remained an influential agent in and for the Dutch cause—an agent to whom Dutch (poet-)politicians would naturally have an easy introduction.

On the strength of what Sidney reported, Rogers was sent back to the continent on 26 June 1577 [2] to consolidate the Queen's dealings with the Protestant Princes. This was his third trip that year, but now, for the first time, he went independently as her Majesty's ambassador.

During Sidney's journey Rogers had spent most of his time at Dordrecht with William of Orange treating 'gravissimis de causis'. Only once had he managed to hurry across to Leiden, but Dousa, to his deep regret, was absent and there was no way of following him to Utrecht. Two letters telling of his fruitless call [3] are further evidence of their regular exchange of verses, books, and literary news, with Lipsius—still at Louvain—as their closest literary companion. Though he was to meet Dousa at the Prince's Court that summer, the next few years were to leave a *hiatus* in their correspondence, so Rogers wrote to Ortelius in 1580 [4].

The relatively unimportant Rogers was the Queen's representative for the Low Countries for the year 1577 in order to further her attempted league as inconspicuously as possible. [5] 'Serenissimae Reginae legatus clarissimus atque

---

[1] See M. Wallace, *Sir Philip Sidney*, 1915, p. 184; and especially D. E. Baughan, 'Sir Philip Sidney and the Matchmakers', *Modern Language Review*, XXXIII, 1938, pp. 506–519.

[2] See Bakhuizen van den Brink, 'Het Convent te Frankfort', p. 250.

[3] D. Rogers to J. Dousa, Leiden, 25 April [1577]; D. Rogers to J. Dousa, Dordrecht, 3 May 1577 (B. M., MS. Burney 370, f. 10, f. 11).

[4] D. Rogers to A. Ortelius, London, 16 January 1580: '[*Lipsius and Dousa*] a quibus miror me hoc triennij spatio nihil accepisse, cum saepius ad ipsos scripserim' (Hessels, I, no. 92).

[5] See p. 49, note 1.

integerrimus vir, vetus amicus utrique communis, Dominus Rogerius', as the Dutch psalmist Dathenus (Pieter van Daeten) styled him in a letter to Walsingham [1], was instructed to attend on William of Orange, whom the Queen had asked to counsel him with advice in the same letter in which she had expressed her gratitude for 'l'honorable treictement que vous a bien amplement raccompté le . . . Sieur de Sidney' [2]. In July he travelled with the Prince from Alkmaar to Enkhuizen accompanied also by Van der Myle, Dousa, and Marnix. Rogers did not fail to report how they had inquired after Leicester, Sidney, and Dyer. [3] There, too, were Buys and George Gilpin. A summary of the whole setting which prophesied the pre-Leicesterian embassies of 1584 and 1585 is contained in a report to Leicester of 3 October—the liberation day of Leiden:

I find the Prince the most desirous in the world of your Lordship's coming over, and it is the string he daily harps on . . . We fell to speak of persons to supply your room, to which I named my good Lord of Warwick, your brother, or if that might not be, Mr. Philip Sidney, both men so agreeable to his Excellency as in a world I would not have made a choice to his better contentment . . . [4]

Rogers then went to Germany where he held, unofficially, a most prominent position at the Frankfort Convent of September 1577. [5] He stayed, of course, with Languet, who had recently written to Sidney that 'here, towards the evening, arrived Mr. Daniel Rogers, who, as soon as he said he had a letter for me made my anger [with your negligence in writing] to cool down' [6]. 'Meanwhile', he added in another

---

[1] P. Dathenus to F. Walsingham, Franckenthal, 27 December 1577 (Lettenhove, X, no. MMMDCCX).

[2] Queen Elizabeth to William of Orange, Greenwich, 24 June 1577 (P.R.O., SP 70/145, f. 152).

[3] D. Rogers to F. Walsingham, Hoorn, 20 July 1577 (*Cal. S.P. for. 1577–1578*, no. 38).

[4] [W. Davison] to R. Dudley, Brussels, 3 October 1577 (*Cal. S.P. for. 1577–1578*, no. 293).

[5] See Bakhuizen van den Brink, 'Het Convent te Frankfort', pp. 257–258.

[6] H. Languet to P. Sidney, Frankfort, 12 August 15[7]7 (*Huberti Langueti epistolae ad Philippum Sydnaeum*, Leiden, 1646, no. LV[I]). See Appendix II, no. 30.

letter, 'we enjoy his sweet company and often make mention of you'. [1]

It is very likely that Rogers' verses 'on the portrait of the illustrious young man Philip Sidney' [2] belong to this date, the more likely because this unique poem on so controversial a subject as a Sidney portrait [3] seems to match the lost and yet so famous Veronese painting which Sidney had had specially done for Languet in 1574. Of it we know two things: firstly, that 'the features are on the whole well drawn, but that it is far more juvenile than it should have been: you [Sidney] will probably have looked like that when you were twelve or thirteen' [4]; secondly, that 'it would have been more agreeable if your expression had been more cheerful when you sat for the portrait: the artist has represented you sad and mournful' [5]. Rogers turns both youthfulness and sadness into some kind of a compliment, but avoids the description of Sidney as a gallant young gentleman:

Well then (may Divine Youth long encircle with soft down those cheeks wherein it resides), who painted you, o Sidney, in such a unique manner, and who spread this rosy charm lightly over your face? Who enlivened your forehead with expression, your eyes with radiant beams? Whose art has given your lips that keen expression? Has Zeuxis returned to this earth from the underworld? Have you derived that splendour from the fingers of Apelles?

But no, whoever it was that drew you with such art, he was greater than Zeuxis, he was a greater Apollo. For truly, the figure lives, and you, Sidney, live in it; who would have thought a human hand to be capable of it?

When I look at that image, so like your own nature, it looks

---

[1] Ibid., no. LIX. See Appendix II, no. 31. In a poem addressed to Languet, written on 10 December 1577, Rogers refers to 'Belius, Rogeriusque,/Antistansque tuis meisque amicis/Sydnaeus patriae iubar amorque' (Hertford MS., f. 363ᵛ).

[2] Hertford MS., f. 216. See Appendix I, no. 3. A reference to this poem in *H.M.C. Report Hertford* put Miss Siebeck on the track of Rogers' verses, but being unable to locate them she concluded: 'man musz sie vorläufig als verschollen betrachten'. See Siebeck, *Das Bild Sidneys*, p. 100.

[3] See A. C. Judson, *Sidney's appearance*, Indiana Un. Press, 1958.

[4] H. Languet to P. Sidney, Vienna, 11 June 1574 (*Langueti epistolae ad Sydnaeum*, no. XXXII). See Appendix II, no. 32.

[5] H. Languet to P. Sidney, 6 June 1575 (Ibid., no. XLII). See Appendix II, no. 33.

back at me with eloquent eyes. But oh, why is it muter than a silent fish, why does it not speak? It imitates your habits, for you are a follower of Pythagoras' praised silence, you seem to hear much and to speak little. The rest corresponds completely: the difference lies only in this, that you speak little, but that your picture is always mute.

The abundance of state papers of 1577 and the following few years bear testimony to active diplomacy between the two countries, with Rogers as an untiring go-between. The network of literary contacts was meanwhile being enlarged. One letter from Rogers to Dousa could refer, among others, to the following variety of topics: his delight to see the Prince in good health; his regret on having missed Dousa at Wechel's house for the Frankfort Fair; the intention of Willem Silvius—soon to be appointed printer to the States and to the University of Leiden—'to migrate to us with his printing office' [1]; his fear that Dousa's *Basia* 'though inscribed in our name' will not escape censure; his imminent departure to England; and dinner with the Prince's preacher Villerius (De Villiers) who reported the London printing of Buchanan's 'Tragedia Johannis'. [2]

Some lines in the Album of Bonaventura Vulcanius [3], future Professor of Greek at Leiden, and three poems printed in Goltzius' *Thesaurus* of 1579 [4] indicate that Rogers' pen continued to produce a regular flow of verses. He also appears to have thrived as a diplomat. One important indication of this is the *ad vivum* painting of William of Orange which was presented to him, some time after 1 April 1578, by the Prince himself. [5] Sidney exhorted Languet 'still more to

---

[1] See C. Clair, 'Willem Silvius', *The Library*, 1959, pp. 192–205. Cf. particularly N. Carenzoni to F. Walsingham, Brussels, 12 October 1577 (*Cal. S.P. for.* 1577–1578, no. 333).

[2] D. Rogers to J. Dousa, Antwerp, 16 Januari 1578 (B.M., MS. Burney 370, f. 12). See Appendix II, no. 34.

[3] f. 29, Antwerp, 14 March 1579 (Brussels, Bibl. Royale; transcription, Leiden, Univ. libr., MS. BPL 1912).

[4] *Thesaurus rei antiquariae huberrimus . . . per Hubertum Goltzium*, Antwerp, 1579, pp. 198, 199, 208.

[5] The portrait was discovered not long ago at Blair Castle (see E. M. Meijers, 'Prins Willem van Oranje', *Mededelingen uit de Civitas Academica*, no. 5/6, Leiden, 1952). A contradictory inscription on the panel men-

love my Rogers for my sake' [1], unnecessarily, it seems, for
the two were constantly together, especially in Duke Casimir's
circle. Languet sailed to England for the first time in 1579—
'Languet must make himself ready to pass the seas in his old
days' as Rogers put it [2]—and when Casimir, who vainly
requested Sidney to be his companion and counsellor, also
crossed the Channel, Rogers had the honour to be with him.
As early as 1577, actually, Wilson had thought Rogers fit for
a prominent position: 'I woulde wyshe upon my revocation
that some choyce man myght succeade [as ambassador]. Mr.
Davyson, Mr. Wyndebanke or Mr. Rogers woulde wel
answer the place' [3].

It is impossible here to draw a proper outline of that inter-
change of scholars, poets, printers, and ambassadors which
took place in the Netherlands in the late seventies. This was
the time between the Pacification of Ghent and the final
secession of 1581, during which William of Orange held his
triumphal entries in Flanders, while Louvain in the south
became Spanish and Amsterdam in the north chose sides with
the States. Literary events often interacted with political
developments. When Duplessis—for the second time after
the Massacre of St. Bartholomew—visited England in
1577/78 where 'ses plus confidens amys estoient messire
Françoys Walsingham, secretaire d'estat d'Angleterre, et sir
Philippes Sidney, filz du vice roy d'Irlande, nepveu du
comte de Lecestre, et depuis gendre du dict seigneur Wal-

tions, among other things, that it represents the Prince aged 45 at Dort
on 1 April 1572. It does not actually say that Rogers received the painting then and there, although this seems implied. 1 April 1578 is presumably the correct date: because on that day, when William of Orange
was really 45, Rogers visited him at Dort (see *Cal. S. P. for. 1577–1578*,
nos. 736, 744, 749)—the Queen's military aid being forthcoming at
last, thanks, probably, to Rogers' negotiations. Rogers already owned
three paintings of the Prince in armour and so requested an informal
portrait, 'as large as Marcus [Geraerts] has painted me' (D. Rogers
to A. Ortelius, Norwich, 19 August 1578; Hessels, I, no. 76).

[1] P. Sidney to H. Languet, the Court, 10 March 1578 (*Works*, III, no. 34).
See Appendix II, no. 35.

[2] D. Rogers to F. Walsingham, Ghent, 14 January 1578 [o.s.] (*Cal. S.P. for. 1578–1579*, no. 516).

[3] T. Wilson to F. Walsingham, Brussels, 1 May 1577 (Lettenhove, IX, no. MMMCCCCXIV).

singham, le plus accomply gentilhomme d' Angleterre' [1], his aim was no doubt political. Unfortunately he left without 'obtaining that which would have been salutary to the Christian common-wealth' [2], but not before he had inspired an illustrative series of translations: Philip Sidney began an English rendering of the *De la Verité de la Religion Chrestienne* [3] and Languet a Latin one, while Lucas de Heere, the designer of Orange's Flemish entries, also joined the ranks of Duplessis translators with the *Tractaet van de Kercke*, dedicated to the Prince [4]. At this time, too, as a result of political shifts, Lipsius moved from Louvain to Leiden, where for the next ten years his lectures were a major attraction in the Faculty of Arts. Even the writings of Marnix—to give one more example—were subject to the present tide. His English interest, to judge by the one English book in his library, Stow's *Chronicles* [5], was almost certainly non-literary. But in 1578, the year when he drew his device 'Repos Ailleurs' in Dousa's Album [6], the year when Leicester asked Davison:

comende me also veary hartyly to Monsieur Saint-Allagonde, and excuse me that I wryte not to him now, for I am mallincolly; and I wyshe full oft that he were here, as, yf shall seme good that any further dealing be with Hir Majestie, I wyshe he may come befor all others, as I think, if he had bin here, the matter had gonne better; [7]

in that same year Marnix's famous anti-Catholic satire—in its turn a manifestation of the same critical interest in church matters—was translated by George Gilpin, Rogers' successor with the Merchant Adventurers and a recent friend of Languet's [8]. It was published soon after as *The Beehive of the Romishe Churche*, and dedicated by the printer to Philip Sidney

---

[1] *Mémoires de Duplessis-Mornay*, I, p. 117.

[2] See p. 57, note 1.

[3] *A Woorke concerning the trewnesse of the Christian Religion*, London, 1587. The translation was completed by Arthur Golding.

[4] The letter dedicatory is dated at Antwerp, 28 June 1580.

[5] *Catalogus librorum bibliothecae ... Philippi Marnixii Sancto-Aldegondij*, Leiden, 1599, p. v.

[6] Leiden, University Library, MS. BPL 1406, f. 97.

[7] R. Dudley to W. Davison, 9 March 1577 [o.s.] (Lettenhove, X, no. MMMDCCCXI).

[8] Cf. H. Languet to P. Sidney, Cologne, 22 October 1578 (*Langueti epistolae ad Sydnaeum*, no. LXX).

himself. It is astounding that this general 'migration' concerned such a limited number of participants. In this migration we may recognize one trend out of many within the general revaluation of religious commitments among the intellectuals of those years. This was a gradual process and naturally of so private and often confusing a nature that in many cases it remains exceedingly hard to define the convictions of these men—singly or as a group—at any particular stage of this development, while a reliable indication of its necessarily great influence on their thoughts and activities is seldom found.

At Leiden, meanwhile, the University was beginning to show signs of life thanks in some degree to a sudden decline of both Heidelberg and Louvain. Not only could it welcome its first English student, John James [1], a fellow of Trinity College Cambridge and later a physician in Leicester's household, but also the arrival of a younger contingent of Dutch students —some of whom were soon to appear in an Anglo-Dutch context.

Among them was Dominicus Baudius, who had come to read theology but was later to return to Leiden, first as a poet and law student, and then as professor of History and *Eloquentia*. His biographer is clearly right in assuming that 'the eight months which Baudius spent in Leiden as a student in 1578 . . . exercised a most decisive influence on his life'. [2] For Baudius, a refugee's son whose mother had recently moved to Protestant Ghent, was quick to join the literary circle of Lipsius, Dousa, and Van Hout. And in making good friends with Dousa's son Janus and with Georgius Benedicti, he was already on the way to become a prominent figure in the coming generation of Leiden writers.

As one of that 'gathering and assembly of those within the new University of Leiden who are exercising themselves in Latin or Dutch poetry' [3] he shared those early days of literary trial to which only letters and some later editions of collected

---

[1] Registered on 21 September 1578 (Leiden, Senaats-archief, *Volumen Inscriptionum*).

[2] P. L. M. Grootens, *Dominicus Baudius*, diss. Nijmegen, 1942, p. 8.

[3] See p. 38, note 4.

verse bear testimony. Though little remains, there is reason to suspect some development, even in vernacular writing. Dousa's Album is found to contain a number of Dutch sonnets inscribed in 1578, [1] the year when Van Hout started an Album of his own [2] and gave it a Dutch verse-introduction; of 1578 also, a translation of Horace's 'Eheu fugaces' survives, [3] and in 1579 Van Hout wrote a Dutch sonnet—on the dullness of Dutch wit—in Ortelius' Album [4]. One should hesitate as yet to talk about 'the new poets' in connexion with that small Leiden circle. That these poems survive only in Albums emphasizes their private and informal character.

There is an interesting resemblance here to the obscure beginnings of 'new poetry' in England. In 1578 Harvey penned his flattery of the poet-courtier Sidney in a little book which, probably because it included an early poem of Dousa,

---

[1] By Th. Leeuwius, Leiden, 24 August 1578 (ff. 44—44ᵛ). In his first sonnet the writer recalls how often Dousa has listened to his poems ('. . . ghy' die u ooren ionstich / Zoe dicmaels hebt verleent to myn gedicht onkonstich, / . . .'), the second contains a compliment on the amazing poetic gifts ('Ghy die soe meesterlick u' liere cont doen clincken, / Dat t'al verwondert es, van sulken soet accoort, / . . .') of Dousa who has graced his Album with a Dutch and a Latin lyric ('U poetycks gesanck, dat gij in beyde taelen / In duijtsch end' in Latijn, seer constich hebt gedicht, / . . .'). It is not uninteresting, however, that a fellow-poet, De Heere, at the time of the Ghent entry looked upon Dousa as *the* Latin poet, whereas he found reason to suggest that Marnix should write of the Prince's glories in pious verse or prose in various languages: 'Dat Aldegond dan in Prose oft in schoon dicht, / (Want hy kantt even wel) en in verscheyden tale, / U wonderdaden groot, gheleerdelick verhale: / Op dat God zy gheeert, end kercke ghesticht. / En' dat Douza voort ga, na zijn schuldighe plicht, / En zijngh in zijn Latijn, als eenen Nachtegale' (*Beschryvinghe van het ghene dat vertoocht wierdt ter incomste van d'Excellentie des Princen van Oraengien binnen . . . Ghendt, den xxix. Decembris 1577*, Ghent, 1577, sig. B4).

[2] Leiden, Lakenhal Museum.

[3] A. van Loo, Album Amicorum, (Leiden, University Library, MS. BPL 1753), f. v.

[4] Subscribed: 'Tot een merc-teyken vande gewisse ende onbeveynsde vruntschappe mitten . . . Heere Ortelio binnen dezer stad Leyden . . . zeeckeren tyt geleden begonst ende vulmaect zyn de bovengeschreven nederlandsche verskens hier gestelt dezen xxvᵉⁿ Slachmaent . . . by zynen ende aller const-liefhebberen Dienstwilliger Jan van Hout' (Ortelius, Album, p. 231).

was circulated even in Leiden. [1] At that time the literary discussions of the English group will have assimilated the poetic theory which Sidney was soon—after Gosson's *Schoole of Abuse* in 1579 had provided the occasion—to formulate in the *Apologie for Poetrie*. The *Shepheardes Calendar* was the only contemporary English poem mentioned in the *Apologie*— as having 'much *Poetrie* in his Egloges, indeed woorthie the reading, if I be not deceived'—not, perhaps, because it had been dedicated to Sidney, but because Spenser had already put some principles of the theory into practice. The English circle was probably even less of a formal 'school of poetry' than that of the Leiden writers whose literary status was on the whole more professional.

The absence of anything like a record of their literary discussions at Court makes it difficult to grasp the actual setting for 'the new poetry' in England, but fortunately one useful account survives. This unique document, a long Latin elegy by the well-informed Rogers, outdoes Harvey's Χαῖρε both in length and in its personal touch. In more than one respect this only contemporary, though brief, 'Life of Sidney', deserves a more careful examination than its poetic qualities would warrant. [2] It is more than a happy coincidence that Rogers wrote his 'To Philip Sidney, a young man of renowned wit and virtue', in the then political centre of Dutch Protestantism, Ghent, on his last day there with Hubert Languet, 14 January 1579. There is reason to imagine that Rogers wrote it in the presence of Languet, and that he showed the result to those near and interested—Casimir, Marnix, and probably quite a few others.

[1] Harvey, *Gratulationum Valdinensium Libri Quatuor*, London, 1578 (Harvey, *Works*, I, p. xxxvii ff.). Book III is entitled Χαῖρε, *vel, Gratulationis Valdinensis Liber tertius*, and dedicated to Lord Burghley to whom Dousa addresses an ode on p. 5. Since Dousa, while paying compliments to Lord and Lady Burghley, apologizes for his youthful effort, its date of composition must be 1572 when Dousa visited Lord Burghley with an introduction from Hadrianus Junius (above, p. 25). The book later turned up in the auction catalogue of the libraries of Georgius and Janus (the Younger) Dousa as 'Gabrielis Harveij Carminum libri 4. [4°]' (*Catalogus librorum Jani ac Georgii Dousarum*, Leiden, 1604, sig. F 1ᵛ).

[2] Hertford MS., f. 42ᵛ ff. See Appendix I, no. 4. The poem is to some extent complementary to Thomas Moffet's *Nobilis* of 1593 (ed. V. B. Heltzel, *Huntington Libr. publ.*, 1940).

The elaborate opening and its typical concern with the
divine representation of Eliza's Court speaks for itself, and
may recall an actual pageant on the Queen's birthday,
possibly in 1578 when Rogers was at Court:

Now you reside at Richmond with its golden tapestries, the noble
work of King Henry VII, adorned with its row of varied turrets,
washed by the eddies of the Thames as the water runs past.
There the curved ceilings shine with gold leaf, there an opulent
refinement fills every room. And there, o Sidney, when the
Queen keeps Court and celebrates her birthday, there—I am
happy to say—you share the pleasures of ethereal life and see
the heavenly choruses coming and going.

First you see how Religion comes to keep Divine Eliza company,
graciously occupying the space by her right side. On the left
She sits who rules with equal scales, the dear keeper of our parental
soil. Prudence stands in front and gives good counsel of life: they
both temper the passions. Then comes brave Constancy who
fortifies the mind and holds forth the laurel wreath towards
victorious heads. Meanwhile you will see the Graces competing
with the Muses in making sweet melodies, with their voices, or
on strings and flutes.

In their midst she sits who embraces these divine beauties,
Eliza, and her love takes nourishment from their nectar. It is
worth hearing this singing of goddesses and letting the attentive
ear drink in their sacred hymns.

Need I speak of the bevy of illustrious Heroines, ready o
Royal Nymph, at your command? Outstanding among them,
o Sidney, your mother[1] and sister[2] on both of whom the Queen
bestows the greatest care. With them is the Countess of Sussex,[3]
remarkable for her fine wit; to you she is almost another parent
in proximity. And also among these Nymphs is Lady Huntington,[4] faithful sister of your mother, and a second mother to you.
But with what beauty does Lady Russell[5] surpass them all: she
is the goddesses' equal in wit, features and manners.

Let me remain silent about the others who are yours through
friendship or the closer bond of consanguinity. Their gifts are so
great that I fear our Thalia may only lessen their great virtues.

---

[1] Mary, daughter of John Dudley, Duke of Northumberland; in 1551
married Henry Sidney.

[2] Mary Sidney; in 1577 married Henry Herbert, Earl of Pembroke.

[3] Philip's aunt Frances, daughter of Sir William Sidney; in 1555 married
Thomas Radcliffe, 3rd Earl of Sussex.

[4] Philip's aunt Catherine, daughter of John Dudley, Duke of Northumberland; in 1553 married Henry Hastings, 3rd Earl of Huntingdon.

[5] Elizabeth, daughter of Sir Anthony Cooke; in 1558 married Sir
Thomas Hoby; in 1574 married John, Lord Russell.

For who could celebrate you with due praises, Lady Knollys, [1] who are second in beauty only to the divine sceptre-bearer? Who can properly sing your praises, Lady Howard, [2] noble ornament of the House of Norfolk? No one could aptly speak of your qualities, Lady Stafford, [3] for unequalled you flourish in gifts of grace and beauty—If Naso lived, he would sing of these ladies in triumphant verses, Naso, first laurel of the Pelignian land; and that Albius [Tibullus], knight of the Ausonian nobility, would not prefer his mistress Nemesis to such beauties, nor would you, refined Propertius, have always been concerned with Cynthia alone if you had seen such as these. My Muse has often urged me to speak of them, but sounds halt in my mouth, and fade.

This deviation leads up to a compliment for Sidney's own poetic gifts: it is of interest not only that the first item in Rogers' enumeration of Sidney's qualities should concern 'the poet', a not so common appreciation of that time, but also—to be examined later—because of the way Rogers discusses it.

Worthy they are, I think, to be celebrated by the voice of Phoebus, or of you, Sidney, or of you, Dyer. For yours is not a body without a heart, [4] nor were you only born in an illustrious family.

Jupiter has inspired you with a rare genius, the eloquence of Suada has taught your tongue. Whether you wish to speak out in Latin, or prefer the accents of Gallia, or rather express your feeling in Italian speech, nobody could do it more gracefully or better than you. But when your [poetic] passion seizes our arts, then how abundant are the streams in which your wit flows forth.

What did the Weird Sister sing as she spun the first threads of your life? Allow me briefly to touch on the things which the one Parce once ventured to speak as she stood by your cradle.

Before the most interesting part—an account of the past six years—Rogers, adopting the accepted epic introduction, brings in an emphatic prophesy of Sidney as the puritan leader.

---

[1] ? Lettice, daughter of Sir Francis Knollys; c. 1561 married Walter Devereux, Earl of Essex; in 1578 married Robert Dudley, Earl of Leicester (and so in 1579 was Philip's aunt); c. 1589 married Sir Christopher Blount.

[2] Mary, daughter of Thomas, Lord Dacre of Gillesland; in 1576 married Thomas Howard, son of Thomas 4th Duke of Norfolk, future 1st Earl of Suffolk.

[3] Dorothy, daughter of Henry Stafford, 1st Baron Stafford; married Sir William Stafford of Grafton.

[4] Horace, *Epist.*, I, iv, 6. The letter was addressed to Albius Tibullus.

It would be you, she prophesied, who, born of great ancestors, would surpass your great descent by the nobility of your mind; whom every goddess would honour with her own special gift, and who would be sacred to Virtue, the Muses, and the gods.

Here the man is born, she said, who will travel to many countries, who will become familiar with the manners and minds of the world; who will be master of the arts of peace and war alike, who will ever, at pleasure, control both powers. Under his leadership Religion, dressed in modest rites, will firmly and with a pure voice establish God in his churches! With his support Themis will protect equality of rights: and he will win the esteem of Queens and Dukes. Him, Virtue and Fortune will raise in common agreement, and him they will place in the highest position.

Thus she spoke: and so as to make the words she had uttered come true, she offered your lips pure kisses as a libation.

Those words have indeed come true, and the Parce has not spoken in vain: every word has been fulfilled as prophesied. When you had only just been born, a swarm of bees took you from the cradle and poured their honey on your lips. Then the eloquent Muses shaped you with their own hands: they cultivated your tongue and your manners. Each vied with the other to adorn you with her gift, to leave all her tributes in your cradle. Gracious Venus gave you beauty, the Graces wit, and Pallas took care of your judgement and eloquence. Hence all those remarkable rich gifts of your heart, at which old men stand amazed in great admiration.

Rogers makes no reference to Sidney's life before the beginning of his period abroad, the Grand Tour in terms of a continental Protestant education. [1] Apart from one of the very few extant allusions to Sidney at Paris during the Massacre, the passage reveals quite definitely where Sidney met Languet and what Languet taught him at Vienna.

Then the *Genius* took you to distant countries, and taught you what to gain from the regions of France: here, too, you were when malicious Gallia allowed her own father, Coligny, to be killed by an unholy woman [*i.e. Catherine de Medici*], when the town of Paris raged at the children, girls, mothers, and old

---

[1] Cf. the same subject, if in even more general terms, in Harvey's Χαῖρε: 'At tua sunt privata magis Praeconia: Te, te / Gallica Nobilitas; te, te Germanica valde / Admirata fuit; te, te novus Induperator / Mirifice coluit: (celebris Legatio multum / Addiderat decoris): tam forti pectore, tanto / Judicio, tam spectata virtute refertum, / Tot literis Juvenem: Stephanus tibi multa trophaea / Ingenii statuit: Languetus plura: sed unus / Plurima Banosius, nives signanda lapillo: / Banosius, pars magna animi, bona portio nostri.' (Harvey, *Works*, I, xxxvii).

men, who were her own offspring. But when you were exposed
to such great dangers, the Gods commanded you to go and
visit the states of Germany. There you heard what arts are
taught by holy Sturmius, the leader and father of the Aonian
herd. Full of which, you wished to view the land of Italy, in
order to learn whatever the Latin states could teach you. Then
you stayed with great fascination in Austria, and with wandering
eyes you have seen the country of Bohemia. In those regions you
began your friendship with Languet, Languet with his firm
knowledge of law. He guided you through the histories and
origins of states, he was the tutor who determined your judgement.
I think that you might even have thought of visiting the
Antipodes if the Queen had not recalled you to your native soil.

Rogers proceeds to describe Sidney's intended life of action
(before his difficulties with the Queen over Anjou), and
sheds new light on Sidney's military ambitions in an evocative
representation of his life at Court. Perhaps one should not
read 'Stella' into his 'mixing with Stars', but the revealing
passage on Sidney and the foreign ambassador compensates
for the absence of Penelope Rich.

All the things which you have seen in your early manhood have
been added to your subtle senses, you blessed man: they have
made you the more welcome at powerful Courts, and the more
esteemed in your opinion, o Royal Eliza.
Need I speak of how the Queen selected you when you were
in the very flower of youth, selected you alone among numerous
grown-up men. To pronounce her words before the face of
the great Caesar she sent you, and to you she confided the deepest
secrets of her mind. Even Germany was no less amazed at your
accomplishments than your own country had been—and rightly
so. Leicester himself could not have loved you better than Casimir,
the Palatine, loves you. When he was about to lead his powerful
phalanxes to war, he asked you to be the sharer of his fortunes.
For your blood does not freeze in a sluggish heart, but you are
skilful in the duties of war and peace alike. We know with what
immediate enthusiasm you wanted to be hei soldier when the
Queen fitted out her fleet against the enemy. We also know at
what great expense the spirit of war made you choose armour so
that Duke Casimir would be able to proceed to the Netherlands—
for truly, a spirit of greater constancy than would be in so tender
an age rose up in you, and wisdom flowed forth with fine eloquence.
Must I speak of how warmly, on your return from the Roman
Emperor's Court, you were welcomed by the whole realm—
which, recently your country, had now almost become your house—

while the Queen commanded you to remain in her presence: and so, whether she walks with wandering steps through the green fields which one sees from the nearby Court of Richmond, or whether she takes a walk through the sunny gardens, you are there, faithfully ready to wait upon her Majesty. If it pleases the goddess to ride into the gay fields, you will mount your horse and presently keep your Mistress company. And when an ambassador from a distant country arrives she first commends him to your good care. And whatever you are doing, you must be close to the Queen, whether she is seriously occupied or pleases to be merry. O fortunate man, who as the servant of Eliza can mix with Stars—yea, goddesses. And need I speak of how often she merrily chirps with you, and of how that Royal Nymph delights the company with her ready wit. By condescending to favour your wishes, how much your obedient services must please her.

Let me add how ready both your uncles are there to smooth your path to the true height of great honour: Warwick's zeal for Mars, Leicester's for Jupiter, both of them fathers and reliable supporters of their country. These two cast their light, like twin Stars, before their nephew, and shine like the Lesser Bear on your ship's stern. Yea, there, also, is your father, the leader from the land of Inverna; so that nothing is left for you to wish for. Whatever number of accomplished men are with you, warriors and scholars, the Court beholds none greater than these three.

He refers next to Dyer and Greville as Sidney's best friends, showing that their friendship was based on more than common literary interests. What is more, Rogers does not even record the arts as an item of their discussions, but only law, religion, and moral philosophy: although poetry as defined in the *Apologie* is the obvious next step and synthesis of their philosophizing.

Nor are you without a faithful and happy circle of companions in whom, in close friendship, there abounds a pious love. In divine virtue Dyer, keeper of judgement, storer of wit, excells. Next comes Fulke whom you have known since the earliest days of manhood, Fulke, dear offspring of the House of Greville. With them you discuss great points of law, God, or moral good, when time permits these pious studies. You are all ornaments of the Court, its favourites almost—the Royal Court (Nemesis be my witness) is therefore dearer to me.

If you were to allow us to be loved as one of them, that were enough, that is the culmination of my wishes.

But where does my love for you drag me in my simple verses? Desist, Muse, such matter should properly resound in heroic verse. But it is because I, while executing the Queen's commands in this part of Belgium, have joined Languet—your Languet, and also mine. Frequently we talk of you, Sidney, and love commands me to write to you of our talks about you.

Am I wrong, or do you also—in spite of distant separation—feel the same, and does it sound from here agreeably in your ears? But I conclude and leave the rest to the Muses so that you will not say I cannot bear my happiness.

Not as a poet, therefore, but by means of his poetry do we find Rogers in a sense entreating admission to the courtly sessions of Sidney, Greville, and Dyer. The request is so bold that one has good cause to wonder whether it had not already been granted. At any rate, this Ghent *Elegia* suggests that Daniel Rogers was particularly familiar with Philip Sidney during some of the most interesting years of the literary development of both countries.

VI

THE ECLIPSE OF ROGERS

Rogers' opportunities for mediation between English and Dutch literary circles were unfortunately brought to an abrupt end in 1580. His travels had often taken him through dangerous regions. Only recently, in the early spring of 1578, there was a rumour that he had been taken prisoner. On hearing it, Melissus (in Nuremberg) had immediately sent two worried letters, one to Ortelius in Antwerp [1] and one to Dousa at Leiden, begging for news about Rogers 'for whom my love is extraordinarily great' [2]. Davison, however, could report that 'some of the Prince's horsemen, arriving by chance, had . . . rescued him and conducted him on his way' [3]. But on his way to Rudolph II and the Duke of Saxony in 1580 Rogers was less fortunate [4]. He was imprisoned and put under the guard of that same Maarten Schenk—at the time on the Spanish side—on whom Leicester was to bestow such exceptional honours at Utrecht on St. George's Day 1586 [5].

The news soon spread, and his gaoler, eager for a liberal ransom, did little to prevent it. Its effect was remarkable in that it moved to activity the pens of those learned gentlemen who had so far figured as his closest 'intellectual friends'

---

[1] P. Melissus to A. Ortelius, Nuremberg, 25 March 1578 (Hessels, I, no. 74).

[2] P. Melissus to J. Dousa, Nuremberg, 25 March 1578 (B.M., MS. Burney 370, f. 79). See Appendix II, no. 36.

[3] W. Davison to W. Cecil, Antwerp, 29 March 1578 (*Cal. S.P. for. 1577–1578*, no. 749).

[4] His instructions were dated 7 September 1580 (B.M., MS. Harl. 33. C. 9, f. 327). For a description of the captivity of Rogers and subsequent political activity, see J. N. Bakhuizen van den Brink, 'Daniel Rogers, Engelsch gevangene te Breedevoort, 1580–1584', *De Gids*, 1943, I, pp. 26–37, 82–96. The documents quoted in this chapter are not found in the article.

[5] J. Stow, *The annales*, London, 1615, p. 716.

rather than cause any serious political disturbance. It is curious, also, that the earliest (surviving) letter concerning his captivity should be addressed to Sidney and written by Languet who reported from Antwerp that 'our mutual friend Daniel Rogers, whom your Queen has sent to Germany, has been taken prisoner by bandits near the town of Cleves, and abducted to the castle of Blyenbeck which belongs to Maarten Schenck' [1]. Languet's point in writing was plain: for, he continued, 'it is your business to procure his liberty, since the Prince of Orange can do nothing about this case, the men who have seized Rogers being his most embittered enemies.' That Sidney did intervene on behalf of 'communis noster amicus' seems plausible when one finds that it was probably his father-in-law Walsingham who at last undertook negotiations. Rogers needed this concern, for Schenk's own instructions illustrate only too well how powerless he desired his prisoner to be:

Monsieur et frere Son Excellence m'a commandé de vous escrire que l'Intention et volonté unicque de son Excellence est que l'ambassadeur [D. Rogers] de 'Angleterre prisonnier soit par vous estroitenant tenu et gardé en sa chambre, sans y admettre personne pour communicquer avecq luy, et sur et sur tout porter soing que ne luy soit permis d'escrire a personne. Item que vous faciez courir le bruit que Ledit prisonnier est transporté ailleurs.[2]

'We are very worried about Mr. Rogers here,' Camden said to Ortelius, 'and I am anxious to know whither you will direct the force of your inventiveness.' [3] But as long as no

---

[1] H. Languet to P. Sidney, Antwerp, 22 October 1580 (*Langueti epistolae ad Sydnaeum*, no. XCVI (= XCIV)). See Appendix II, no. 37. Cf. B. de Mendoza to the King of Spain, London, 23 October 1580: 'Rogers ... has been captured ... because they saw he was burning some papers. The Queen has written to the prince of Parma about it, without sending word to me.' (*Cal. S.P. Span. 1580–1586*, no. 50).

[2] M. Schenck to Duke of Anholt, 20 November 1580 (B.M., MS. Cotton Galba C VII, f. 97); heading 'The very woordes of Skinkes Letter transelatyd out of Douche into Frenche'.

[3] W. Camden to A. Ortelius, Westminster, 22 November 1580 (*V. Cl. Gulielmi Camdeni epistolae*, ed. Th. Smith, London, 1691, no. IX). See Appendix II, no. 38; Cf. W. Camden to T. Sackville, [January 1580] (ibid. no. X): 'Accepisti, opinor, ut ille ... abductus fuerit in Westphaliam, jam tertium mensem detentus'.

effective measures were taken, Rogers was left to his own devices. Languet continued his alarming reports:

The roads along which one goes into Germany are infested with bandits, so that no one dares to expose himself to them. Our unfortunate Rogers experienced this to his great disadvantage, and I am very unhappy about his situation. He has recently succeeded in deceiving his appointed guards to escape from there with the help of some woman, but he was stayed, and I learn that he is now detained in even closer custody than before. [1]

Languet repeated the case of 'Daniel Rogers, our mutual friend, who honours you to an exceptional degree', to George Buchanan in a letter from Delft, where he spent the winter, 'only three hours' distance from Leiden, or *Lugdunum Batavorum* as they already say, where Justus Lipsius and the Poet Janus Dousa live, learned and famous men'. [2]

The sad chorus of anxious friends was not a little strengthened by the poet Melissus. Verses to George Gilpin—twice successor to Rogers [3]—included a request for royal instructions to act on the prisoner's behalf. [4] It showed his genuine interest in a man to whom he often referred in his poems, to whom he dedicated some elegant lines on the swans of the Thames, [5] and whom, moreover, he was to select for an honourable part in the opening lines of a book of poetry addressed to the Queen:

I want the witnesses of my verses to be both SIDNEY and ROGERS. [6]

Gilpin was not the only one to whom Melissus looked for support, but Dousa and Lipsius were also enlisted:

I am forced to be idle and yet to hear at a distance in my unwilling ears the iron chains and cruel fetters of Rogers in his captivity, and through the silent air to ply the mute plains of Pegnitz with my weeping complaint... Who will report to me

---

[1] H. Languet to R. Beale, Delft, 15 February 1581 (B.M., MS. Egerton 1693, f. 46). See Appendix II, no. 39.

[2] H. Languet to G. Buchanan, Delft, 20 February 1581 (*Buchanani epistolae*, pp. 83–84). See Appendix II, no. 40.

[3] First with the Merchant Adventurers at Antwerp, now as her Majesty's ambassador in Germany.

[4] 'Ad Georgium Gilpinum, Reginae ad comitia Augustana legatum' (Melissus, *Schediasmata*, 1586, p. 440).

[5] 'Ad Danielem Rogersium Reginae Angliae legatum' (ibid., pp. 163–164).

[6] Ibid., p. 165. See Appendix II, no. 41.

—and when?—that cheerful ROGERS' chains have been broken, and that he may at last in liberty enjoy the open air?[1]

By now everybody knew about his predicament—except some gentleman in Groningen who still hoped to get three travelling noblemen introduced to him on their arrival in England [2]. But in spite of whatever pressure may have been exercised, his relief was not procured. Plantin, for instance, was obliged to notify Buchanan that autumn about a delay in publishing a selection from his works, owing to the absence of Rogers [3]. The most personal efforts, meanwhile, seem to have come from his sister, who appears to have married into another literary family, the Proctors [4]. For when it looked as if his captive brother-in-law Daniel would have to endure the hardships of another winter, James Proctor appealed to Walsingham in these moving terms:

My humble dutye to your honour considerid, my poore wyfe being sister to mr Daniell Rogers, (whoe as your Honour dooth well know,) was an yarnest suyter allmost all the last wynter, as well to your selfe, as to the rest of the honorables of her majesties prevy counsayle, for her sayd brother beyng sent of her majesties affayres beyonde the seas, and now a presoner in thoes partes; to be inlarged; all which suytes and travell as yet hath taken smale effecte or none, for the poore man continueth a presoner still in most miserable case, sethence which tyme: his poore sister hath once more renewed her suyte to her majesties owne personn. and to the rest of the counsayle, being alltogether at the counsayle table: and booth of her Majestie and them hath recevid most gratious and comfortable promisses; all this was donn in your honors Absence, which was no smale grefe to the poore wooman, for that her gretest trust was in your Honour. not withstanding this, the poor man continueth still A presoner without all hoope of deliveraunce, with out comfort any way, saving in god aloune; his lodging not swete, without Lyght, nether bookes, penn, ynke,

---

[1] 'Ad Ianum Dousam Nordovicem, et Iustum Lipsium Iscanium' (ibid., p. 417). See Appendix II, no. 42.

[2] A. Freijttagh to A. Ortelius, Groningen, 12 August 1581 (Hessels, I, no. 109).

[3] C. Plantin to G. Buchanan, Antwerp, 7 October 1581. (*Correspondance de Christophe Plantin*, ed. J. Denucé, Antwerp-The Hague, 1916, VI, no. 953). Perhaps Rogers was in possession of the MSS., and the intended editor.

[4] Among them are John Proctor, historian, and author of the *Historie of Wyates Rebellion*, 1584, and Thomas Proctor, author, and editor of e.g. *A gorgious Gallery of gallant Inventions*, 1578.

or paper, his diet worse then I dare for shame speake of; and every day worse and worse; in consideration where of, he hath found the meanes to signify unto me, and other of his frendes of his miserable estate, praying us to become humble suyters unto your Honour for his inlargement, which as we subpoose must be wrought by your good meanes, and that wheras two hundred poundes was appoynted, by your Honour to be deliverid unto him by the governour of the Inglish howse at Antwarpe, whereof he hath recevid as yet but fyftie poundes his humble suyte is that your Honoures commandeme[nt] may be renewed, and the money to be deliverid to such as he shall appoynt there to receve hit, for his relese, or other wyse there is no hoope of his lyfe to continue any time, and thus leaving all the rest to your ryght honourable good consideration, very sorry and ashamed to truble your Honour with so many wordes, I leave you to god. [1]

'Poore man' indeed, for in spite of repeated attempts by Leicester and Walsingham to have Mendoza, the Spanish ambassador in London, imprisoned as a hostage, [2] it was to be January 1584 before a collection was held to pay for Rogers' return [3]. And—with Melissus still pressing Dousa 'see that I know whether Rogers has been freed' [4]—it was a further year before Joannes Sturmius, once Sidney's teacher, could at last write this cheerful note to Walsingham:

Behold! Even before you, I have seen your and my Rogers: of whom I have so frequently written to you . . . I was grateful and happy to hear Mr. Rogers' confession about your benevolence

---

[1] J. Proctor to F. Walsingham, 19 November 1581 (P.R.O., SP 12/150, f. 64).

[2] B. de Mendoza to the King of Spain, London, 19 February 1582: '. . . Before Leicester left the Council to discuss the detention of Rogers and the Queen's writing on the subject, Leicester and Walsingham again voted as before, to the effect that if the Prince [i.e. Parma] did not at once release him I should be arrested. Cecil, on the other hand, said that there was a great inequality between my person and that of Rogers, besides the fact that I was here as an ordinary ambassador, and must be considered as such, whereas Rogers was only a servant of the Queen sent with letters' (Cal. S.P. Span. 1580–1586, no 213). See also Bakhuizen van den Brink, 'Daniel Rogers', pp. 86–88.

[3] See Lords of the Council to Archbishiop of Canterbury, Greenwich, 28 January 1584 (B.M., MS. Lansd. 982, f. 136).

[4] P. Melissus to J. Dousa, Paris, 20 October 1584 (B.M., MS. Burney 370, f. 63). Melissus had heard from Gilpin meanwhile that even the Emperor, Rudolph II, was endeavouring to liberate Rogers: see P. Melissus to A. Ortelius, Nuremberg, 20 March 1584 (Hessels, I, no. 123).

and interest and patronage towards him: I am certain that you
can imagine for yourself how grateful I am—I do not say 'have
been' for I shall always be grateful.
First of all I thank God for his deliverance from long and great
oppression. Next I am grateful that he first came to me before
returning to you, believing and trusting that you would give
him the greater preferment since his dangers and anguish, too,
had been the greater on account of you: so that this prolonged
sadness would be compensated by greater happiness: and therefore, o let me soon have a letter from you—not a fatal, killing
letter, but one that is happy and festal . . .
[P.S.] You must divert our Rogers with a good wife [1] before his
grey hairs become more numerous. [2]

Full of expectations as to the justice of his cause he travelled
home, and on his way to England another man of influence
and mutual friend of Walsingham and Rogers, Christophorus
Ehemius, Duke Casimir's Chancellor, gave him a rather
similar letter to deliver [3].

But, strangely enough, Walsingham, whom one might have
imagined as duly embarrassed over the unnecessary advers-
ities of one of his most loyal adherent, seemed hesitant to
support his client. Since his past extremities would have made
Rogers reluctant to continue his former career, it is surprising
that Walsingham soon destined him for another continental
visit, without much improvement. Rogers wrote verses on
Nonsuch [4], and a letter to his 'approved patron' Walsingham
to make it quite clear that 'truelie it is highe tyme, that some
better consideration weare had for my advancement' [5], but
in vain. Then, a little later, he saw his chance when the
prebend of Windsor was available, and made his claims still
clearer in this desperate appeal:

No man knoweth better, then your honor, in how great affayres
I have bene employed this. 18. yeares, and how I have not used
my selfe after the common devotion, as also, how littell recompence
I have felt. The present neede in which I presently am, after my

---

[1] Rogers indeed married in 1587: see p. 11, note 2.
[2] J. Sturmius to [F. Walsingham], Northeim, 29 January 1585 [n.s.]
(Hessels, II, no. 213). See Appendix II, no. 43.
[3] C. Ehemius to F. Walsingham, Heidelberg, 9 February 1585 [n.s.]
(Hessels, II, no. 214).
[4] 30 September 1585 (*Cal. S.P. dom. 1581–1590*, no. 182).
[5] D. Rogers to F. Walsingham. 24 October 1585 (P.R.O.. SP 12/183,
f. 50).

so great and longe calamitie, constrayneth me to crave your favour and ayde at this tyme. . . . my present neede, requireth present helpe. God strengthen your honour. [1]

Melissus, in London at the time, composed a poem in commendation of him, which somehow found its way into the State Papers. [2] The Queen intervened and offered him the treasureship of St. Paul's, but Rogers insisted on the prebend of Windsor, and rightly added: 'I doo not doubt, but that [inserted your Honour iudgeth] I have deserved better recompence, then a prebende.' [3] What exactly followed is not quite clear, but probably resulted in some form of a compromise. He was not sent back to the Low Countries, but was made a Clerk of the Privy Council in 1587, and travelled to Denmark on diplomatic business a few times.

In February 1591 Daniel Rogers died, 'whereupon his body, accompanied by an Herald or two, was buried on *Shrove Tuesday* the 16th of the same Month near to that of *Nicas. Yetswiert . . .* in the Church of *Sunbury* near to *Hampton Court* in *Middlesex*.' [4]

It takes no far-fetched theory to explain the almost total disappearance of Daniel Rogers from the Anglo-Dutch scene after 1580. Leicester, when Governor General in the Netherlands, at certain critical moments sent repeated requests for this Dutch expert:

I would gladly have Daniell Rogers here, for some good service which I thincke he is fitt for. Yf you fynde that her majestie meane to continue me in service here, I hartely pray you that Daniell Rogers may be sent to me. [5]

[1] D. Rogers to F. Walsingham, 16 January 1586 (P.R.O., SP 12/186, f. 9).

[2] 'D [. . .] RSIO ALIIS [. . .] ROGERSI, / Quibus est honos in aula / Potior, potissimas nunc / Habeamque agamque grates? / Tibi quid? Tibi profecto / (Nec enim nego aut negabo) / Potiore laude grates / Tribuentur. Efficis pol / Studio evidentiore / Operaque promptiore, / Ut ego hospes insularis / Aliis queam inquilinis / Agere atque habere grates: / Ideoque te, ROGERSI, / Studij ob peculiaris / Animique signa, patrem / Vocitare Gratiarum'. Greenwich, 20 January 1586 (P.R.O., SP 12/186, f. 32).

[3] D. Rogers to F. Walsingham, The Court, 13 February 1586—not 3 February 1583 o.s. as calendared (P.R.O., SP 12/168, f. 2).

[4] Wood, *Athenae Oxon.*, I, p. 247.

[5] R. Dudley to F. Walsingham, The Hague, 11 February 1586 (*Correspondence of Robert Dudley*, ed. J. Bruce, p. 83).

But Rogers was obviously no longer interested in the hazards of the enterprise, and presumably disgusted with those men at Court on whom the political union depended. For all his personal zeal and all his labour had only resulted in one disappointment after another, an appalling lack of interest in the cruel treatment of her Majesty's envoy (perhaps even more so after the death of his main advocate, Languet, in 1581), and a still more infuriating display of ingratitude on his return. It is revealing, meanwhile, to note that those few who appear to have remained personally concerned for him throughout were his humanist friends in England, Germany, and the Low Countries: Buchanan, Camden, Sturmius, Languet, Melissus, Ortelius, Dousa, Lipsius. The extent of his influence is indicated by their reactions to his imprisonment.

Though he occasionally had opportunity to display his interest in foreign visitors, and though his name did not vanish altogether from their books of verse [1], within the unprecedented opportunities for greater Anglo-Dutch literary contacts which were to present themselves in 1586 Daniel Rogers was never to play the leading part which 'that great Daniel, the envoy of the most glorious Elizabeth Queen of England, no less remarkable for his literary prowess than for his courtesy,' [2] had deserved, more than anyone else.

---

[1] E.g. J. Dousa the Younger, 'Ad Danielem Rogertem . . . cum a diuturna captivitate apud hostes liberatus esset', and another epigram on Rogers (*Poemata*, 1704, p. 183); some references in Dousa's *Elegiarum Liber*, 1586; and Baudius, in 'Ad Thomam Baronem de Burgh' (*Carmina ad Petrum Regemorterum*, 1587).

[2] J. Radermacher to J. Cool, Middelburg, [25 July 1603] (Hessels, I, no. 330).

PART TWO

SIR PHILIP SIDNEY

I

LEIDEN VISITS ENGLAND

ONE should in all fairness admit that the Anglo-Dutch political alliance of 1585 was an inevitability rather than the fulfilment of a long-cherished general desire. Both partners had first exhausted all possibilities within their traditional French policies. Anjou had been a last chance, and the episode, a meeting-ground for Anglo-Dutch political and non-political interests[1], had in its more promising stages seemed a happy compromise. It must have been doubly painful for Rogers to have been imprisoned at a time when all eyes were fixed on a liaison different from the one which he and his party were known to support. But that policy, too, proved a *débâcle*. A general re-orientation was inevitable, and became even more urgent when William of Orange was assassinated in 1584.

Dousa sailed for England immediately after that date to investigate in an unofficial capacity the chances of an English union, while at the same time Henry III of France was approached with an official offer of sovereignty over the Netherlands. The latter's refusal left the disturbed States without an alternative, and the small but persistent faction of English-minded politicians [2]—Dousa among them—

---

[1] See F. A. Yates, *The Valois tapestries*, London, 1959.
[2] The activities of this 'faction' and their share in the Dutch festivals for the Earl of Leicester in 1585/86 are to be treated in a Sir Thomas Browne Institute study by R. C. Strong and the present writer.

whose history went back to the seventies, that is to 'the days of Rogers', without serious rivals. Even if the Queen refused the open commitment of a Dutch crown, an Anglo-Dutch union was only a matter of time and the Protestant Walsingham-Leicester-Sidney (-Rogers) approach the only immediate, if slightly unpopular, solution. The surrender of Antwerp—ironically by one of her great champions, Marnix—caused Elizabeth at last to decide in favour of the Protestant-league policy. The sending of Leicester and Sidney to the Low Countries, therefore, was the logical outcome of a party-policy which had been established in readiness for the day when the Queen would sign her treaty with the Dutch ambassadors [1] and her historic *Declaration* [2].

An increase of literary contacts was one of the most likely consequences of the foregoing development, especially as they had been initiated by those very men who were now to take the lead in political matters. But it is wrong to assume that political and literary contacts remained strictly interdependent. As in the days of Rogers' imprisonment when literary friends had been faithful in spite of a decreased official interest, Leicesters future loss of popularity was not to result in a termination of literary relations.

This may to some extent be explained by remembering that Dousa's circle, though central in the forthcoming Anglo-Dutch relationship, can never really be identified with the policy of an English Puritan party. The participation of liberal Leiden in the welcoming of English Protestant leaders seems the result of established affinities with English humanists rather than a mere bid for new patronage. Thus, so mixed an assembly—Lipsius, a liberal Catholic, Dousa, truly Erasmian, and the anti-Roman-Catholic Van Hout—could appear as 'Leicestrians' in 1586, yet avoid involvement in the embarrassing Leicester *coup* in Leiden of the following year and dishonour when the English episode proved an altogether unfortunate *interregnum*.

---

[1] 2 October 1585.
[2] *A declaration of the causes mooving the queene to give aide to the lowe countries*, 1585. Also in Latin, French, Italian, and Dutch: London, Amsterdam, Delft, Dordrecht, 1585. Cf. Bachrach, *Huygens and Britain*, p. 87.

Moving freely within the limits of political developments, a small group of Leiden poets visited London in the summer and autumn of 1585 and were at last enabled to meet their fellow English poets. Of this group only one, Dousa, leader of the representatives of Holland, was on diplomatic business. But in his train and that of the other official speakers was a host of unnamed young men from Holland, France, and the Protestant parts of Germany and Denmark, who had crossed the sea to finish their education in the courtly setting of a foreign embassy. Among them was Dousa's oldest son with his great friend Dominicus Baudius and another close companion of their undergraduate days, Georgius Benedicti (who had already spent some time at Cambridge).

It will be necessary to isolate carefully those few who matter from the rest of that spectacular crowd. The four from Leiden to begin with, who had left a regretful Lipsius behind, found faithful Rogers waiting for them instead: 'ye gods,' Lipsius wrote,

how I have wanted to come, how I should still want to come. How is our Rogers? I envy you because of him, and him because of you; we would have chatted, we would have conferred, daily, whenever we could, as long as we could. [1]

Their contacts with Sidney were closer than ever: 'please,' Lipsius continued in this same letter, 'convey all my respects and love to Burghley, Sidney, and Dyer'. To these names should be added that of Melissus who 'had sailed from Dieppe to England in the autumn of 158[5] to offer his poems to the Queen at Richmond, and there remained with the Court that winter' [2]. He was to leave again early in 1586 'after he had visited the Universities of Oxford and Cambridge and the libraries with their rich stock of old books, at which journey his travelling companion was Hieronimus Groslotius Lislaeus, a French nobleman who had been educated under George Buchanan [3] at the same time as the youthful King of Scotland,

---

[1] J. Lipsius to J. Dousa, Leiden, 1 September 1585 (B.M., MS. Burney 370, f. 35). See Appendix II, no. 44.

[2] J.-J. Boissard, *Icones quinquaginta virorum illustrium*, II, Frankfort, 1630, pp. 33–34. See Appendix II, no. 45.

[3] Another Buchanan-England-Leiden link of the same year is the case of Adrian(us) Damman(t), future translator of Du Bartas, who, when in

James VI.' It is evident that this Groslot(ius), too, was to play his literary part in the social engagements of these months.

Originally, Benedicti's presence in England had no connexion with Leicestrian politics at all. Shortly after Baudius had returned to Leiden in the autumn of 1583, the twenty-year old student from Haarlem had gone off to Cambridge [1] where he remained until some time after the arrival of the Dutch ambassadors two years later [2]. The opening lines of Benedicti's epitaph—he died prematurely in 1588—recall these Cambridge years:

> Hic est hic Benedictus ille, carus
> Dousae, Lipsiadaeque, Iunioque;
> Quem Batavia tota, quem Britanna,
> Quem Germanica perstrepunt Lycaea. [3]

At Cambridge Benedicti himself had composed his *Carmina* on the death of Orange which appeared in 1585. His return to Leiden did not coincide with Leicester's journey, for it would be 28 March 1586 before Groslotius had occasion to write to Dousa about 'much beloved young Georgius Benedicti who is leaving us, much to our regret, at the bidding of his patrons.' [4] But he was in England and so happened to join the chorus of Leiden poets who used the winter of 1585/86 to sing the praises of the Queen, of Leicester, and of Sidney, [5]

England (1584/85), accepted the invitation of Dousa and Paulus Buys (below, p. 150, note 1) to become Professor of Ethics at Leiden (1586–88). For some time he was the States' ambassador in Scotland, and he is said to have been a tutor to various young gentlemen at the request of Buchanan.

[1] On 28 September 1583 he inscribed the Album of Jan van Hout (f. 38) as 'Anglia petens'. Dousa wrote a farewell-*carmen* (*Epodon ex puris iambis libri II*, Leiden, 1584, sig. C 5), a draft of which survives in a Leiden copy of his *Epigrammata* (see above, p. 37, note 1).

[2] Cf. G. Benedicti to J. Dousa, Cambridge, 26 August 1585 (B.M., MS. Burney 370, f. 13).

[3] P. Scriverius, 'Georgii Benedicti tumulus' (G. Benedicti, *Poemata Posthuma*, Leiden, 1601, p. 39).

[4] H. Groslotius to J. Dousa, London, 28 March 1586 (B.M., MS. Burney 370, f. 4). See Appendix II, no. 46.

[5] G. Benedicti, *De Rebus gestis Principis Guilielmi*, Leiden, 1586: pp. 44, 53 (the Queen), 46 (the Queen's portrait in J. Ortel's house), 45 (the Queen and Leicester), 47, 53, 58, 60 (Leicester), 47, 54 (Sidney; see Appendix I, nos. 9, 10).

although Benedicti's laudatory contributions were yet to remain somewhat impersonal.

Not so with Baudius, who, in his autobiography, was subsequently to recall that 'towards the end of that month [*i.e. June 1585*] he accompanied the splendid legation which the States then sent to Queen Elizabeth, there made the acquaintance of many men of renowned fame and dignity, but was of all most dear to Philip Sidney'. [1] It will soon become evident that there was some truth in this assertion by a man who would later affirm 'to have in his studies imitated three men above all, the three Philips', Duplessis, Sidney, and Marnix. [2]

A central position must be reserved for Dousa, whose leading part in the Dutch embassy had been anticipated by his unofficial mission of the preceding year, 1584, when, apart from his formal duties, he will gladly have fulfilled the customary request which Lipsius had sent him: 'please greet the gentlemen Philip Sidney and Dyer on my behalf.' [3] Nor did he forget his concern for mixing the *utile* and *dulce* when travelling in an official capacity. In his Album one can see the steady widening of his English circle: Richard Mulcaster, the renowned educationalist, Richard Thomson, 'Dutch Thomson', the biblical scholar, Andrew Melville, the great Scottish theologian and divine poet, and three others on a single day (26 August), viz. Sidney's adventurous friend Archibald Douglas, the Italian Scipio Gentili, and William Camden, whose verse read:

Ut Douzam Camdenus amet, miretur, honoret,
Douziaci genii dosque, decusque facit. [4]

Dousa could therefore claim to have friends in more than one quarter when, soon after his appointment as historiographer of Holland and University Librarian, he returned to England

---

[1] D. Baudius, *Epistolarum Centuriae tres*, Leiden, 1636, sig. *6ᵛ. See Appendix II, no. 47.

[2] Ibid., I, viii (p. 34). See Appendix II, no. 48.

[3] J. Lipsius to J. Dousa, Leiden, 23 August 1584 (J. Lipsius, *Epistolarum selectarum centuria prima*, Antwerp, 1605, p. 78). See Appendix II, no. 49.

[4] These six inscriptions in Dousa's Album occur on ff. 142ᵛ, 140, 131ᵛ, 120ᵛ, 136ᵛ, 141ᵛ. Camden's verse also occurs in his volume of drafts, now in the B.M. (MS. Add. 36, 294, f. 14).

in 1585—an event which his *cliens* Benedicti was not slow to record in a 'Gratulatio' [1].

Nothing would have been more unlike a true humanist than to visit foreign parts empty-handed. Thus one finds Dousa bringing his recently printed *Petronius Arbiter*, and offering it to Sir Philip Sidney, the greatest 'arbiter' of all, with an appropriate Ode [2]. Dousa had actually dedicated a commentary on this book to Sidney's intermediary, Rogers, only two years before. The London meeting had been prepared by many an earlier contact.

Although it is easy enough to imagine that an exchange of thought would take place under these circumstances, it remains difficult to prove or even indicate what this literary traffic in fact comprised. The problem does not become any the less if one moves from an academic world and its well-preserved correspondence to informal incidents in courtly surroundings. The more fortunate, therefore, that one or two such incidents have left enough traces to allow an attempt at their reconstruction.

One is the Latin translation which Janus Dousa the Younger is known [3] to have made of a sonnet by Henry Constable [4]:

Blame not my hearte for flying up so high	Ne, quod te celso fugiat per inane volatu,
Sith thow art cause that it this flight begun	Cor precor ah misero saevius ure mihi.
For earthlye vapoures drawne up by the sun	Culpa tua haec; vestri pennis sublatus Amoris
Comets become and night-suns in the skie	Mortali ignotas cogitur ire vias.
	Ac velut halantes coeli ad confinia fumos
	Cynthius aethereis usque trahit radiis,

---

[1] Benedicti, *Poemata Posthuma*, p. 31.
[2] Dousa, *Odarum Britannicarum liber*, p. 21. See Appendix I, no. 5.
[3] See J. G. Scott, 'A Latin Version of a Sonnet of Constable's' *Modern Language Review*, XX, 1925, p. 462.
[4] H. Constable, *Poems*, ed. J. Grundy, Liverpool, 1960, p. 121; Dousa, *Rerum caelestium*, pp. 79–80. In later editions Dousa's', last two lines read: 'Est tua lux ignis, nostrum quae attraxit amorem, / Et qui summa petit, est meus ignis amor'.

My humble hearte so with
thy heavenly eye
Drawen up alofte all low
desires doth shun
Rayse thow me up as thow
my heart hast done
So during night in heaven
remayne may I

Unde trabes flammasque creet,
dirosve Cometas,
Aut crine accendat lampada
flammifero;
Affixam sic ante solo lux enthea
mentem
Sustulit, ut superis inserat ordinibus:
Hic ubi, sacratae radiant velut
astra Coronae,
Fulgurat ardoris sic quoque
flamma mei.
Quin igitur tellure etiam me
tollis inerti,
Ne patiar mentis flebile disci-
dium.
Sic mihi tu coelum, coeli sic
lumine nobis
Continget totis noctibus usque
frui.

Blame not I say againe my
high desire
Sith of us both the cause
thereof depends
In thee doth shine in me
doth burne a fire
Fire drawes up others and
it selfe ascends
Thyne eye a fire and so
drawes up my love
My love a fire and so a-
scends above.

En interum clamo: effectus
utriusque caloris
Expendens, pectus mitus ure
meum.
Idem nos ignis, in te qui fulgurat, urit:
Secum cuncta trahens ignis, ut
attrahitur.
Ignis more tuum ad sese trahit
omnia lumen;
Utque ignis, noster summa pe-
tissit amor.

Dousa's translation first appeared in print in 1591, as the
twelfth *carmen* of his ''Ἐρωτοπαίγνιον'. Since Constable's
Diana was not published until 1592 (and no copy is recorded
in Dousa's library [1]), Dousa the Younger must have translated
from a manuscript. This need not have been given to him by
the author himself, who, incidentally, has recently been
recognized as a Protestant politician [2]. There is no evidence

---

[1] See p. 61, note 1.
[2] Cf. [Constable,] *Examen pacifique de la Doctrine des Huguenots*, Paris, 1589
(see *Poems*, introduction pp. 31–33). Constable's conversion to Roman-
Catholicism in 1590 meant his final answer to the frustrating problem
of the Reunion of the Churches for which he and so many others of his
generation—such as Lipsius and Hotman—had worked.

that either the poet or his father, Sir Robert Constable, followed Leicester to the Low Countries in 1585/6 [1], although at the time of Dousa's London visit Henry Constable may well have been in England to receive Walsingham's instructions for his next continental journey [2]: his familiarity with the background to Leicester's campaign as revealed in *A short view of Cardinall Allen* (1588?) [3] supports this supposition. But the fact that Constable is never mentioned in the letters and poems of the Dousa circle makes it unlikely that any degree of intimacy existed, so that the manuscript may have reached the younger Dousa through other channels. The translation—which, incidentally, testifies to Dousa's knowledge of the English language—thus presents some interesting problems. Why should he have selected this truly 'conceited' love-poem by a writer who had no direct links with the Dutch, and why a sonnet addressed to the legendary Penelope Rich, Sidney's Stella? And who could have shown it to him?

The key to this curious Stella-Constable-Dousa connexion appears to be a Frenchman, Jean Hotman. [4] Hotman, whose father François—a good friend of Dousa the Elder's—had been offered a Leiden Chair in 1578 [5], was a former tutor to the children of Sir Amias Poulet, English ambassador at Paris in the late seventies. Through his connexions at Oxford he had entered the English Court, where his familiarity with the Sidney-Leicester circle [6] brought him to the post of secretary to Leicester. In this capacity he was to spend the years of Leicester's Governorship in Holland, where the Hotmans already had numerous influential friends. Orange's widow, Louise de Coligny, was not the least important of

---

[1] See p. 114, note 4; and the lists in Tenison, *Elizabethan England*, VI, pp. 45–47, 204–213. Considering their rank and social status (see Constable, *Poems*, p. 20) the absence of their names in the various rolls and musterlists seems sufficient proof that neither of them went with the English forces to the Low Countries in 1585/6.

[2] See *Poems*, p. 23.

[3] Ibid., pp. 24–26.

[4] Miss Grundy is of the same opinion (ibid., p. 31, note 2) but gives no details.

[5] J. Dousa to F. Hotman, Leiden, 20 October 1578 (*Francisci et Joannis Hotomanorum epistolae*, Amsterdam, 1700, p. 97).

[6] Cf. *Hotomanorum epistolae*, no. 103.

these: François Hotman had commemorated her father in his *De Furoribus Gallicis*. [1]

Not only does the name of this *intimus* of Sidney frequently occur in the verses of both Dousas, but it was equally familiar to both Penelope Rich and her 'other admirer', Henry Constable, who had also written verses to Louise de Coligny on her father's death. Various references to Constable, for instance in connexion with some controversial treatise of the poet [2], survive in Hotman's correspondence. Lady Rich continues to appear until the early seventeenth century when we find Hotman hoping to use her influence to receive from King James I the promised reward for his French translation of the Βασιλικὸν Δῶρον. [3]

One published and five unpublished letters of Penelope Rich to the Hotmans, in one of which she apologizes for her 'mauvase escriture' because she has lost her 'fidele guide [*Mrs. Hotman?*] en la lange françois' [4], show, in spite of the somewhat general terms of the short notes, that they were close friends. One of them contains the following lines:

J'ay envoié une letre à ma clarté, et un autre à hilliard lequel je desire monsieur hoteman de doner à luy, et de prandre de luy mon pourtrait, et de la doner à monssieur l'ambassadeur . . . [5]

It may be worth noting that only two references to the lost Hilliard miniature of her are known [6], one of which is the sonnet 'To Mr. Hilliard upon occasion of a picture he made of my Ladie Riche' by Constable himself. The other letter (also preserved at Haarlem) is more eloquent still. In it Lady Rich makes a mischievous display of her London friends and

---

[1] Edinburgh, 1573.

[2] P. l'Oyseleur de Villiers to J. Hotman, Middelburg, 14 May 1590; and [Middelburg], November 1580 ('Correspondance de Jean Hotman', ed. P. J. Blok, *Archives du musée Teyler*, Haarlem, II, xii, 1911, nos. 107 and 109).

[3] J. Hotman to ? , n.p., n.d. (*Hotomanorum epistolae*, no. 115).

[4] P. Rich to Mrs. Hotman, n.p., 8 October, no year (Haarlem, Teyler Museum, MS. Hotomaniora, no. 43).

[5] P. Rich to Mrs. Hotman, n.p., n.d. (ibid., no. 45). Two other letters are also to Mrs. Hotman (nos. 41 and 44), n.p., 10 September and 11 September, no years. The fifth unpublished letter is to [Jean] Hotman (no. 42), London, 1 May, no year.

[6] See R. C. Strong, 'Queen Elizabeth, the Earl of Essex, and Nicholas Hilliard', *Burlington Magazine*, CI, 1959, p. 146.

admirers: Paul Choart, Seigneur de Buzanval, Henry of Navarre's ambassador in London; Horatio Palavicino, the diplomat-financier; Philip Sidney's brother Robert; Henry Constable; and Hotman himself, whom she admonishes 'to love his wife and be constant, with all the others', until the return of 'la plus constante de ceux qui sont nommez en ce papier, hors mis une, Penelope Riche'. [1]

No date is given in this epistolary gem—which Hotman rightly preserved among his more serious letters—but 1589 [2] is probably correct. It is useful to remember, however, that as early as 1585/6 or possibly earlier these same men worked closely together on behalf of Navarre when the combined English, French, German, and Dutch summer campaigns for 1586 and 1587 were being prepared in London.[3] Whether Lady Rich played an active or merely decorative part at such an early date is uncertain, but she may have been on the scene. It seems justified, at any rate, to surmise that the setting of the 1589 letter had existed for some years, thus providing a fitting background to the translation of Constable's sonnet, which was probably made through Hotman's mediation in the younger Dousa's 'period of English interest'. This period was limited, as we shall see, to the years 1585–6 only; but in it we find young Dousa expressing such sentiments as:

This rude song, my Muse, you must carry to our Hotman. . . . It will take you two days before you reach Arnhem . . . where you will find him busy writing or studying, or relaxing has mind by reading or walking. And if he receives you well and kindly, then, if Hotman should send you to him as well, you will venture with less fear and trepidation to submit yourself to the judgement of the learned Sidney. Beware of hastily importuning the polite ears of Sidney, and make sure that you do not obstruct his business

---

[1] P. Rich to J. Hotman, n.p., n.d. (Hotman, 'Correspondance', no. 108).

[2] Blok gives 1590?, while Miss Grundy, who quotes the letter on p. 28 of Constable's *Poems*, tentatively dates it 1589.

[3] Cf. De Buzanval to R. Dudley, London, 4 April 1587: 'J'ay entendu par le sr. Hotman présent porteur, l'affection, de laquelle procédez à l'advancement de l'affaire du roy de Navarre . . .' (Leicester, *Correspondentie*, II, no. 275). See L. Stone, *An Elizabethan: Sir Horatio Palavicino*, Oxford, 1956, pp. 109–152; Constable, *Poems*, pp. 21–33. Palavicino, with Van Meteren as one of his agents, also sponsored Leicester's campaign (Stone, *Palavicino*, pp. 191–192).

and occupations. But if he will somehow have leisure, free from all cares and worries, then o Muse, then remember to approach him— but reverently and with modesty . . . [1]

Concerning the small group of poems in which the Constable 'adumbratio' is found, Dousa in his 'Ad lectorem' of 1590/1 writes that he will not apologize for their lack of refinement because many of them 'slipped out three years ago' when their author was only 'sixteen or even fifteen years old'. [2] Considering, therefore, firstly Dousa the Younger's brief though active interest in English letters and his literary contact with Sidney's milieu through Jean Hotman at the time of Leicester's Dutch campaign, secondly the French Huguenot background to Lady Rich's courtly clique in which Constable's poems originated (perhaps well before 1588 [3]), and, finally, his own allusions 'To the Reader', there is reason to believe that Dousa's rendering was made in about 1586, and that it went back to a copy—necessarily in MS.—which he will have obtained at the time of his youthful visit to the Protestant Court of England in 1585. As regards Dousa the Younger's acquisition of this material, Hotman's close friendship with Sidney's Stella [4] (or Constable's Diana) and his familiarity with these French-minded poet-politicians leave

---

[1] Dousa, *Poemata*, 1704, p. 186–187 ('Ad nostrum hoc rude carmen Hottomannum / I perfer mea Musea, . . . Labor est duum dierum / Priusquam venias ad Arnemum urbem . . . Illic invenies vel occupatum / Scribendo studiisve, vel legendo / Relaxantem animum vel ambulando. / Quod si te excipiat bene & benigne, / Audebis minus anxius tremensque / Docti judicium subire Sidnei; / Si te illuc quoque mittat Hottomannus. / Sed ne tempore non tuo politas / Sidneii properes caveto ad aures, / Neve seria & occupationes / Ejus impedias vide impudenter. / Sed si quando animum ociosum habebit / A curisque molestiisque cunctis, / Tunc accedere tunc memento Musa / Illud, sed reverent[e]r & pudenter . . .').

[2] Dousa, *Rerum caelestium*, sig. *5^V ('in quibus impolitiam quorundorum non excuso, praesertim cum magna eorum pars iam ante triennium mihi decimosexto, aut etiam decimoquinto aetatis excederit'.)

[3] Constable's secular poems all appear to have been written in the 1580s. It seems unreasonable to suppose that he became an expert love-sonneteer only after his earliest dated connexion with Lady Rich in 1588, when he wrote a sonnet on the birth of her daughter.

[4] On Sidney's Stella and Dousa the Elder's 'Ad Stellam et Philastrum amantes '(*Epigrammata*, p. 48), see J. G. Scott, 'The names of the heroines of Elizabethan sonnet-sequences', *RES*, II, 1926, p. 159.

little need to wonder how and why some of the *Diana* poems
came to the notice of his best friends in Holland—including
the son and companion of ambassador Dousa, who translated
one of them in admiration of the poetry, if not of that incom-
parable Lady herself.

This was not the only English poem which the young
Dousa translated. His 'book of love-play', the ' 'Ερωτοπαίγνιον',
consisted of twenty *carmina*, followed by one ' 'Triumphus'
and five Dutch 'Epigrammata'. The first two *carmina* had no
special title, nos. 3–7 were headed 'Ex Graeco', and 8–11
'Ex Graeco Meleagri'. No. 12 (the Constable translation)
was not subtitled but headed by the words 'Adumbratum de
Anglico Henrici Conestabilis', with 'Carmen XII' under-
neath. The later editor of his Complete Poems [1] therefore
regarded not only 'Carmen XII' as an imitation of Constable, but also the following numbers 13–21, and typo-
graphically gave all ten the appearance of belonging together
for that reason.

In the absence of further demonstrable parallels—no
extant Constable poems match the numbers 13–21—one
would be inclined to regard the editor's attribution as a
mistake. But then one discovers that the first (Dutch) sonnet
of the five 'Epigrammata quaedam Belgico idiomate' which
follow immediately after is a literal translation of another
sonnet by Constable [2]:

Thyne eye the glasse where I behold my hearte	U oog is een glas, daar mijn hart is ingegreven,
Myne eye the windowe through the which thyne eye	Mijn oog een tralie is, door welken openbaar
May see my hearte and there thy selfe espie	U stralend' oog mag sien mijn hart, end'hoe gy daar
In bloudie coloures how thow paynted art	Met een bloedig penseel ge-schildert zijt na 't leven.
Thyne eye the pyle is of a murdering darte	U oog is eene pijl, daar meenig over sneven;
Myne eye the sight thow takst thy levell by	Mijn oog is het versich, daar gy by mikt eenpaar
To hitt my hearte and never shut'st awrye	Dat nimmermeer de scheut kan wiggen hier of daar:
Myne eye thus helpes thyne eye to worke my smarte	Dus helpt mijn oog u oog, dat 't mijn mag so doen beven.

---

[1] Gulielmus Rabus, Rotterdam, 1704.
[2] *Poems*, p. 117; Dousa, *Poemata*, 1704, p. 163.

Thyne eye a fire is both in heate and light	U oog is een klaar vyer en licht end'hette beyde:
Myne eye of teares a river doth become	Mijn oog van tranen heel ver- gaat in een Rivier.
O that the water of myne eye had might	Og dat mijn oogens vloet had mogen als ik schreyden
To quench the flames that from thyne eye doe come	De vlammen blussen, welk spruyt uyt u oogen fier!
Or that the fire thats kindled by thine eye	Of dat het brandig vyer ge- sproten uyt u oogen
The flowing streames of myne eye would make drye	mijn oogkens waterstroom uyt hadde kun[n]en droogen.

Although the other four Dutch sonnets again have no obvious parallel in any extant Constable sonnet, it might be argued that Dousa's 'Epigramma III' also looks like an *adumbratio*:

Prometheus, for stealing living fire	Gelijk als Pyrrhas [1] Oom der Gooden gast, ten laast,
from heavens King, was iudg'd eternall death,	Om dat hy had gerooft d'on- sterffelijke vonken,
in selfe same flame with unrelenting ire,	Heeft moeten hangen aan der hooge Steenrots honken,
bound fast to *Caucasus* lowe foote beneath.	Daar in sijn hert den Gier met bek en klaauwe raast;
So I, for stealing living beau- ties fire	So ik die van mijn Lief gespijst werd en geaast,
into my verse, that it may alwaies live,	Om dat ik uyt 't gesicht en vriendelijke lonken
and change his formes to shapes of thy desire,	Haar oogs tot mijn behoef ge- nomen heb wat vonken
thou beauties Queene, selfe sentence like dost give.	Daar mijn hert door verquikt zou worden metter haast,
Bound to thy feete, in chaines of love I lie,	Van u Cupido fel verscheurt werd wreedelijken,
for to thine eyes I never dare aspire,	Ben ik zo schuldig dan dat gy niet met mijn pijn
and in thy beauties bright- nes doe I fry,	Te vrede zijnd'u gaat by eene Gier gelijken,
as poore *Prometheus* in the scalding fire.	En hebt genomen voor mijn altijt by te blijven?
Which teares maintaine, as oyle the Lampe revives,	O groote deerlijkheyt? want wanneer zal van mijn
Onely my succour in thy favour lyes. [2]	Dit hartknagig gequel ooyt Hercules verdrijven?

[1] Editions of Dousa here include a footnote: 'Prometheus'.

[2] *Poems*, pp. 202–203. A Scottish version also exists. It may have been written (see Constable, *Poems*, p. 29, note 3) by the same Archibald Douglas who, with Gentili and Camden, wrote in the elder Dousa's Album on 28 August 1584 (see above, p. 81).

The most logical conclusion, therefore, is that the whole series of *carmina* XII—XX, 'Triumphus' (XXI), and the following five Dutch sonnets were translated or at least derived from Constable's love poetry. This need not be contradicted by the absence of the majority of their originals. We know that Dousa the Younger used a mansucript which was circulated privately before a number of poems were printed. Constable's original set of *Diana*-poems may therefore have included many others which now only survive in the Leiden *adumbrationes*. In conclusion, this printed collection of Dutch love sonnets and other poems was one result probably of the pre-Leicestrian embassy of 1585, and perhaps entirely a translation from the English.

Hotman acted as a link between Dousa the Younger and Constable. It would not be difficult to find, through Hotman, other names which would widen the London circle considerably. These names will, of course, help to define the original Sidney-Leiden group to which Hotman, for one, truly belonged. 'How much laughter have we shared in jest and wine,' Dousa was to write to Groslot, 'I, Hotman, and you, together with Melissus'; and, he added, the fifth member who used to enlarge their carefree 'quadrumvirate' was Rogers, or 'ipse Sidneius pater elegantiarum'. [1]

Again through Hotman, the 'quadrumvir', one may associate Scipio Gentili with the Leiden visitors a little more closely than an inscription in Dousa's Album need imply. Both his Leiden sojourn in the winter of 1582/3 [2] and his printed paraphrases of the Psalms [3] and Tasso translations (some dedicated to 'the outstanding poet' Sidney [4]) may have brought the Italian refugee into contact with Dousa's circle; and perhaps through his brother and Jean Hotman he became acquainted with Sidney—on the birth of whose

[1] Dousa, *Odarum Britannicarum liber*, p. 44. See Appendix II, no. 50.
[2] He was registered on 12 October 1582, on the same day as one Dominicus Goyvaerts of Antwerp with whom 'Scipius Gentilis Picentinus Italus stud. Jur.' also shared rooms. The *Alb. Rec.* of 1583 records them as 'wech' (i.e. 'gone').
[3] *Paraphrasis aliquot Psalmorum Davidi*, London, 1581; *In xxv. Davidis Psalmos epicae paraphrases*, London, 1584.
[4] See Buxton, *Sidney*, pp. 152-3, 157.

daughter Elizabeth he wrote and published in 1584 the poem *Nereus*. Some seven years later, in a letter addressed to 'my Scipio', Hotman still had occasion to recall 'the *carmina* which so pleased our Sidney'. [1] Indeed, it is evident that Scipio, the poet 'whom all England admired' [2], was a familiar name in 1586 both as a talented writer and as a legal scholar [3]. His brother Alberico was the great pioneer of international law, who, with a letter of recommendation from Leicester, had been registered at Oxford University in 1581 on the same day as Jean Hotman. [4] This Gentili's early publications, a few years before his Oxford appointment as Regius Professor of Law, had included books dedicated to Leicester, Dyer, and Palavicino. [5] On 21 July 1585, coinciding with the Dutch and French negotiations with the Queen, he dedicated his *De Legationibus libri tres* to Sidney whom he describes, while defending Leicester [6], as the ideal ambassador. The history of Alberico's book re-introduces Hotman, for *De Legationibus* was based on the legal advice which those two Protestant refugees had given to the Privy Council concerning the disputed criminal immunity of the Spanish ambassador, Mendoza, in 1584. [7] Thus Scipio Gentili's name in Dousa's Album emphasizes the fact that contacts between Sidney's circle and the gentlemen from Leiden were no longer exclusively dependent on one or two earlier friendships.

In this way new names continue to appear. For example,

---

[1] J. Hotman to Scipio [Gentili], Basle, 10 December 1592 (*Hotomanorum epistolae*, no. 111). See Appendix II, no. 51.

[2] Id. to id., Basle, 12 February 1593 (ibid., no. 108). See Sppendix II, no. 52.

[3] See G. H. J. van der Molen, *Alberico Gentili and the development of international law, his life work and times*, diss. Amsterdam, 1937, pp. 42-43.

[4] 6 March 1581 (ibid., p. 47).

[5] See ibid., pp. 47-48.

[6] See E. Rosenberg, *Leicester patron of letters*, New York, 1955, pp. 289-92, who argues that there are significant similarities between this printed defence and Sidney's own MS. defence; cf. also Buxton, *Sidney*, p. 157. The dedication mentions Dyer and shows that John James had assisted Alberico in preparing his publication.

[7] See Van der Molen, *Alberico Gentili*, pp. 49-50; and *De Legationibus*, 1594, ed. Oxford 1924, II, pp. 21a-37a.

Dousa's Ode on the Queen's birthday [1] to Alexander Neville, future editor of the Cambridge poems on Sidney's death, enumerates ten scholars, some previously mentioned, some 'new', yet every one of them in some way connected in England with Sidney and Rogers, or in Holland with Lipsius and Dousa. They are Abraham Hartwell, the antiquary, Andrew Melville, Alexander Dickson from Cambridge [2], Scipio Gentili, Richard Mulcaster, Abraham Ortelius, the future 'Arminian' professor Peter Baro [3], Georgius Benedicti, William Whitaker the Calvinist theologian [4], and William Camden. It seems to follow that the number of 'secondary participants' in the Anglo-Leiden meetings of 1585 is not strictly limited.

The poetic traces of their English visit, as far as the Leiden group is concerned, are too numerous for discussion. If Dousa wrote Latin verses on the Queen's birthday, so did his son [5]. Dousa wrote a poem to Sidney when offering a copy of *Petronius Arbiter*, and his son used Sidney's appointment as Governor of the isle of Walcheren as the occasion to make a similar poetic effort. Dousa the Younger addresses Sir Philip Sidney—like others had done at the time of the 1577 embassy to Germany—as 'princeps Philippus Sidnaeius, Henrici Hiberniae proregis filius', and writes:

---

[1] 'Oda V. Celebratio natalis regii. Ad virum vere nobilem Alexandrum Nevyllum Anglum, amicum non è multis' (Dousa, *Odarum Britannicarum liber*, p. 26 ff.).

[2] One of Dickson's works was later printed at Leiden by Thomas Basson: A. Dicsonus, *Thamus*, 1597. In the same year Basson produced: H. Scepsius, *Defensio pro Alexandro Discono*. See the present writer's *Thomas Basson, English printer at Leiden*, Leiden, 1961.

[3] Cf. G. Benedicti to J. Dousa, Cambridge, 26 August 1585: '... Per quem hac scribo, Doctor Baro est ... vir, ut ipse facile cognosces, summi iudicii & doctrinae. Is, quum Londinum cogitaret, & imprimis ad te, nominis tui & Clariss. viri D. Lipsii fama commotus ...' (B. M., MS. Burney 370, f. 13). On the origin of the term 'Arminian', see Bachrach, *Huygens and Britain*, pp. 72–77.

[4] Cf. J. Lipsius to J. Dousa, Leiden, 1 September 1585, on receiving a letter from Whitaker and a delay in answering Baro (ibid., f. 35).

[5] *Britannicorum Carminum Silva* (printed after the *Odarum Britannicarum liber*), p. 51.

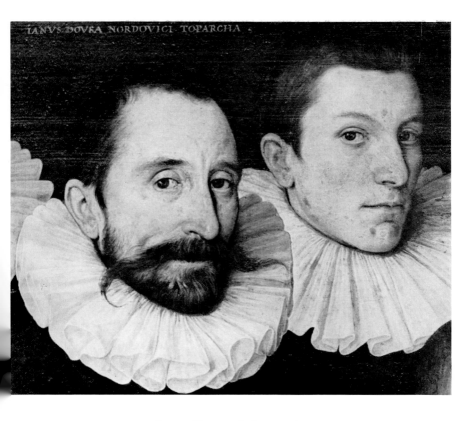

4. Janus Dousa, father and son.

From a family portrait
by Roeloff Willemsz. van Culemborg.

O Sidney, to whom Pallas has given her own arts, Hermes eloquence, Mars valour, Cynthius the art of poetry, whom Suada has granted her very essence [1], Plutus richess, Cypris beauty, the Graces wit; where should I begin to sing your praises and the eminence of your wit (your skill in Latin and Greek will surely be honoured in greater peotry than this) . . .? [2]

This is not very fortunate verse, supporting the conclusion that poems in praise of Sidney tend to become more stereotyped with the growth of Sidney's own reputation. It is, for instance, almost impossible to see anything personal in the elaborate Sidney-Ulysses comparison with which the young Dousa continues. Of course, there is a convention behind it, and the social distance between 'Princeps Sidnaeius' and the eldest son of 'Jonkheer' Jan van der Does must be taken into account. Or was his extreme formality, one might almost say reverence, an artificial means towards establishing a relationship of the same nature as client and patron with 'the common *Rende-vous* of Worth in his time' [3]?

Let us turn to his friend Baudius first. Any Maecenas was welcome to this brilliant lawyer-theologian-historian whose inclination towards the bohemian life necessitated his having rich patrons. Dousa, on some occasions, was one of them. Though probably a most unreliable character, his ready wit, drinking habits, and pleasant conversation made Baudius good company, an opinion held by even so retiring a scholar as the great J. J. Scaliger [4]. In any case, apart from writing

---

[1] Cf. Ennius, *Annales*, 308.

[2] See Appendix I, no. 7.

[3] Greville, *Life of Sidney*, p. 34.
To the list of dedications to Sidney in Berta Siebeck's *Das Bild Sidneys*, the following should be added: *The Castle*, London, 1581 (see Tenison, *Elizabethan England*, IV, 1933, p. 120); *The History of Cambria*, transl. by H. Lloyd, ed. D. Powel, London, 1584 (ibid., V, 1936, p. 95); *Declaration of the King of Navarre*, [transl. by C. Desainliens *alias* Holliband] London, 1585 (ibid., IV, p. 42); S. Gentili, *In XXV Davidis Psalmos epicae paraphrases*, London, 1584 (see 'Sir Philip Sidney 1554–1586—List of Exhibits', Oxford, 1954, no. 58); T. Bright, *In Physicam Gulielmi Adolphi Scribonii animadversiones*, Cambridge, 1584 (ibid., no. 94); N. Monardes, *Simplicium Medicamentorum ex Novo Orbe Delatorum Historiae Liber Tertius*, transl. by C. Clusius, Antwerp, Plantin, 1582 (see F. W. T. Hunger, *Charles de l'Escluse*, The Hague, 1927, p. 154). Cf. also below, p. 122, note 2.

[4] See J. J. Scaliger to J. A. de Thou, 9 March 1591 (J. J. Scaliger, *Lettres françaises*, ed. P. T. de Larroque, Paris, 1879, p. 281).

the customary poems on the Queen [1], he used his time successfully enough to provide the financial basis for a life of leisure. In September he pointed out to Lipsius that lack of occupation had now led to habitual inertia. [2] A little later he sent Sir Philip Sidney a poem begging his patronage in no uncertain terms. [3] In November Sidney sailed for Zeeland and arrived at Flushing on the twenty-first of that month. From there Baudius sent this other letter to Lipsius, a remarkable document not only illustrating the working of Baudius' mind but also throwing some curious light on the conditions in the *familia* of a 'Maecenas':

They say that friends mean wealth. Thatt his is true I daily experience. Because, either through some happy fate of mine—as I persuade myself to believe—or on account of my own merits—which, however, I do not wish to arrogate to myself—I may freely rejoice in having met with numerous special friends whose works and courtesy have always been most honourable and useful to me. I leave out all the others, but this one man I must speak about, Dousa, I say, and Mr. Rogers, through whose kind offices it has been achieved (nothing more desirable could have fallen to my lot) that I am received into the *familia* of the illustrious knight Sir Philip Sidney. Should I, to you, bring to mind his wisdom, kindness, and his other gifts?

Our wit is incapable of describing the bounds of such praises,
Nor can it celebrate such men in proper verse.

And yet, I do not know why, here I am a mere nobody, as they say; not indeed because I like it, nor, I believe, through any fault of mine, except perhaps because of some slight rustic bashfulness. And so, in order to content my mind where I can, I earnestly request you, my Lipsius, that you will relieve the shyness of my nature, by including, when you send him a letter, some indications of your love for me: indications of those things which you, too, can say about me without an infringement of the truth: I trust that I shall honestly answer for your affirmations. I tell you, there is nobody more accessible to you than he is, for he burns with admiration for you. And so, if you will do this, you will not make me love you still more warmly (for my love for you has nowhere to increase), but you will achieve that I owe you more, and at the same time can do more to repay you this debt. Farewell.

[P.S.] Again I beg you, my Lipsius, what I have already im-

---

[1] Baudius, *Carmina*, pp. 34, 48; see also below, p. 95, note 4.

[2] D. Baudius to J. Lipsius, London, 25 September 1585 (*Sylloges epistolarum*, ed. P. Burman, Leiden, 1727, I, no. 252).

[3] See Appendix I, no. 8.

plored you concerning the sending of this letter to this place. I am here at Flushing in the house of Van der Beke, the Pensionary. I should really prefer you to send various letters of the same kind at different times. I shall only bring him one, and if more of them should arrive I shall keep the others. My regards to Donellus, and also to the Van Hout family. Farewell, my precious friend. [1]

The revealing parts of this remarkable letter are the references to Dousa, Rogers, and Lipsius and their actual relationship to Sidney. Whatever one may think of Baudius' pathetic request, this was an instance of a Leiden man whose literary friendship with Dousa and Rogers gave him access to Sidney, the *Heros* as he called him, and whose personal introduction to the Englishman's *familia* was a demonstrable result of the long Rogers-Dousa-Sidney friendship of many preceding years. His literary intimacy with Lipsius, which was real enough in spite of that unfortunate letter, could make Baudius a somebody in the eyes of one whom 'the Universities abroad ... accompted ... a generall *Maecenas* of Learning' [2]. Here was a future Leiden professor, whom various generations were to allow no small merit as a neo-Latin poet, finding a patron in Sir Philip Sidney, and consequently travelling in his company for the few remaining months of the latter's life.

One is somewhat doubtful about Baudius' later statement [3] that his verse 'Oratio Sub Persona Belgarum' [4] was instrumental in persuading the Queen to support the cause of the Dutch embassy of 1585. Nor is it certain that Sidney's munificence satisfied Baudius' demands. He wrote another poem, probably on new year's day 1586, praising his patron for a love of poetry, but concluding with the inevitable request that 'you, o good Maecenas, will deign to lift up your insignificant pupil, and lead him away from a slothful life'. [5]

---

[1] D. Baudius to J. Lipsius, [Flushing, November/December 1585] (Leiden, Univ. Libr., MS. BPL 885, copied 'E codice Parisino Nouv. acq. Lat. 1554, p. 10'). See Appendix II, no. 53.

[2] Greville, *Life of Sidney*, p. 33.

[3] See p. 81, note 1.

[4] Baudius, *Carmina*, p. 48 ff. A MS. copy of this poem is preserved in the B.M. (MS. Burney 371, f. 127); on the preceding fol. is a MS. copy of Baudius' 'Ad Guilielmum Caecilium Borlaeum', which was also printed in the *Carmina* (p. 96 ff.).

[5] See Appendix I, no. 11.

Sidney would no longer have to be content with minor verses
as a reward:

> I shall arm myself to speak in histories about great deeds,
> I shall sing of Dudley the hero, and I shall sing of you, o Sidney,

promises Baudius as he enters the beginning of 1586, ready to
draft the Sidney epic.

It seems possible that Dousa the Younger—though in his
case not for financial motives—also followed the first English
contingent and sailed with the new Governor of Flushing, for
his presence in London at any later date cannot be proved
with certainty.

His father, on the other hand, stayed behind with a small
group of diplomats long after the other ambassadors' return to
The Hague. Their concern, no doubt, was to hasten the
speedy execution of her Majesty's promises, and to advise
the English campaigners. During the month which elapsed
between Sidney's departure and Leicester's sailing, the
'quadrumvirate' of Dousa, Hotman, Groslot and Melissus, with
Rogers as an additional member, was in its most active state.

Melissus, it will be remembered, had travelled to England
that year to offer his poems to the Queen. 'His poems' must
have been a shorter manuscript copy of the *Schediasmata
poetica*, printed in 1586 but dedicated to the Queen 'at Paris,
August 1585' [1]. This was by no means his first poetic presentation to Elizabeth. Three years earlier he had, from Augsburg, written her an *Ode pindarica*, and the very dedication
of that *Ode* had included a reminder that 'you have before
this received my *Schediasmata* [of 1574-5]'.[2] Of the *Ode
pindarica* two copies had been sent to George Gilpin 'the
Queen's ambassador to Rudolph II', one with a poem written
on the first fly-leaf in which Melissus requested his friend to
present the book to Elizabeth and then

to let me know with a felicitous sign what she orders me to execute.
You will dedicate me—for what I am worth—to the celebration
of her fame, I am all ready to serve England. [3]

---

[1] *Schediasmata poetica. Secundo edita*, Paris, 1586, sig.ā iij.
[2] *Ode pindarica ad Elisabetham*, Augsburg, 1582, verso title page. See
Appendix II, no. 54.
[3] *Ode pindarica*, B. M. copy pressmark 11.408. See Appendix II, no. 55.
The poem was afterwards printed in the *Schediasmata*.

Encouraged perhaps by some 'felicitous sign', Melissus had now come to England with two volumes of poetry addressed either to living persons or to his courtly mistress 'Rosina'. The volumes were divided into 'books', and each book was preceded by a poem to Elizabeth. In perfect agreement with the subtle fashions of Eliza's court his mistress of perfection, Rosina, was the mirror of those ideals of courtly love exemplified by the Virgin Queen. Rosina was, so to speak, Melissus' Tudor Rose:

AURORA, hail. Each day when my eyes beheld your beauty I felt happy, for thus I thought clearly to see ELISA, that learned, cultured Queen of England, and in her living image my ROSINA, whose fame lies enwrapped in many shining books of songs, long celebrated by a thousand poets' verses. [1]

Whether it was by his ability to address the right people in the proper fashion, or by his familiarity with numerous English writer-politicians, Melissus appears to have found the English Court hospitable. No doubt his long-established friendship with the Sidneys, Philip and his brother Robert, to whom he devoted another poem in the 1586 *Schediasmata*, increased the delights of his London sojourn. This poem, an elaborate plea for simplicity to be fashioned after the unpainted naturalness of sweet Diona and Diana, was at least a more personal tribute than the formal verses of his colleagues. [2]

Close friends already, [3] Dousa and Melissus, like Rogers and Sidney, shared a literary Parisian background and thence a particular interest in modern literature. Neither of them hesitated to recognize their spiritual kinship, while praising the happy Fate that had brought them together under so favourable circumstances.

> Quae Fortuna duos junxit in Anglia?
> Quis dexter Genius? quod Genio favens
>   Exoptabile sidus?

---

[1] *Schediasmata*, 1586, [I], p. 184. See Appendix II, no. 56.
[2] See Appendix I, no. 6.
[3] See their correspondence in B.M., MS. Burney 370. Also, Dousa had dedicated his *Schediasma succidaneum*, Antwerp, Plantin, 1582, to Melissus. The *Poemata* edition of 1609 includes *Elegiarum juvenilium sive cupidinum libri duo*, dedicated to Melissus in a letter dated Leiden 1576.

writes Melissus in the autumn of 1585. To share the delights of our conversations, he continues, 'your son is with you, a boy of lively wit, whom Melpomene has deemed worthy her loving care by teaching him the fine arts of the Muses, whom she has made a Latin poet of great merit'. You, the ambassador, find the Queen divinely agreeable to yourself and your cause of liberty. 'The virgins of The Hague prepare with tender hands the golden gifts for Dudley their leader . . ., Leiden expects you, too, and meditates an eternal epic in honour of you as much as of Leicester. But do not go so soon, Lord of Noordwijk.'[1] This poem of Melissus was to be included in an anthology entirely devoted to Dousa[2]—no slight honour for a living poet—and Dousa writes to Melissus in much the same manner[3].

Meanwhile arrangements for Leicester's departure were under way and Dousa was ready to precede the Lord Governor, in order to assist perhaps in the preparations of his festive welcome. Towards the end of November both Melissus and Groslotius wrote in Dousa's Album.[4] Soon afterwards, probably early in December, Dousa was notified that

I and Groslotius will see you before you go, as we promised yesterday. Therefore, my dear Dousa, let us know what hour would suit you and not be inconvenient to you and your time-schedule. If you expect to be asked for a repast we shall wait for you afterwards, and then we shall come to attend the ship with mutual good wishes. A poem may follow you and your son.[5]

The poem followed indeed, recalling how

your faithful friends stood on the riverbank when the tide went out, myself, Rogers, and Groslotius, following the Poet with sincerest wishes.[6]

---

[1] Melissus, 'Ad Janum Dousam' (B.M., MS. Burney 370, ff. 69–70). See Appendix II, no. 57.

[2] *Encomia Dousana . . . Edita a Ioanne Posthio*, Heidelberg, 1587, p. 6.

[3] 'Ad Paulum Melissum Schedium Francum, Comitem Palatinum et equitem, laureatum q. Poetam, Civem Romanum' (Dousa, *Odarum Britannicarum liber*, p. 37).

[4] Ff. 122[V] and 123.

[5] P. Melissus to J. Dousa, London, [December? 1585] (B.M., MS. Burney 370, f. 118). See Appendix II, no. 58.

[6] Melissum, 'Ad Nerea' (ibid., f. 76; printed in *Encomia Dousana*, p. 8). See Appendix II, no. 59.

After Dousa's safe arrival [1] Melissus tarried in England a little longer. Few letters survive, but they imply a continuous correspondence between Melissus, Hotman, Dousa, and Sidney. When Dousa sailed—for Flushing, it would seem—Melissus asked him to give his 'kindest regards to Philip Sidney, whom I have known so well for many years'. [2] Early in the new year he sent his old friend via Hotman a 'munus', which was in all likelihood his printed *Schediasmata*:

I was glad to learn from your letter, my Hotman, that Sidney liked my present. I wish I had the good fortune to see him here; my negotiations at Court would be concluded very much more quickly and conveniently if he were present... Greetings again to Lipsius and Dousa and the other friends. [3]

Nevertheless he could write to Walsingham a week later that

my reason for writing is to inform you of my departure to France... Nothing keeps me here any longer, except waiting for a passport which I shall need at the harbour: I hope that Mr. Secretary Nicasius [4] has already made it to be written out and signed by the Queen's hand.

If any letters from my old friend Sir Philip Sidney should be sent to me, I should like to have them forwarded. [5]

Though the 'quadrumvirate' was thus broken up, some events, as we shall see, would again unite them. The first immediately presented itself in the death of the inspiring leader to whom they all had reason to feel indebted: 'as I am writing this,' said Groslotius in a somewhat belated letter to Dousa, 'I receive the news that Pierre de Ronsard has recently died, our principal *vates*, inferior only to Du Bartas' [6]. The literary world was deprived of one of its foremost leaders. And every one of the London circle of the preceding months, English or Dutch, French or German, could claim to have lost a great teacher, and, in some cases, also an old friend. Many

---

[1] Cf. J. Gruterus to J. Dousa, Rostoch, 27 April 1586 (o.s.) (B.M., MS. Burney 371, f. 156).
[2] See p. 98, note 5.
[3] P. Melissus to J. Hotman, London, 12 February 1586 (*Hotomanorum epistolae*, no. 92). See Appendix II, no. 60.
[4] In 1587 Rogers' father-in-law: see above, p. 11, note 2.
[5] P. Melissus to F. Walsingham, London, 19 February 1586 (P.R.O., SP 12/186, no. 71). See Appendix II, no. 61.
[6] H. Groslotius to J. Dousa, London, 28 March 1586 (B.M., MS. Burney 370, f. 4). See Appendix II, no. 46.

years separated Ronsard's death from their days of literary apprenticeship in Paris, from the time which Rogers had recalled in a poem to De Baïf:

when I visited your house, Baïf, and you would read me the graceful delights of your Muse,

with Ronsard, whom

I see before me singing your poems with his refined voice. [1]

The ode which Melissus now wrote on Ronsard, to be included in the *Tombeau recuelli de plusieurs excellens personnages*, was composed in London in February 1586, soon after Rogers had reported the news of Ronsard's death; and it was his last poem devoted to French matters. It has been observed that in his 'Ode de obitu Ronsardi' Melissus weeps 'avec plus de sincérité que certains compatriotes du maître. Le génie de Ronsard et les principes dont la Pléiade avait vécu étaient déjà fort démodés dans cette jeune poésie, qui se ralliait autour de Desportes; ils n'avaient rien perdu de leur prestige pour l'imagination toujours fraîche de Melissus.' [2] Certainly, Ronsard's undiminished prestige to Melissus may account for some of the tears, and it is curious that the two poets whom he introduced in this same ode in order to share the grief were Rogers and Dousa. [3] The German, the Englishman, and the Dutchman, who had been equally inspired by a poetic example which was then a quarter of a century old, must have looked slightly old-fashioned in the company of the other 'excellens personnages'. The French eulogized a man who had been 'a pioneer in his day'. Melissus' poem, on the other hand, serves to remind us of how far Dutch, English, and German poetry still lagged behind.

It may not be inappropriate to consider at this point a few questions connected with the development of vernacular poetry in England and Holland. When confronted with such quantities of Latin verse a modern reader will find himself

---

[1] Rogers, 'Jano Antonio Baifio' (Hertford MS., f. 291). See Appendix II, no. 62. Cf. De Nolhac, *Ronsard et l'humanisme*, pp. 217, 219.

[2] De Nolhac, *Melissus*, p. 90.

[3] An epitaph on Ronsard is ascribed to Dousa in B.M. MS. Sloane 2764, no. 38.

prejudiced in favour of vernacular writing. [1] This is curious because the authors themselves seemed hardly conscious of any such problem of preference. Sidney himself never apologizes for English poetry as opposed to Latin writing, nor does he reveal an impulse to defend the English language against a tyrannical insistence by scholars on Latin. His very examples of great contemporary authors are almost exclusively Latin poets, and he omits the 'obvious' point in favour of a vernacular, even in a *Defense* which was so clearly written for an English public. 'Latin or English' was not one of his problems, and his assertion is simply that English was no less suitable a medium for poetry than any other language.

To understand the Dutch interest in English writers it is worth considering for a moment how much they knew of the language and literature of Britain. The prestige of English and Dutch as literary languages was only just being established, although by 1585 some men in both countries had begun to indicate or prove the merits of their mother tongue in comparison with other 'vulgar speeches'. Though it should be noted that a philological interest for its own sake was developing at the time, the motive for learning a modern language other than French would often have been, in the case of scholarly poets, that of wanting to read other literatures. We know that Sidney had some acquaintance with German, but the absence of a literary reason for mastering the tongue Languet had advised him to learn may have accounted for his abandoning these exercises [2]. One is of course rarely told about proficiency or motive, but when Dousa the Younger translated Constable's sonnets into Dutch as well as Latin, and did so with more than average skill, this can only be evidence of a good knowledge of the languages. We may assume, perhaps, that all the Leiden visitors of that year learnt 'literary English' to varying degrees of fluency. One poem by the same Dousa [3] suggests that he knew Sidney's *Arcadia*, and he was not necessarily an exception. Sometimes

---

[1] On this prejudice, see J. Sparrow, 'Latin Verse of the High Renaissance', *Italian Renaissance Studies*, London, 1960, pp. 354–367.

[2] See P. Sidney to H. Languet, Padua, 4 February 1574 (Sidney, *Works*, III, no. 11).

[3] See Appendix I, no. 17. See pp. 157–158.

writers attribute proficiency in foreign languages to their contemporaries, but one cannot be too careful. Melissus, we are told, 'apart from his own language, which is high German, and those which are taught at school and in the Universities, was very fond of Italian, French, Spanish, and also Dutch and English.' [1] Melissus himself, however, allows us to see this tribute in the right proportions in a letter to Dousa while both were in London: 'if I stay here any longer, I shall make an effort to learn English'. [2] And that was only two months before he left England.

Conversely, in 1586 there is the problem of whether any of the English knew Dutch—i.e. low Dutch. But before that time such questions never seem to occur in an Anglo-Dutch context—at least we never hear of them. Nor, in some cases, is there any need to create the problem.

It has never been thought strange that foreign writers should have unanimously praised Philip Sidney in his capacity as a poet, [3] not only in 1585/6 but even at the time of his German embassy much earlier [4]. Had they all read his English works, his *Astrophel and Stella*, his *Psalms*, and also his greatest piece of poesy, the *Arcadia?* Perhaps at one time, but certainly not in 1577, before these works were written. It is obvious that his admirers had more than these English books in mind. Rogers has given the answer at a very early date when, declaring his poetic inability to do justice to the wonders of Eliza's Court and calling them a subject befitting 'the voice of Phoebus, or of Sidney, or Dyer', he said of Sidney:

Whether you wish to speak out in Latin, or prefer the accents of Gallia, or rather express your feelings in Italian speech, nobody could do it more gracefully or better than you. [5]

Much later Groslotius was to make the same point and even add another item, Greek, to his specified account of Sidney's multilingual Muse:

Second to none he was in the arts of the *Camoenae*; witness his English, Italian, Latin, French, and Greek poetry: such laurels deck

---

[1] J. J. Boissard, *Bibliotheca*, III, p. 29. See Appendix II, no. 45.
[2] See p. 98, note 5.
[3] See Appendix I, nos. 2, (4,) 6, 7, 11, 12, 13, 18, 19, 21, 28.
[4] See Appendix I, no. 2.
[5] See Appendix I, no. 4.

so great an image, to me they are as many burning torches of life; because of them, for ever he shall live. [1]

Groslotius—though a Frenchman—gives pride of place to Sidney's English poetry, as does Rogers when he emphasizes the particular abundance of the poet's wit 'when your passion takes possession of our [*i.e. English*] arts'. But almost equal tribute is paid to his (now lost) achievements in Latin and Greek, French and Italian. Perhaps Thomas Moffet thought of these same literary compositions when he discussed Sidney's *oeuvre* under the heading 'adolescentia'. [2]

This completes our picture of a renaissance poet who without these other accomplishments would have looked strangely disloyal to his own ideal of a complete courtier. As a practising amateur-polyglot he was as true to the model as any other respectable member of the Republic of Letters. This also helps to explain why he was recognized as a *confrère* by many a foreign poet whose skill in the English language or interest in 'Areopagitican' experiments is easy to doubt. We must therefore assume that Sidney's concern with English poesy and the authority with which he compared its merits had their foundation in his practice in non-English verse. This he had probably written with greater ease since he was able to draw from the established tradition of the 'literary languages'. Some Dutch writers were to pursue the same course, which the Pléiade poets themselves had indicated (after the example of Du Bellay) by using Latin and Greek for literary composition as much as the vernacular. And even Ronsard, the French renovator, began ambitiously as a Latin poet and never deserted the humanists' world [3].

It follows that language barriers did not arise. Nor can the half-truth be maintained that 'Sidney est le seul écrivain anglais de son temps qui ait joui d'une réputation européenne; toutefois, celle-ci était fondée non sur ses ouvrages qui, de son vivant, ne furent pas connus sur le Continent, mais sur sa personnalité de gentilhomme ami des lettres.' [4]

In approaching their underestimated vernaculars, Sidney's

---

[1] See Appendix I, no. 13.
[2] Moffet, *Nobilis*, ed. Heltzel, p. 10 and notes on pp. 116–117.
[3] Cf. De Nolhac, *Ronsard et l'humanisme*, pp. 78, 243.
[4] Poirier, *Sidney*, p. 258.

circle and the Leiden poets ran almost completely parallel. In this only did they differ: that in a non-academic setting of Ladies and Courtiers, the English works of Sir Philip Sidney had a better chance of survival, while the classical spirit of the University of Leiden would take better care of non-vernacular manuscripts. In fact, the survival of manuscripts was determined more by the above practice than by relative merit.

Towards the end of the crucial year 1585, Robert Dudley, Earl of Leicester, at long last sailed for Holland to join his nephew and lead the Queen's forces in the foreign field.

They were both preceded by the formal adulation of the four Leiden poets, who were seconded by one Arnoldus Eick(ius) from Utrecht. This peculiar versifier—perhaps another unofficial member of the Dutch legation—wrote and printed two 'Elogia' [1], one to Leicester, and one to Sidney which he subtitled *De vera nobilitate*. The Sidney eulogy, a set of 'Odes Horatianae', was dedicated to the author's son Justus; although the tract was really addressed to the sitter for the portrait 'of true nobility', since Eickius signed his pages of exalted *clichés* with:

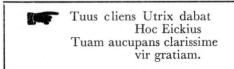

> Tuus cliens Utrix dabat
> Hoc Eickius
> Tuam aucupans clarissime
> vir gratiam.
>
> [2]

His odes, unfortunately, deserve no further inspection in respect of either contents or merit. The end of a bombastic 'To the Reader' includes the line: 'may Dousa, the Attican Muse, support me in this with greater force'. A reader of the

---

[1] *Elogium . . . Roberti, comitis Leycestrii . . . Recognitum & auctum. Ad serenissi-mam reginam . . . Elizabetham. Cum Elogio . . . Philippi Sidnei . . . Seu De vera nobilitate*, Utrecht, 1586. According to B. Siebeck (*Das Bild Sidneys*, p. 67, n. 2) an *Elogium Philippi Sidneii* appeared in 1585; the same seems implied in the present title's 'Recognitum & auctum'.

[2] Evidently, the writer wanted to take no risk and printed these lines just so, index and all.

copy which is now preserved in the British Museum [1] was provoked to add in manuscript a distich 'to the critic':

Dousa, who will to reprove this *vates* and accuse him of a wart, hiding the while the large tumours of his monstrosity? [2]

So acid a contemporary comment relieves us from the task of discussing the Utrecht pamphlet. Its subjects, however, Leicester and Sidney, deserve more attention. For in the opening weeks of 1586 Holland was to witness an uncommon yet at the same time truly 'renaissance' spectacle, the triumphant entry of the chivalry of England headed by two noblemen who were known to be, the one a principal patron of letters, the other a renowned poet.

[1] B. M. pressmark 837. h. 7. (2).   [2] See Appendix II, no. 63.

ENGLAND VISITS LEIDEN

By 1585 the Netherlands could no longer, as they had done when Sidney wrote his 30th sonnet,

Trust in the shade of pleasing Orange tree. [1]

Orange was dead. Antwerp was lost to the Spaniards, and the northern Provinces appeared too disorganized to resist armed pressure from the South without help and leadership from outside. To many Dutchmen the arrival of Leicester must have seemed a happy solution after years of unsuccessful negotiating. But rather than speculate on the tangle of motives, sentiments, and misunderstandings which attended the opening months of his Governor-Generalship, we must concentrate on some English writers who came with him 'to trail a pike' in the Low Countries.

Two aspects of Leicester's campaign offer a special problem because they imply what seems a patent contradiction. On the one hand there is the undeniable fact that these months happened to be the first meeting of really large numbers of Englishmen and Dutchmen from every social layer, and that this very encounter had to a large extent been prepared in a political milieu of poets, patrons, and professors. On the other hand we find the general assumption that the 'literary soldiers' in Leicester's forces were then, for once, so busy discussing politics as to forsake the Muses. On closer inspection this assumption seems untenable. Ten years or more of preparations on various levels had led up to the Earl's arrival. They had been, above all, years in which a political relationship had been steadily built up by literary activities. Throughout the recent embassy, which was only a finale to the introductory period, poets had been active. Within the relatively small, but select, circle of these humanists an ideal had been established. The πρᾶξις now remained, for which

---

[1] Sidney, *Astrophel and Stella*, xxx.

an opportunity at last presented itself. Sidney came, as a learned soldier, and, in the words of his companion and best friend Greville, 'this one man's example, and personall respect, did not onely encourage Learning, and Honour in the Schooles, but brought the affection, and true use thereof both into the Court, and Camp.' [1] Baudius has already helped us to disprove 'that he had little opportunity for patronage' [2]. Needless to say, Sidney was not the only *literatus* in the camp. On the contrary, it shows the campaigners' *vertu* to find so many men of culture in their leading ranks. Very few are outside the scope of this context.[3] Even Leicester's physician was that first English graduate of the young University of Leiden, John James.[4]

Before moving from Court to Camp, the English leaders went on an introductory tour, travelling with Leicester on his Progress. When the new year began—on 1 January in the Dutch calendar—they were all assembled in the Province of Holland with half the distance of the magnificent entries

[1] Greville, *Life of Sidney*, p. 34.
[2] Buxton, *Sidney*, p. 167.
[3] A borderline case is Sir Henry Norris' son Edward, Sidney's lieutenant, particularly famous for his quarrel with Count Hollock. Edward Norris deserves mention for having rendered, as the only known Rogers translator, Rogers' 'Ad Franciscum Thorium medicum et poetam' of 2 May 1570 into English verse. It may not prove his ability as a sonneteer, but is certainly a good example of another 'literary soldier' in Holland, who was, moreover, a friend of Rogers'.

> The Quayle that unto Pelops plaines doth flie,
>   And leaves of famous Phare, the parched soyle,
>   Amids her course, behold, overcome with toyle,
>   She falles, and on the seas, doth flotinge lye.
> Her force her fayles, het hart beginnes to die,
>   She reddy semes to vewe the Naiades seate,
>   Yet she at last with winges the sea(te) to beate
>   And with her feete the waves to cutt doth trie.
> Triumphinge she, and hoysinge fethered sayles,
>   To Tyndars cost arives, her force avayles:
>   Marck thy wel Thore, whoe though opprest by fate
> With vertues giftes thy selfe shoudst rayse agayne,
>   Which stil (allthough thy fortunes fail,) remaine:
>   Shew this, and overcome thy Destines hate.
>   (Hertford MS., f. 149ᵛ)

[4] See pp. 59 and 129.

still to cover. The next station was to be Leiden, an hour's ride from The Hague where Leicester was to keep his Court. Whatever could happen to his political *Secours*, the literary side to its background warranted another personal meeting, not in London this time but as a return visit in the one University of Holland. It would have been as unlike these English gentlemen not to have looked forward to the occasion as it would be cynical to doubt that some Leiden scholars at least were eager to entertain them.

What was the situation in Leiden meanwhile, as far as poetry was concerned, and, more particularly, how had Van Hout's ambitious Dutch programme progressed? He indeed must keep his central position, not only because four of the leading Latin poets had been away for some time, but also because the general distinction between 'Latin Dousa' and 'Dutch Van Hout' was still valid in 1586 [1]. Nor had the past five years been as barren as the rare survival of Dutch verse might lead one to think.

In 1581 a number of students had occupied rooms in Van Hout's house: Jacobus (van) Walraven, Jan (or Justus) van Ryswyck, Theodorus (or Dirc) (van) Lyfvelt, Winant Micault, and Van Hout's own son Bartholomeus. Each of them was registered in the Faculty of Arts, except Micault, and none is known to have left with a degree. It has been suggested [2] that some of Van Hout's followers are perhaps to be found in this group. Lyfvelt, it is true, later made himself a minor name in Dutch literature for translating Du Bartas, [3] but the others have successfully hidden themselves in the remotest regions of Van Hout's obscure 'gathering'. A notable exception is Jacobus Walraven from Hoorn, not a youthful undergraduate but a man who had given up his profession

---

[1] E.g. an 'Elegia' by Dousa (uniting the names of Giselinus, Rogers, Lipsius, J. Grotius, Leovaeus, Walraven) which includes the following lines: '. . . Seu Patrio vultis, Latio seu Carmine dici, HAUTENUS patrium Carmen, at Ausonium / DOUSA canet vobis: . . .' (Dousa, *Elegiarum lib. II*, Leiden, 1585, pp. 4–5).

[2] See p. 36, note 1.

[3] *De eerste weke der Scheppinge der Werelt*, Brussels, 1609.

at an advanced age [1] in order to hear the lecturers of Leiden. Dirck Volckertszoon Coornhert, the Haarlem poet, was the first to compliment him on his decision when, as early as 1582, he selected him for the dedication of his *Comedie van de Rijckeman*. There Walraven is pictured as a man whose only desire is to live for the *bonae literae*. An appropriate dedication it was, for nothing appears to have pleased Jacob more than the pursuit of vernacular poetry. His efforts, like Van Hout's, are now almost entirely lost; and also like Van Hout's must have been fairly continuous and not without merit, if one may judge by one quite pleasant 'Ode' which appeared in 1584, preceded by a Dutch sonnet of Dousa's and another Dutch ode by Van Hout, among the prefatory matter of the famous *Spieghel der Zeevaerdt* [2]. For the rest he was in the non-publishing amateur tradition.

Janus Gruter(us), a Dutchman with an English background [3], friend of Dousa and of Rogers [4], and in 1602 Melissus' successor as Librarian at Heidelberg, was then no longer in Leiden. Nevertheless he must also be included, if only *in absentia*. It remains difficult enough to give the future Wittenberg Professor of History his rightful place in the development of Dutch literature of the preceding five years, but it is possible to revive his share in its dark origins. In April 1586 Gruterus wrote to Dousa as follows:

I live 'in otio sine negotio', and really have begun to despair that I shall be able to keep my former name among men of letters.

---

[1] His actual age is often discussed as a problem, but the Leiden *Volumen Inscriptionum*, in which his name was entered on 9 November 1579, gives it very clearly: 35.

[2] L. Jansz. Waghenaer, *Teerste Deel van de Spieghel der Zeevaerdt*, Leiden, 1584, sig. A4.

[3] His mother, Catherine Tishemin (see fig. 1), taught him Greek and Latin. Born at Antwerp in 1560, he reached Leiden via Middelburg, Antwerp, and Cambridge. He was created 'Dr. Juris' on 31 May 1584. In 1593 he did not accept a Leiden Chair when it was offered to him. (See C. G. Jöcher, *Allgemeines Gelehrten-Lexicon*, Leipzig, 1750)

[4] Cf. J. Gruterus to D. Rogers, Danzig, 11 November 1585 (P.R.O., S.P. 12/193, no. 30), which includes a Latin poem. Gruterus' *Pericula*, Heidelberg, 1587—in which the 'Harmosynes, seu ocellorum liber' (pp. 167 ff.) was dedicated to Dousa—has no reference to Rogers, but includes poems to and from Ortelius, Vulcanius, Clusius, the Dousas, Lernutius, Lipsius, and others.

Yea, even that sweet composing of sonnets is quite abandoned; and I who once dared to pronounce these triumphant words [. . . [1]] am now prepared to leave it—and do leave it—to the least of all mortals. But I have chatted enough. Give the task to others, if you like. Greetings to your son, whom I would have sent a *Carmen*, but the last stanza has not come off yet. [2]

This reveals an early share in Van Hout's programme of Dutch poesy. Moreover, the same letter includes the (mediocre) sonnet in which he boasts of the perennial fame his Dutch Muse would bring him and which contains such statements as 'it was I who first translated Roman verses'—a statement of some historical importance, although the sonnet itself is also a translation. [3]

Printed evidence must come from a Dutch rendering of Lipsius' famous treatise *De Constantia* which Plantin's son-in-law Moretus (Jan Moerentorf) had prepared soon after its appearance in Latin. Walraven had undertaken a translation also, 'not without consulting the author' [4], but had abandoned

---

[1] Here a sonnet was inserted: see note 3.

[2] J. Gruterus to J. Dousa, Rostock, 27 April 1586 (o.s.) (B.M., MS. Burney 371, f. 156). See Appendix II, no. 64.

[3]
  Myn werc heb ic voldaen, veel harder dan fyn stael,
    veel hooger dan t'steyl spits der vuyriger pilaren.
    D'welc noch des regens plas, noch t'grof getal der jaren,
    noch Aquilo's gedruys sal brengen totten dael.
  Mijn beste' & meeste helft in Libitina's dwael
    men niet bewimplen can, maer met een vlug moet varen
    hoog henen door de locht, & so sich openbaren,
    voor yder man, glyc s nachts de maen aen shemels sael.
  Mijn lof men hooren sal van daer Auroras wagen
    Swart Indien verclaert, tot daer Apollo's ros
    zyn sweetich hayr comt in de weste zee af vagen.
  Ic was die eerst het dicht vertaelde der Romeynen.
    Steect op dan vry den hals, melpomenè, & het bos
    myns hoofs wilt met den rueck eens lauriers treflyc reynen.

The sonnet is an almost literal translation of Horace, *Od.*, III, xxx. Another sonnet, 'ut vocant', is on f. 161 of the same MS., to Dousa the Younger, [Amsterdam], 7 September [1587]; under this verse (on fever) Gruterus wrote: 'I am sorry and ashamed to have written it, for it is even worse than I thought'—but then he *was* in bed with a fever himself. A. J. van der Aa, *Biographisch Woordenboek der Nederlanden*, Haarlem, 1852, makes mention of 500 unpublished Dutch sonnets by Gruterus but gives no further information.

[4] Whetstone, *Honourable reputation* (see below, p. 139), p. 4. See Appendix II, no. 65.

the project when learned Moretus was found to be engaged on the same task. In 1584 the Leiden House of Plantin published an edition of *Twee boecken van de stantvasticheyt*. This book was exceptional in that its prefatory matter included four Dutch poems, by Van Hout and Gruterus. The former contributed an interesting 72-line ode 'Op de Standtvasticheyt des achtbaren vermaerden ende hoochgheleerden Iusti Lipsii', while Gruterus, future dedicatee of the younger Dousa's ''Ερωτοπαίγνιον', offered three Dutch sonnets full of curious images and idioms. The beautifully printed book truly and gracefully represented the new Leiden poets.

All these minor indications naturally lead one to the conclusion that during the five years preceding the arrival of Leicester's literate companions, there was an increase of enthusiasm for a modern Dutch poetry, for translations, and for such forms as Odes and Sonnets, but always in an informal manner. In 1584 the Amsterdam Chamber of Rhetoric published at Leiden a treatise advocating the proper use of a pure mother tongue. [1] This their poet Henric Laurens Spiegel rendered in (Dutch) verse [2] and dedicated to the University of Leiden, arguing that they should introduce the use of vernacular in the University, and praising Van Hout as the great champion of this innovation. There is an obvious connexion here with the 'General Table of Rhetoric', a large single sheet on which the broad rules of Dutch composition were arranged diagrammatically with simple examples to each item, issued by Plantin at Leiden in 1585. [3]

The prestige of Dutch, in other words, was gaining ground rapidly; and it even found 'scholarly justification' in a special preface 'On the Worthiness of the Dutch Language' by the scientist Simon Stevin, the first Dutch academic engineer. Stevin's *Beghinselen des waterwichts* of 1586 was written in the vernacular to prove the supreme clarity of northern

---

[1] *Twe-spraack van de Nederduitsche Letterkunst*, Leiden, 1584. See *Geschiedenis van de letterkunde der Nederlanden*, III, Bois-le-Duc, 1944, pp. 44–50, 307, 395—396.

[2] *Ruych bewerp der Redenkaveling*, Leiden, 1585.

[3] *Een alghemene Tafel voorbeeldende alle de stucken van Dialectika of Redenkaveling*. Of this neglected broadsheet a copy exists in the Royal Library, The Hague (pressmark Pamfl. no. 760).

Dutch. [1] It is curious to note how all this resembled similar developments in England.

The leading poets and patrons on both sides of the Narrow Seas knew one another either personally or by report even before they met in Leiden on 12 January 1586. We know of varying degrees of intimacy between Leicester, Sidney, Gilpin, the Dousas, Lipsius, Baudius, and Hotman. With almost equal certainty we may assume that many of the others had heard much about their respective hosts or guests and that there were few complete strangers.

The scarceness of documentary evidence, however, makes it necessary to proceed most cautiously. What can be noted is that these few preceding weeks probably were the ones about which Walraven speaks in his description of how he and young Dousa together with Van Hout and François van Brouchoven (the bailiff of Leiden) seriously undertook to learn English [2]. Nor will they have been the only ones to do so, for towards the end of January their teacher was officially permitted to 'hold school' for the public, the first English language school in Leiden, and probably of Holland, too. The teacher was an English refugee, Thomas Basson, who had recently set up a printing press in a house of Plantin's almost opposite the University building, the first Leiden press to do English books. [3] In the case of Van Brouchoven, and to a lesser extent also of Van Hout, their sudden enthusiasm could be seen in view of the approaching English army as entirely utilitarian. But, since University members were exempted from billeting, that would not be the concern of Walraven and Dousa and an unknown number of others, who had no business with common soldiers and might use their French or Latin for conversation with the officers. Their motive, in short, was an interest in the English, their

---

[1] *De beghinselen des waterwichts . . . duer Simon Stevin van Brugghe*, Leiden, 1586. Sig. bB 1: 'Uytspraeck vande weerdicheyt der duytsche tael'.

[2] George Whetstone, *The honourable reputation of a souldier*, Leiden, 1585, p. 11. See below, p. 139.

[3] Except for Paedts's 1582 edition of Stanyhurst's *Aeneis* (below, p. 139. note 2). For Basson, see above, p. 92, note 2.

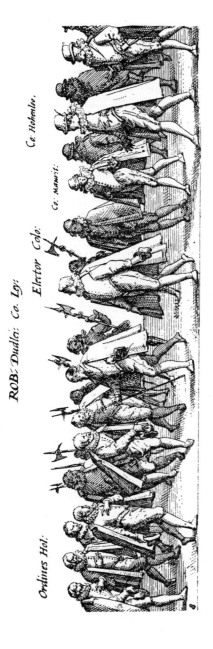

Figure 2

Leicester welcomed in The Hague. Sidney probably walks between the
Elector of Cologne and Prince Maurice.

From *Delineatio Pompae Triumphalis*, 1586.

language, and even in some special cases their literature.

An early contingent of English cavalry had meanwhile reached the town, and Van Hout's major worry was to find suitable accommodation for the imminent arrival of Leicester and his large train. A letter which he was to write the General soon after this first visit shows that he had some reason to be concerned:

We have been extremely gratified to hear of your Grace's resolution also to keep his Court in this town for some time, which will be a great honour to this city.

And since we are duly desirous to find the best lodging and accommodation for your Excellency's Grace and his suite, and desirous also to prevent all the irregularities which have occurred before and make sure that nobody will be encumbered beyond his means, therefore we have sent our delegate to you . . .; [1]

then followed a request for the complete roll of Leicester's suite, stating the number of beds required according to rank and number of servants. This letter becomes doubly interesting because the roll has survived [2]. Exact information about Leicester's retinue is known since the billeting lists, both Van Hout's earlier versions and the improvements, are extant. [3] These specify who visited Leiden, when, in whose house, and 'with how many beds'. [4]

As a leading light in the town's Chambers of Rhetoric and as an experienced writer of interludes, Van Hout will also have had a hand in the preparation of pageants. Verses and mottoes were painted on cardboard, houses along the main route were hung with tapestries, sand was sprinkled on the slippery pavement, and all was prepared for the distinguished visitor.

At last, on 12 January, the colourful procession reached the south gate, Leicester mounted on a white horse. Van Meet-

---

[1] Burgomasters of Leiden to R. Dudley, Leiden, 18 January 1586, in Van Hout's hand (Leiden, Gemeentearchief, *Missiveboeck begonnen 1581*). See Appendix II, no. 66. An impossible transcription is given in the *Correspondentie van Robert Dudley*, ed. H. Brugmans, Utrecht, 1931, I, no. XXI.

[2] Leiden, Gem. arch., Secretarie Archief no. 1059[1].

[3] Id., no. 7885.

[4] A complete list of names will be published elsewhere (see p. 77, note 2).

kercke [1], one of the Dutch representatives in the 1585 embassy, was there to meet him. Whether it is true that Van Meetkercke bowed so deeply as to fall from his (famished) horse, as a Catholic observer maliciously noted [2], is hard to prove and unkind to believe. Whatever the actual welcome was like, Leicester went honourably escorted to his residence in the 'Prinsenlogement' from where he could see the fireworks along the Rapenburg canal and some of the 157 pitchbarrels and 1725 torches and faggots which were burned in the celebrations [3]. On the other side of the Rapenburg he will have noticed the old chapel which the University had recently occupied.

This ys a goodly town and very strong, and most loving people,

he wrote to Walsingham [4].

Leicester's entry into Leiden at long last enabled Van Hout to see the gentlemen of whom his two best friends, Dousa and Lipsius, must have spoken often and warmly. Not only could he meet them, and perhaps try his elementary English, but being in charge of the accommodation he could favour one of them with his own spare rooms. The delightful result is that Town Secretary Van Hout, ignoring perhaps the stricter rules of courtly protocol, entered on the billeting list at his address the name of 'Sir Philip Sidney, Governor of Flushing, with seven beds' [5]. Thus, almost next door to the Town Hall and in the same street as Professor Lipsius, Sidney spent his first days in Leiden in the house of the town's most active poet. In all probability he remained there until after Leicester's second and longer visit (21 January), or left and then returned to the same address, where he also appears to have lodged when the Governor General came for a third visit to Leiden on 10 March.

---

[1] For Van Meetkercke's background and English connexions, see Bachrach, *Huygens and Britain*, pp. 150–151, 154.

[2] F. Dusseldorpius, *Annales*, ed. R. Fruin, in *Werken, uitgegeven door het historisch genootschap*, III, i, The Hague, 1893, p. 208.

[3] Leiden, Gem. arch., *Tresoriers Rekeningen 1586*, ff. 654–655ᵛ.

[4] R. Dudley to F. Walsingham, Leiden, 13 January 1586 (*Correspondence*, p. 49).

[5] Leiden, Gem. arch., Secr. arch. no. 7885, '3', f. 11. See Plate 6.

The Earl's official entry was brief and formal in spite of all the attendant gaiety which Van Hout had arranged in his honour. His second visit nine days later, however, was more spontaneous—the result, no doubt, of a felicitous first meeting—and perhaps therefore the more rewarding to us.

He came with increased numbers of attendants this time and even brought his musicians and players. [1] Excepting Rogers, Melissus, Groslotius, and Benedicti (who was still at Cambridge or London), 'everybody' was present. Sidney lodged at Van Hout's house in the Breestraat, the Dousas in their town-residence at the Oosterlingplaats (now Garenmarkt), Leicester on the Rapenburg, Lipsius in his Breestraat home, Walraven in his corner house on the Steenschuur, and Hotman with Pouwels Vos, the Pensionary. Even George Gilpin, now with Van Brouchoven, had followed them, and so probably had Baudius.

The University, though free from billeting, was ready to entertain the cultured guests. Seventeen days before, they had decided to send the *Rector Magnificus* to The Hague as their official delegate while the Senate stayed behind. But when the Earl arrived, Professors and Curators in full academicals lined up in twos and formally greeted him in front of their Academy. [2] An austere procession it was, as if to underline the pages of Latin verse which their respectable Muse had offered the foreign patron. Even the heavily bearded Professor of Greek, Bonaventura Vulcanius, presented twenty-six lines of poetry. [3] The University, in short, was polite and duly expectant.

Leiden had numerous Catholics, and Leicester will have been popular with few of these. That, in a way, was fortunate, because it is due to the hard feelings and the diary of one of them that an indication of what went on in Leiden has come down to us. The following entry should in all fairness be given in full:

---

[1] Some new material on this first visit of English players to the Low Countries has come to light but will require special treatment.
[2] See *Bronnen*, I, p. 42.
[3] Leiden, Univ. Libr., MS. Vulc. 103, II.

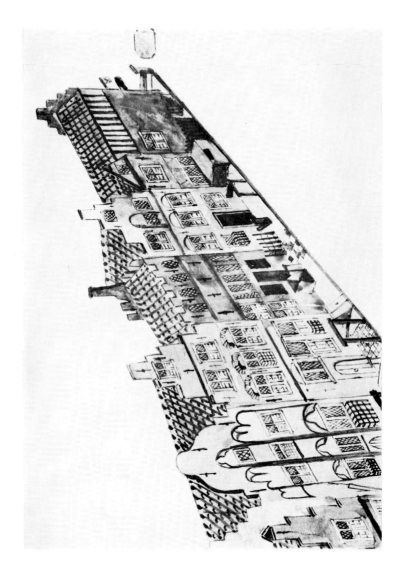

6. Sidney's Leiden residence in January 1586: the house of
Jan van Hout (fourth from the left) on the Breestraat near
'the blue stone' (upper right corner).

From a contemporary water-colour on parchment.

MORIBVS ANTIQVIS   ÆTAT. 40.   Aᵒ 1577

7. Justus Lipsius in 1587.

Engraving by Hendrick Goltzius.

When he [*i.e. Leicester*] was in Leiden, he wanted to see that famous University and there to hear Justus Lipsius, *literator* of great repute, publicly explaining Tacitus' *Agricola*.

He went accompanied by the son of Antonius, the pseudo-king of Portugal [1], and other noblemen. After the lecture he invited Lipsius to a repast; for he resided not very far from there in the sacred monastery of St. Barbara which Orange had already occupied before him; there he could be seen with the aforesaid son of Antonius and the pseudo-bishop of Cologne [*i.e. Gebhard Truchsess*], banqueting his way through the holy days of Lent [2] at a table exceedingly well-furnished with meats. [3]

Lipsius' lecture must have been for many an enlightened member of his courtly English audience an occasion of some significance in the sequence of Anglo-Leiden literary contacts. Seated or standing in the 'greater auditory', the English nobles and their friends together with the Leiden *doctores* and undergraduates listened to the pride of the Academy lecturing on Tacitus (his special subject) in that characteristic pose seen in the Goltzius engraving [4], a book in one hand, and the other on the head of Mopsus, his favourite dog [5].

Much of Lipsius' fame rested on his *De Constantia*—a theme, incidentally, the propagation of which many were to hold against him when he moved to Louvain five years later. 'Lipsius,' said Fynes Moryson in 1592, 'whom I loved for his Booke of Constancy, did bereave me of this hope, when I came to the Low-Countreys, by his inconstant flight to the Spaniards' [6]. But flying to the Spaniards seemed as yet far removed from Lipsius' mind. Perhaps it was during this English repast that he made his host a present of the renowned treatise, a copy of which with the author's autograph in-

---

[1] E.M. Tenison (*Elizabethan England*, IV, p. 42, facs. p. 24) has proved that *The explanation of the true ... tytle, of ... Anthonie ... At Leyden In the Printing house of Christopher Plantyn, 1585* was a translation by Claude Desainliens (*alias* Hollyband, the schoolmaster) and printed in London, not Leiden.

[2] This of course refers to Leicester's third Leiden visit in March 1586.

[3] Dusseldorpius, *Annales*, pp. 209-210. See Appendix II, no. 67.

[4] See Plate 7.

[5] An epigram on Mopsus: Lipsius, *Epistolarum ad Belgas centuria I*, Antwerp, 1605, p. 53.

[6] Moryson, *Itinerary*, 1617, ed. Glasgow Univ. Press, III, 1908, p. 372. For the interesting implications of this 'Constantia', see Bachrach, *Huygens and Britain*, pp. 35-44.

9

scription to the Earl of Leicester still exists [1]. For the rest we can only guess as to the actual circumstances under which they met and talked in the days of which Lipsius wrote: 'The Earl himself, and Sidney, too, we have had with us; the *Princeps* is indeed an honourable, benign, Heroic man: the other, his kinsman, son of his sister, has remarkable prudence and wisdom.' [2] The visit proved to him the truth of his earlier pronouncement when he had said, with special reference to Sidney:

Blessed is England in this, that its nobility is truly noble, educated as it is in studies of *virtus* and *doctrina*. [3]

---

[1] See the catalogue of 'A Loan Exhibition depicting the Reign of Queen Elizabeth', 1933, no. 368. I am indebted to Mr. R. C. Strong for this information.

[2] J. Lipsius to H. Ranzovius, Leiden, 5 April 1586 (*Hotomanorum epistolae*, misc. no. 5). See Appendix II, no. 68. It is sometimes said that Sidney was with Lipsius at the time of the letter, but the Latin has 'apud nos habuimus'.

[3] J. Lipsius to J. Dousa, Leiden, 1 September 1585 (B.M., MS. Burney 370, f. 35). See Appendix II, no. 44. Cf. p. 7.

III

FRIENDSHIP AND FRICTION

'You ask me in earnest, illustrious Philip Sidney, what I think about the pronunciation of Latin— whether this 'German manner' which we now use is the true one, or some other, which (like so many things) has died out long ago and since lain hidden under the darkness of ignorance and ancientness. It is a delicate and subtle question'.[1] Thus wrote Lipsius on 17 March. Whether Sidney's 'subtle question' had arisen at Leicester's luncheon or in the house of Van Hout, it was appropriate that he should have put it to the Leiden expert—many years, incidentally, after Languet had advised him to continentalize his insular Latin diction [2]. The question was one result of the Englishman's academic sojourn, and more specifically of Leicester's second visit. So was the treatise *De recta pronunciatione Latinae linguae dialogus* [3] which Lipsius immediately [4] sat down to write and soon after the 'third visit' dedicated to Sir Philip as a formal professorial presentation to a foreign patron. The booklet, which was to enjoy a wide popularity [5], perhaps contributed to Lipsius' renown in England of which Bonaventura Vulcanius was to speak in later years [6]. It certainly represented

---

[1] J. Lipsius to P. Sidney, Leiden, 17 March 1586 (Lipsius, epistle dedicatory to *De recta pronunciatione;* see below, note 3). See Appendix II, no. 69.

[2] See H. Languet to P. Sidney, Vienna, 22 January 1574 (*Langueti epistolae ad Sydnaeum,* no. XI).

[3] *De recta pronunciatione Latinae linguae dialogus,* Leiden, F. Raphelengius, 1586.

[4] Cf. J. Lipsius to J. A. Thuanus, Leiden, 30 January 1586: '... Damus nunc et edimus De Pronunciatione Latinae Linguae Dialogum, ...' (Lipsius, *Epistolarum selectarum centuria secunda miscellanea,* Antwerp, 1605, p. 131).

[5] A new edition appeared in the following year in *De vera pronunciatione Gr. et Latinae linguae,* Paris, H. Stephanus, 1587.

[6] See *Delitiae poetarum belgicorum,* IV, p. 571.

the Sidney-Leiden contacts in their most promising days. What is more, it put Sidney and Lipsius together in print, in an Anglo-Dutch-Latin context. Lipsius has frequently shown himself, as in those letters of 1584 and 1585 when Dousa was in England to forward his greetings, an admirer of that 'Flos Angliae', as he had once called him,[1] and one who was eager to be remembered by him. The *De recta pronunciatione* was another result of earlier contacts.

It is possible to suggest when the two first met. Since it was neither in Holland, because Sidney's first Dutch visit (1577) preceded Lipsius' arrival, nor in England, where the professor had never been, one must look for an occasion when their paths had crossed elsewhere. It appears that they could have seen each other on only one earlier occasion. In March 1577 Sidney, 'son of the Viceroy', had travelled to the imperial Court via Brussels (where he stayed with the ambassador Sir Thomas Wilson) and Louvain (where Don John of Austria resided). There at Louvain was Professor Justus Lipsius, whose name should have been enough to attract the studious Sidney. Failing that, somebody else could have arranged an introduction, for with the English travellers, it will be remembered, was Lipsius' friend Daniel Rogers. From what we know about Rogers, he would have been delighted to introduce his friend to young Philip Sidney on that 6th of March 1577. If Rogers was responsible —and there is enough reason to suggest he was—this is yet another instance of his influence on the curious pattern of Anglo-Dutch relations of 1586.

Considering the dedication of *De recta pronunciatione* as a token of Lipsius' frequently repeated respect for the scholarly English nobleman, one cannot help noticing how singularly unrelated politico-religious principles and literary friendships could be: the differing views of the much-maligned Lipsius and of Sidney, the Protestant hero, must have been obvious to all. Let us also note that the Leiden scholar took his Dialogue even less seriously than he cared to state in the epistle dedicatory, although it was ambiguously implied. Sidney's question, he remarked, was 'subtilis' and 'tenuis',

---

[1] See G. Whetstone, *Sir Philip Sidney*, 1587, epist. ded.

'subtle and delicate', but what he really meant was 'slight'. For in his correspondence, unknown to Sidney, he casually referred to his little treatise as 'tenue in re tenui opus, nec dignum meliori ... aure' [1]; and in another letter confessed to have written 'levi manu, ut in re levi' [2].

But still, *De recta pronunciatione* was a fair beginning:

... What then will be my aim? To render you a service, Sidney: because it would be rude, or impudent rather, to refuse anything to a man whom the very gods ... have refused nothing. Do I refer to excellencies of appearance? You have been created both for physical strength and elegance. Of your mind? You are most erudite, and wit and judgement abound in you. Hardly anything is wanting in you that Nature and Fortune can provide. Forsooth, you are gifted: the more so because you do not abuse it, like the majority of that aristocracy, and turn it to ambition and pomp: but you make it contribute, where you can, to yourself and to the common weal. And this privately and publicly, in gown and in armour: with that lively force of mind everywhere sufficient, you are the favourite of Mars and never desert the rites of Sophia and the Muses. What Archilogus once proudly asserted, you can say with still better reason:

Although I am the servant and admirer of the god of war,
I yet retain the famous gifts of the Muses.

But I only touch on the fringes of your accomplishments without penetrating into them. Because I be hold your virtues in the same way as we look at sacred things: in silence rather than with applause. Your virtues I admire, but cannot pursue: I should almost say, adore without adorning.

O bright star of your Britannia (on whom Virtue, the Muses, and the Graces have vied with one another to shine), graciously accept this slight and dull piece of work from me, and let the value of this gift for a while be judged in the temple of Fame. Not, however, as a true and legitimate present: but as a hostage, and as a warranty of another work. Other things are worthy of you and myself: these I shall compose and dedicate, if I shall live: and thus may I live.

Be greeted by Lipsius, who wrote this at Leiden.[3]

Lipsius' present, therefore, though 'tenuis', was only a first instalment of future service to be offered to his 'bright star of Britannia'.

---

[1] See p. 119, note 4.
[2] J. Lipsius to P. Villerius F., Leiden, 1 April 1586 (Lipsius, *Epist. sel. cent. sec. misc.*, p. 131).
[3] See Appendix II, no. 69.

Equally defined by a long history of Anglo-Dutch-Latin antecedents, and perhaps not nearly so 'slight', was Dousa's
Odarum Britannicarum liber ad D. Elisabetham [1] which must have
appeared at about the same time. It is difficult to separate
its significance as a political pamphlet and its 'mere literary'
interest. One suspects the *Odae* to have served precisely that
dual purpose. They were dedicated to the Queen, and not
to Sidney as is sometimes supposed [2], while their being
reprinted in *Musae Errantes* thirty years later [3] suggests some
non-political value as well. At the time of his *Odae*, Dousa
also issued a volume of elegies and epigrams. [4] Some of these
were similarly connected with English affairs, especially the
third Elegy, 'To Paulus Buys [5] his colleague and companion
in the English embassy' [6]. The laudatory *Encomia Dousana*
of 1587, it will be remembered, were to a certain degree due
to Dousa's third London visit, and may to some extent be
regarded as a *liber adoptivus* to his *Odae* and *Elegiae* of the
preceding year. Finally, his son contributed a *Britannicorum
Carminum Silva* to the father's *Odae*. It is evident that the Muse
of Noordwijk could not have been more devoted to the

---

[1] Dousa, *Odarum Britannicarum liber ad D. Elisabetham. Item Iani Dousae
Filij Britannicorum Carminum Silva*, Leiden, F. Raphelengius, 1586. Cf.
Benedicti, *De rebus*, p. 54, on receiving a copy from Dousa.

[2] E.g. Siebeck, *Das Bild Sidneys*, p. 183.

[3] *Musae Errantes*, Frankfort, 1616.

[4] Dousa, *Elegiarum lib. II Epigrammatum lib. Cum I. Lipsii aliorumque
Carminibus*, Leiden, F. Raphelengius, 1586.

[5] Paulus Buys (1531–1594), a Curator of the University, former *Lands-
advocaat* (director of public prosecutions), and a member of the Prince's
Privy Council until the latter's death, played no visible part in the
literary relations between England and Holland. In political matters,
however, this leading member of the Prince's party, who first visited
England in the 1575 embassy, proved pro-English (and anti-French)
throughout his career. This explains his resignation in 1584 when the
French King was called upon for protection, his interest in the 1584
embassy, his part in the 1585 embassy, and his appointment by
Leicester as a member of the Council of State. The Earl's trade
placards of April 1586 estranged him from the Leicestrian party. His
subsequent hostility was to oblige Leicester to imprison him at Utrecht
(see pp. 149–151).

[6] Cf. a 'Gratulatio' by Vulcanius on Buys's return from England (Leiden,
Univ. Libr., MS. Vulc. 103, II).

welfare of a cause which fourteen years of travel, conference, and poetry had helped to promote.

To say that Dousa consciously summarized fourteen years of Anglo-Dutch relations is no exaggeration. For even his dedicatory verse to Queen Elizabeth was nothing else than a revision of the opening twenty lines of that same Ode, beginning

> Queen, issue of great kings,
> Yourself taught by the hand of the Muses,
> Second to none among the Graces . . .,

which had been his first poetic offering to the literary-minded Queen in 1572.[1] It is followed by a letter from Vulcanius to Dousa, dated new year's day 1586. In it the Latin and Greek poet and occasional writer of Dutch translations[2], a relatively new member of Dousa's circle, welcomed the Curator on his return to Leiden. A letter, not in verse, for 'who could have written a poem after you had taken all the Muses across the sea with you?' Now, however, 'reduces tecum Musae omnes', Vulcanius concluded. And so Dousa's book announced 'the return of the Muses'. Five *Odae* he brought home, one on the Queen's birthday, others to William Cecil, Sir Thomas Heneage, Sidney[3], and Alexander Neville. One poem to Groslotius and another to Melissus served as an appendix. His son's contribution was smaller, consisting of verses to the Queen, to Leicester, to Sidney[4], and on a fountain near the Tower. But from a literary point of view the most exciting aspect of Dousa's *Odae* is that here for the first time in the history of Leiden poetry an Englishman contributed verses, not in Latin, but in his own language. Their author, Geoffrey Whitney, was typical also in that he had actually come with the intention of joining the Leiden *vates*.

Van Hout's billeting lists inform us that on 12 January

---

[1] See p. 28.
[2] Some poor translations survive in B.M. MS. Sloane 2764. De Nolhac (*Ronsard et l'humanisme*, pp. 212–3) makes mention of a letter to Vulcanius by Theodor Canter, written at Utrecht on 17 November 1585, to accompany and praise the latest edition of Ronsard's works.
[3] See Appendix I, no. 5.
[4] See Appendix I, no. 7.

1586 'mr Witnay' was given two beds in the house of 'Joncvrou adriane van merwen'.[1] A minor difficulty is the existence of two Whitneys [2] (kinsmen?) both of whom presented them-selves at Leiden on that day.[3] The above 'mr Witnay', however, was Geoffrey Whitney the poet, for his namesake, who travelled with a servant, re-appeared in the lists (with that servant) on 10 March [4], when the poet was a soldier no longer.

Geoffrey Whitney, probably already familiar with Dutch and Dutchmen on account of his Yarmouth background [5], came to Leiden as a soldier (of some standing—'two beds') and spent a few nights there during the first official entry. Before leaving England he had offered a volume of English emblems to Leicester.[6] Coming to Leiden, therefore, as a gentleman-soldier, poet, and *cliens* of the Governor General, he was naturally drawn to seek the company of men like Dousa. The University, moreover, was just across the canal, a minute's walk from the house of Lady Adriana. It looks as if experiences in Leiden meant an untimely end to his military career. For he remained there, or returned very soon, and on 1 March paid a visit to Adrianus Saravia, the *Rector Magnificus*. 'Godefridus Whitneus Junior Anglus' was duly entered in the *Volumen Inscriptionum*. On the same day he rented a room in a fashionable University boarding house behind the huge St. Peter's church: 'Galfridus Wythneus Anglus stud. litt. in edibus lochorstianis' [7], an address which was particularly popular with English undergraduates. This made him a Leiden student proper; and, what is more, the

[1] Leiden, Gem. arch., Secr. arch. 7885, '3', f. 21.

[2] Cf. R. Gottfried, 'The 'G. W. Senior' and 'G.W.I.' of Spenser's *Amoretti*', *Modern Language Quarterly*, III, 1942, p. 543 ff.

[3] 'Mr Witney met een knecht op ij bedden 12-1-86' (Leiden, Gem. arch., Secr. arch. 7885, '3', f. 50ᵛ). 'Mr. Witnay met ij bedden 12-1-86' (f. 21). Whitney's *Emblemes* (see below, p. 132), include poems to two other Geoffrey Whitneys, his father (p. 164) and a kinsman (p. 181).

[4] 'Mr. Witney met zyn dienaer 10-3-86' (Leiden, Gem. arch., Secr. arch. 7885, '5', f. 57).

[5] See H. Green's preface to his edition of Whitney's *Emblemes*, London, 1866.

[6] On 28 November 1585 [o.s.?]; see p. 132.

[7] *Alb. Rec.*, list 1586 (Leiden, Univ. Libr., Sen. arch. 22). See Plate 5.

first to have had some experience in writing English verse.
Another poet interested in vernacular composition had
entered the Dousa circle.

His first contribution, perhaps, was to translate (in an
admittedly unpromising way) young Dousa's welcome to
Leicester into English poulter's measure.[1] Dousa the Elder
gave him the opportunity to show that he could, fortunately,
do better than this.[2] Conspicuously placed at the very be-

---

[1]   Not Rome so ioyed to see Camillus in her waules
When that shee was beseeged rownd, with armies of the Gaules,
As now, most noble Earle, your presence heare doth glad
All Belgica, but most of all doth ioye Batavia sad.
Nor yet like praise was due to him for his deserte,
As to your excellence: who comes with force to take our parte.
Camillus fought to free his lande from forren foe
Wherein his dutie hee perform'de, and countries love did showe
But this is not your land, whose love doth you provoke,
Our liberties, and land to keepe, from force of strangers yoke.
Moreover, he preserv'd, one onely cittie free:
But many Citties, Townes, and men, by yow defended bee:
Wherefore (Renowned Earle) all haile to yow wee saye,
And as yow have begonne, proceede: to tender us we praye.
           (Dousa, *Odarum Britannicarum liber*, pp. 53–54)

[2] IN NOBILISS. ET DOCTIS. VIRI D. IANI DOUSAE A NOORTWIICK
    ODAS BRITANNICAS. *Galfridi Whitney Britanni* CARMEN.
There needes no bushe, wheare Nectar is to drinke:
Nor helpes by arte, wheare bewtie freshe doth bloome:
Wheare Sonne doth shine, in vayne wee lighte the linke:
Wheare Sea dothe swell, the brookes do loose their roome.
    Let Progne cease, wheare Philomela singes,
    And oaten pipe, wheare Fame her trompet ringes.
Then better staye, then simply to commende,
The learned fruites, of noble Dousas penne:
Whose worthie fame, doth to the skyes ascende,
And farre, and neare, is knowne to famous men:
    For when hee writes: Minerva seemes to smile,
    Such is his verse, and eke his sugred stile.
When Nature first his forme did thinke to make,
Shee fetch'd the moulde, from steepe Parnassus hill:
And when that redde Aurora doth awake,
Then was hee borne, which did presage his skill:
    The Muses then, their presentes to him broughte,
    Whome Pallas nurc'de, & great Apollo taughte.
So, what hee writes, both learning, witte, and arte,
Uppon his will eaven at his wishe attende:
His pearles workes do witnes his deserte,

ginning of the *Odarum Britannicarum liber,* Geoffrey Whitney
sang the praises of Dousa, of the Queen, and of Leiden,
perhaps never realizing how strange an innovation the
inclusion of his English 'Carmen' was to the traditional
appearance of Dutch printed Latin poetry.

It is curious to observe the expression of such a serene state
of mutual friendliness in Whitney's well-turned phrases
and find that in only a matter of weeks an open conflict was

> That in his praise, there needes no verse bee pen'de:
>> For Dousas name alone his workes doe grace:
>> And everie one with ioye doe them imbrace.
> But since hee likes of Englande nowe to wryte,
> It stirr'd mee up this slender verse to frame:
> For sweete wee knowe hath alwayes more delite,
> When after sower wee freelie taste the same,
>> So, let these lines your appetites prepare,
>> I but invite, and hee bestowes the fare.
> O Noortwycke blest, with this thy darlinges birthe,
> For by his verse, thy fame thou longe hast had:
> Virgilius made his Mantua live in mirthe,
> Catullus eke, did make Verona glad;
>> And Noortwyck thoughe thou small, and stande alone,
>> Yet nowe thy name, to citties great is knowne.
> Not orely thou, but all Batavia lande,
> And most of all, thou nurce of learned skill,
> Thow Cittie faire, that on the Rheene doest stande,
> Arte famous made by learned Douzas quill:
>> Who to thy praise, doth set thy valour out,
>> When Spayniardes longe beseeg'd thee rownd about.
> But not content these landes alone to praise,
> And make their fame, the azure skye to pearce:
> But that his muse dothe reache beyonde the seas,
> And westwarde mountes for matter for his verse:
>> Wheare hee hath founde within an happie Ile,
>> The onely cause, that doth adorne his stile.
> Which is a Queene, that raignes in regall throne,
> From famous kinges, yspronge of Royall line,
> A pearle of price, a graffe of grace alone,
> Whose heavenly giftes doe make her seme devine:
>> Whose fame hee dothe in goulden verses painte,
>> Eternizing this sacred earthlie sainte.
> Which when thou seest: Then Englande most reioyce,
> Bycause shee is thy gratious soveraigne Queene:
> And prayse the Lorde, with all thy harte and voyce,
> Since other landes, her like have never seene:

to arise between Leicester and Leiden.[1] There were various reasons: Leicester's growing dislike of the magistrates of Holland and his subsequent intimacy with the discontented States of Utrecht; his determination to appoint a professor regardless of the opinion of the Curators of the University; and the extremely ambiguous position of Saravia, the Rector, whose obscure dealings with Leicester at Utrecht rightly roused the Senate's suspicions. But all these reasons were subordinate to the general threat to the academic independ-

Oh happie cause, Lorde Dousa thou hast founde,
 Still write hereon, and never chaunge thy grounde,
And thoughe, that none thy gifte in verse can passe,
Yet shalt thow faile, her graces all to tuche:
Bycause this is that perfecte looking glasse,
That Europe doth with wonder vewe so muche:
 Whoe shewes them lighte, that doe in darknes rest,
 Wherby they see, the waye they maye bee blest.
If all the wittes that ever yet have bin,
To frame one wighte weare wroughte within a moulde:
And Homers Muse, and Virgilles weare therein,
And Ovids eeke with all the Poëts oulde,
 Whoe Nestors yeares, should write both nighte and daye
 With pen of steele that never shoulde decaye:
Yet coulde he not expresse in everie parte,
Her prayses due, but shoulde confesse in fine,
No earthlie man with anie witte, or arte,
Can rightlie praise, the giftes that are devine:
 Then blusshe not thou, althoughe the marke thou misse,
 But beare in mind, shee halfe A goddesse is,
And wheare thy muse dothe after take in hande,
To spread the fame, of Englishe noble peares:
Hereby, thou showest thy love unto our lande,
Wherein I wishe, that thou might spende thye yeares:
 Then should'st thow knowe: both unto prince, and peare,
 Yea unto all, that Dousas name is deare.
Proceede therefore in happie howre I praye,
Still yeelde the fruites, of that thy worthie witte:
And for rewarde, thou shalt bee crown'de with Baye,
And none more highe, shall on Parnassus sitte:
 Wheare at the foote my pen shall sounde thy praise,
 And doe my best, thy name alofte to raise.

(Dousa, *Odarum Britannicarum liber*, sig. *3–*4). The following corrections have been made: 52 giftes] gistes 53 painte,]painte. 61 passe,] passe. 64 muche:] muche. 72 decaye:] decaye.

[1] See W. Bisschop, *De Woelingen der Leicestersche partij binnen Leiden 1586 en 1587*, Leiden, 1867.

ence which was and is one of the most cherished of the University's assets.

If Leicester had been less blind to early warnings, he would have realized some tension at a very early date. On 1 February a new Rector was to be nominated, according to the Statutes by the 'Gubernator Hollandiae', who was now assumed to be Leicester. The following day one of the University's Curators, Paulus Buys—who, completely contrary to his earlier views, was becoming one of Leicester's most determined antagonists [1]—indicated his preference for young Prince Maurice instead.[2] It was finally Leicester, who re-elected Professor Saravia in a letter which Vulcanius read out to the Senate on 8 February [3], Foundation Day. It may be worth noting that Adrianus Saravia, the refugee from Artois, an early convert to Calvinism, had stayed in England for long periods after 1558. In 1564 he taught divinity in the College founded by Queen Elizabeth on the isle of Guernsey, and in 1568 he was Orange's chaplain during the abortive Meuse campaign. Thereafter he returned to London as a minister first of the Walloon then of the Dutch refugee churches. In 1582 he settled at Leiden, where two years later he was nominated Professor of Theology. It is significant that in the summer preceding Leicester's arrival he was again in England. From 1587 onwards, when his position had become untenable in Holland, he again lived in England, where he died in 1613 as Rector of Great Chart in Kent. Saravia, in other words, was more English than French, Flemish, or Dutch.

But the 'Praesidium Libertatis' showed the first real signs of irritation when Leicester disregarded all good custom by trying to give a Chair in Greek to Petrus Rege(l)morterus of Antwerp. The proposal was not new. At one time Dousa and Rogers had supported Regemorterus' application for the employment of 'the fruits of his studies'.[4] But Leicester's

---

[1] See pp. 149–151.
[2] See *Bronnen*, I, p. 42.
[3] See *Bronnen*, I, p. 43.
[4] P. Regemorterus to R. Dudley, London, 26 November 1585: 'Cum ante menses sex illustrissime et excellentissime comes, in alias regiones vocarer: multi viri nobiles ab eo me dehortati sunt, et in primis D.

procedure was awkward and badly timed. On 6 May, the Curators and Burgomasters sent a cold reply, pointing out that there was no vacancy at all, but that they would bear the name in mind for some future occasion. Leicester had meanwhile gone to Utrecht—which was to prove his only reliable stronghold—and being little inclined to let the matter rest a conflict was imminent. A rumour spread that the entire University was to be taken over by the town of Utrecht, where Saravia then stayed—which made him naturally suspect in the eyes of his Leiden colleagues. On 6 May Saravia received an official reprimand for not consulting the Senate, and indeed for being absent. On 6 May, too, Dousa and Buys were sent to Utrecht to act on their University's behalf. On 30 May Burgomaster Van der Werff and Jan van Hout followed.[1] Lipsius had given them a letter to Leicester's Leiden physician, John James, to further the cause of 'Hautenus noster'.[2] On 3 June they endeavoured to force the Lord Governor to commit himself by requesting him to confirm the University Patents.[1] But Leicester persisted and again, towards the end of July, urged the belated appointment of Regemorterus[3], now clearly a matter of principle. Then on 8

Johannes Junius, suasitque ut excellentiae tuae in hac Belgicae expeditione fructus studiorum meorum et operam offerrem. Quam excellentiae tuae usui et gratam fore asseverabat, praesertim in civilibus missionibus, in quibus excellentia tua ijs egebit, qui pro ore et lingua futuri sint. In quo genere vitae ut aliquando quid possemus, decennalis mihi profectio studio varia indagandi suscepta fuit. Quae, si per sacras suas occupationes aditum nobis excellentia tua concedere dignetur, fusius explicabimus. Quin etiam haec omnia a nobilissimo viro Jano Douza D. de Nortwyck intelligere, quando excellentiae tuae visum fuerit, licebit. Et antehac per Danielem Rogerium et fredericum Genebelli intellexit. Denique Deum Opt. Max. rogo, ut excellentiae tuae in dies magis ac magis benedicat, et in salutem Belgicae diu superstitem servet. ... Excellentiae tuae Cliens Petrus Regemorterus' (B.M., MS. Harl. 6993, f. 118). Baudius dedicated his *Carmina* of 1587 to Regemorterus. Johannes Junius was a former burgomaster of Antwerp. Frederico Gianibelli of Mantua, the engineer, is chiefly known for his fireships used during the siege of Antwerp and against the Armada.

[1] See *Bronnen*, I, p. 46.
[2] J. Lipsius to J. James, Leiden, 30 May 1586 (Hessels, II, no. 222).
[3] R. Dudley to the University of Leiden, 28 July 1586 (Paris, Bibl. Nat., MS. Dupuy 699, f. 141). For this information I am indebted to Dr. H. van Crombruggen.

August the University once more rejected his proposal [1]—
obviously *libertatis ergo*.

Of course the University never moved to Utrecht, and,
except for Leicester's political prestige, things remained the
same. But the difference between his warm welcome at Leiden
in January and the feelings caused by the unworthy Rege-
morterus-affair in May was no less emphatic than the change
of heart which drove him from The Hague almost immediately
after his triumphal entry into Holland. This is not the place
to judge his personal responsibility, but two aspects of these
events must be noted. Firstly, that Leicester's Leiden quarrels,
while showing his changing loyalty to those who had for so
long been among his staunchest supporters, were particularly
radical in that they concerned a Governor-Generalship which
had once almost looked like an Anglo-Leiden enterprise.
Fourteen years of liberal diplomacy now seemed wasted,
and the old faction would have to break up, to be replaced,
perhaps, by others. Rogers was absent, Marnix confined to
his house [2], Buys very soon to be a prisoner. Only a very small
minority still cherished hopes of brighter days, like Dousa
who continued to write verses to Hotman in something like
the old spirit [3]. Politically, however, their Anglo-Dutch union
was beyond recovery. The other aspect is that adversity
proved the new independence of Anglo-Dutch non-political
ties. Indeed, not one literary friendship seems to have been
affected by the fate of Leicester's party policy.

The year 1586 was not yet half finished when, in the middle
of these commotions, Sidney marched eastward to begin his
long-delayed campaign, Baudius going with him, perhaps still
hopefully drafting his epic. The University remained where
it was.

---

[1] See *Bronnen*, I, p. 46.
[2] Note, incidentally, Marnix's letter to Vulcanius, written from Seeburg,
of 13 April 1591 with its curious reference to England in connexion
with an edition of the Psalms: '. . . Ex Anglia non esset extra rem aliquid
ejusmodi obtineri: sed jam defuncto Walsingamio, ego neminem
habeo, à quo id sperem posse impetrari. . .' (Marnix, *Œuvres*, ed. A.
Lacroix, Brussels, 1860, no. 57).
[3] See p. [75] in Dousa's copy of *Epigrammata* (see above, p. 37, note 1).

IV

ANGLO-LEIDEN INTEGRATION

LEICESTER'S nephew, then, went south-east to pursue 'that perilous game in forreine soyle'.[1] 'Semiaulicus et semimilitaris' it was, said Hotman to Lipsius (who was then publishing a book for him [2]) in his request for a cheap set of Ortelius' maps for the summer campaign—cheap, because of their 'splendid poverty'.[3] Meanwhile literary Leiden continued as if the campaigners had never left.

A central figure no doubt was Geoffrey Whitney, 'Anglus studens litterarum' since 1 March and living, as we have seen, at the 'Huis te Lochorst'[4]. Ignoring for the present his other friends, we find him surrounded by a small group of students who had chosen the same address.[5] There was 'Gotefridus Wichtinus Anglus' (Wight?), 'Johannes Proost Middelburgensis', and 'Petrus Colvius Brugensis' (Colve): all three had moved into the house on the same day as Whitney. They found three others there already: 'Hubertus Joannis Zierichzeënsis' (Jansz.?), 'Theobaldus Teilinc' of the same town, and 'Johannes de Grave Amsterdamensis' who left in October. On 28 April two Englishmen joined them, 'Robertus Penrudoc anglus', and 'Thomas Whitleus anglus' (Wheteley) who left again before the new *Album Recensionum* list was drawn up early in 1587. Finally, in July, another Dutchman came, 'Adrianus Tas Middelburgensis'.

Some of these students were among his close friends. When

---

[1] E. Spenser, *Astrophel*, London, 1595, ll. 91-92.

[2] Viz. A. Hotman, Πωγωνίας *sive de barba dialogus*, Leiden, 1586, prefaced by a letter (sig. A2) by J. Lipsius to J. Hotman, Leiden, 26 April 1586. Cf. J. Hotman to J. Lipsius, Utrecht, 9 April 1586 (*Hotomanorum epistolae*, no. 93); and note 3.

[3] J. Hotman to J. Lipsius, Arnhem, 17 May 1586 (*Hotomanorum epistolae*, no. 94).

[4] See Plate 5.

[5] As in *Album Recensionum* list 1586.

in 1586 he published an enlarged version of the previous
year's present to Leicester, his *Choice of emblemes* [1], tributes
to and from 'M. Thomas Wheteley' and Petrus Colvius were
included. In the case of Wheteley the compliment may not
have been altogether free from irony, the emblem showing
a man playing chess while his house is on fire, and the text
beginning: 'Awake from sleepe secure...' [2]. Since verses
were dedicated 'to such persons as I [*i.e. Whitney*] thinke the
Emblemes doe best fitte' [3], the other was an undoubted
compliment. Colvius was soon to make his name as a philo-
logist by a highly esteemed edition of Apuleius. Popular
tradition has it that a kick from a mule killed him, at the age
of twenty-seven; but now he was only nineteen and a devoted
arts student, sharing rooms with Whitney, who offered him
the emblem of the two Minervas, one watching, one resting,
and an appropriate verse. [4]

A number of contingencies account for the fact that the
first English emblem-book was a Leiden publication. Its
dedication to Leicester 'presentlie before his Honour passed
the seas into the lowe countries' [3] in a sense prepared its
appearance in Holland, while the fact that the author
remained at Leiden brought it to the notice of the scholars

---

[1] *A choice of emblemes, and other devises, For the moste parte gathered out of
sundrie writers, Englished and Moralized. And divers newly devised, by Geffrey
Whitney*, Leiden, F. Raphelengius, 1586. The title-page advertisement
reads: 'A worke adorned with varietie of mater, both pleasant and
profitable: wherein those that please, maye finde to fit their fancies:
Because herein, by the office of the eie, and the eare, the minde maye
reape dooble delighte throughe holsome preceptes, shadowed with
pleasant devises: both fit for the vertuous, to their incoraging: and for
the wicked, for their admonishing and amendment.' (Ed. H. Green,
London, 1866.)

[2] Whitney, *Emblemes*, p. 208.

[3] Ibid., sig. **3V.

[4] The opening lines are:
> Continual toile, and labour, is not beste:
> But sometimes cease, and rest thy wearie bones,
> The daie to work, the nighte was made to reste,
> And studentes must have pastimes for the nones:
> > Sometime the Lute, the Chesse, or Bowe by fittes,
> > For overmuch, dothe dull the finest wittes.

(Ibid., p. 103.) See figure 3.

of that town—who, incidentally, were well-acquainted with emblem writing and perhaps more emblem-minded than their English colleagues. It was obviously there that Whitney was 'earnestlie required by somme that perused the same, to have it imprinted'. And it was only there that his book could be printed, 'in the house of Christopher Plantyn, by Francis Raphelengius' where all the blocks were ready for use. These were from editions of Sambucus, Junius, Alciatus, and others, best sellers in Plantin's shops, and Whitney's source-material even before he came to Holland.

A choice of emblemes was the major work in English of the Leiden office of great Plantin, printer to the University, 'prototoypographotatos' as Silvius, his predecessor, had once ironically called him in a Latin sentence [1]. Plantin himself had left in 1585, a surprise even to some of his best friends.[2] The Leiden branch was taken over by his son-in-law Franciscus Raphelengius, reputedly a former Cambridge lecturer [3] and certainly Professor of Hebrew at Leiden soon after the printing of Whitney's book [4]. On 17 January 1586 a passport for the Raphelengius family was issued at Antwerp,[5] on 3 March Raphelengius was appointed printer to the University, and on 4 May Whitney's 'To the Reader' was signed 'at Leyden in Holland' before being set up for the prefatory sheets of his collection.

As a curious and well-known compilation, Whitney's devices are deservedly famous. As a monument of Anglo-Leiden relations they exceed in interest the mere patronage of a *Gubernator Hollandiae*—though not, unfortunately, for any outstanding poetic merit. Between the author's arrival in the Low Countries and the publication some five months later, the book underwent three major alterations. Some

[1] W. Silvius to J. Dousa, n.p., n.d. (Leiden, Univ. Libr., MS. BPL 742, f. 42).
[2] See Appendix II, no. 44. Cf. also C. Clair, *Christopher Plantin*, London, 1960, pp. 157-159.
[3] See Whitney, *Emblemes*, ed. Green, p. 270.
[4] He was appointed on 20 June 1586 (see *Bronnen*, I, p. 45).
[5] 'Laisser passer librement françois de Ravelenghien, sa femme, deux enfans, et ung serviteur, avec deux coffres et ung sacq de meubles, vers hollande, ... faict a Anvers le xvij[e] de Janvier 1586' (B.M., MS. Sloane 2764, no. 102).

10

Interdum requiefcendum.
Ad Petrum Ligorium.

(1) J. Sambucus, *Emblemata*, ed. Leiden, 1584, p. 126.

A. Alciatus, *Emblemata*, ed. (2) Leiden, 1591, p. 645.

Infignia Poëtarum.

EMBLEMA CLXXXIII.

Alciatus, *Emblemata*, p. 581. (4)

(3) Sambucus, *Emblemata*, p. 98.

Tempore cuncta mitiora.

Inanis impetus.

EMBLEMA CLXIIII.

Figure 3

Plantin blocks used in Whitney's *Emblemes*. Device 1 was dedicated to Petrus Colvius, 2 to Janus Dousa, 3 to Janus Dousa the Younger, and 4 to Justus Lipsius.

dedications were added 'to certaine of my frendes, to whome either in dutie or frendship, I am divers waies bounde', Dutchmen and Englishmen alike. Secondly, some Latin phrases were added either as glosses or 'to helpe and further some of my acquaintance wheare this booke was imprinted, who having no taste in the Englishe tonge, yet weare earnestly addicted to the understandinge hereof'. Finally, a number of new commendatory verses were inserted on the half-sheet between his prefaces and the text.

First came 'Janus Dousa à Noortwijck'—not the Elder, as one might have expected after Whitney's contributions to the *Odarum Britannicarum liber*, but the Younger, who wrote 'nomine Patris' [1]. But whereas Dousa's verse contained the obvious complimental comparison with other emblematists, Bonaventura Vulcanius, who contributed the second poem, produced a curiously English and therefore more unexpected commendation: 'Una duos genuit GALFRIDOS ANGLIA...', Chaucer and Whitney, one famous already, the other soon. A third commendator was Colvius; then followed two Englishmen with poems possibly of an earlier date. Thus the *Emblemes* appeared preceded by a select chorus of Leiden poets, for whose use it was specially adapted. And Whitney returned their compliments by devoting emblems to the Dousas, to Colvius, to Raphelengius, and also to Lipsius. The absence of one to Vulcanius suggests that he had neither received nor expected the Professor's poem when his official text went to the printer's. For the rest, Whitney's selection of devices shows great care, and frequently close acquaintance with his dedicatees. To characterize Dousa, the poet-soldier, was easy. Whitney chose the poet's 'ensign', a white swan [2],

---

[1] Thus in J. Dousa the Younger, *Poemata*, 1704, p. 205. Green gives verse translations of the prefatory poems in his edition of Whitney's *Emblemes* (pp. xxviii–xxx). The fact that Dousa's son wrote this verse suggests that it was done after 6 May when the father left for Utrecht (see above, p. 129).

[2]   The Martiall Captaines ofte, do marche into the fielde,
       With Egles, or with Griphins fierce, or Dragons, in theire shielde.
       But Phoebus sacred birde, let Poëttes moste commende.
       Who, as it were by skill devine, with songe forshowes his ende.
       And as his tune delightes: for rareness of the same.
       So they with sweetenes of theire verse, shoulde winne a lasting name.

and was considerate enough to give Dousa the full weight of
Latin glossing. But his son—translator after all of Constable's
sonnets—received only two lines of Ovid after twelve lines of
English which conveyed an admonition befitting both him
and the author.[1] Six lines, all in English, recall 'the inward
foe' which Raphelengius had recently seen to 'devoure a
strong cittie' at the siege of Antwerp.[2] Towards the end of
the book Whitney shows his knowledge of Leiden figures
still more clearly by dedicating to Lipsius, the perennial
victim of malice from orthodox-religious quarters, the Alciatus
emblem of 'a dog barking at his shadow in the moonlight'.
Some of his least pedestrian verses gave the old Plantin
woodcut of 'Inanis impetus' an agreeably new appearance.[3]

> And as his colour white: Sincerenes doth declare.
> So Poëttes must bee cleane, and pure, and must of crime beware.
> For which respectes the Swanne, should in theire Ensigne stande.
> No forren fowle, and once suppos'de kinge of LIGURIA Lande.
> (Whitney, *Emblemes*, p. 126.) See figure 3.

[1]
> The grapes not ripe, the travailinge man doth waste,
> And under foote doth treade, as sower, and naughte:
> Which, being ripe, had sweete, and pleasaunte taste
> Whereby, wee maie this lesson true be taughte.
>> Howe simple men, doe simplie iudge of things.
>> And doe not waighe that time perfection bringes.
> For in this worlde, the thinges most faire, and rare,
> Are harde at firste, and seeme both harshe, and sower:
> But yet in time, they sweete and easie are,
> Then staie for time, which gives both fruite and flower:
>> And use our time, and let us still suppose
>> No greater losse, then time that wee doe lose.
> (Ibid., p. 206.) See figure 3.

[2] Ibid., p. 189.

[3]
> By shininge lighte, of wannishe CYNTHIAS raies,
> The dogge behouldes his shaddowe to appeare:
> Wherefore, in vaine aloude he barkes, and baies,
> And alwaies thoughte, an other dogge was there:
>> But yet the Moone who did not heare his queste,
>> Hir woonted course, did keepe unto the weste.
> This reprehendes, those fooles which baule, and barke,
> At learned men, that shine above the reste:
> With due regarde, that they their deedes should marke,
> And reverence them, that are with wisedome bleste:
>> But if they strive, in vaine their winde they spende,
>> For woorthie men, the Lorde doth still defende.
> (Ibid., p. 213.) See figure 3.

Although his unsteady pen hardly deserves the honour, Whitney, too, must have been looked upon as a representative of the new English poetry: not, in all likelihood, as belonging to Sidney's immediate circle, but certainly as one of his sincere admirers. Whitney addresses a verse, without a woodcut, 'To the honorable Sir Philippe Sidney Knight, Gouvernour of the Garrison, and towne of Vlissinge' at the very beginning of Part II of the *Emblemes* where it stands like a hidden dedication.[1] But the crucial passage occurs in the long poem under the Junius block of 'Fame armed with a pen' which he dedicated to Edward Dyer after Sidney had modestly refused it 'as not his proper due':

When frowning fatall dame, that stoppes our course in fine,	The Erle of Surrey, that wrat the booke of Songes and Sonettes.
The thred of noble Surreys life, made hast for to untwine,	
Apollo chang'd his cheare, and lay'd awaie his lute,	
And Pallas, and the Muses sad, did weare a mourninge sute.	
And then, the goulden pen, in case of sables cladde,	
Was lock'd in chiste of Ebonie, and to Parnassus had.	
But, as all times do chaunge, so passions have their space;	
And cloudie skies at lengthe are clear'd, with Phoebus chearefull face.	
For, when that barren verse made Muses voide of mirthe;	
Behoulde, Lusina sweetelie sounge, of Sidneys ioyfull birthe.	Sir Philip Sidney Knighte.
Whome mightie Iove did blesse, with graces from above:	
On whome, did fortune frendlie smile, and nature most did love.	
And then, behoulde, the pen, was bij Mercurius sente,	
Wherewith, hee also gave to him, the gifte for to invente.	
That, when hee first began, his vayne in verse to showe.	
More sweete then honie, was the stile, that from his penne did flowe.	

[1] Ibid., pp. 109–110.

Wherewith, in youthe hee us'd to bannishe idle
    fittes;
That nowe, his workes of endlesse fame, delighte
    the worthie wittes.
No haulting verse hee writes, but matcheth former
    times,

*Horat. lib.
2. Epist. 1.
ad Augustum
No *Cherillus, he can abide, nor Poëttes patched
    rimes.
What volume hath hee writte, that rest among his
    frendes,
Which needes no other praise at all, eche worke it
    selfe comendes.
So, that hee famous lives, at home, and farre, and
    neare;
For those that live in other landes, of SIDNEYS
    giftes doe heare.
And suche as Muses serve, in darkenes meere doe
    dwell;
If that they have not seene his workes, they doe so
    farre excell.
Wherefore, for to extoll his name in what I might,
This Embleme lo, I did present, unto this worthie
    Knight.

. . . . 1

Whitney makes two interesting points. Firstly that he knew
and admired the courtier's 'goulden pen', possibly himself
possessing some of its fruits, and secondly his emphatic
statement that Sidney's gifts were known not only 'among
his frendes' but even 'in other landes' where Whitney would
'extoll his name' for the benefit of poets who 'in darkenes
meere doe dwell'.

In the address of Whitney's *Emblemes* a Leiden audience
was included which had proved 'earnestlie addicted to the
understandinge hereof'. And through the highly fashionable
medium of *emblemata* an Anglo-Leiden student proclaimed
the exemplary qualities of one other writer, Sidney, a known
lover and maker of devices. In a receptive milieu of poets the
first English emblem-book was produced.

A few months later there appeared a booklet, now rare and
almost forgotten, that in a small compass contains a summary of much of this story. It brought together soldiering and

---

1 Ibid., pp. 196–197.

language courses, Dutch, English, and traditional Latin, practical linguistics and Anglo-Leiden 'schools' of verse. And it linked the principal groups of agents: the Dousas, Lipsius, and Van Hout—the English printer-schoolmaster Basson—Gilpin's host Van Brouchoven—Geoffrey Whitney—Leicester himself—the Dutch poet Walraven—and Sidney's eulogist George Whetstone, 'a man singularly well skyld in this faculty of Poetrie' [1]. The book was Whetstone's *The honourable reputation of a souldier* of 1585, translated by Walraven as *De eerweerdighe achtbaerheyt van een soldener* in 1586, and together printed in parallel columns by Paedts—at one time printer of Stanyhurst's *Aeneis* [2]—for Thomas Basson, the publisher [3].

How the English original came to Leiden is uncertain. Walraven in the first of his elaborate prefaces merely speaks of it as 'having been given' to him. At first sight the author's movements do not seem to include a visit to Leiden. George Whetstone is supposed not to have visited Holland before 1587 [4] when he became the assistant of Thomas Digges, Mustermaster General; and then, as an unpopular mustermaster, was killed by a Captain U(ve)dall, the same whom he had recently honoured in his report (at second hand?) of Sidney's last battle [5]. But there is reason to believe that Whetstone did come to Leiden during Leicester's second visit. For at that time two Whetstones were entered in Van Hout's lists:

---

[1] W. Webbe, *A Discourse of English Poetrie*, London, 1586.

[2] Richard Stanyhurst, *Thee first foure bookes of Virgil his Aeneis translated into English heroical verse*, Leiden, 1582. No satisfactory explanation has yet been given for the fact that the Roman Catholic Stanyhurst, then a refugee, went to Leiden (where he was a 'linguarum studiosus' from 1582 till 1583) to have his curious translation published as the first English book with a Leiden imprint. Not one contemporary Dutch scholar or poet seems to have noticed his arrival, and nothing appears to connect him with the main Anglo-Leiden line of exchange. His experimental hexameters—of which no copy survives in the Netherlands—remain the only literary indication of his mysterious visit.

[3] 'Tot Leyden, By Jan Paedts Jacobszoon, ende Jan Bouwenszoon. Anno M.D.Lxxxvi. Men vintse te coop by Thomas Basson Boeckvercoper, woonende tot Leyden opte breede-straet, by de Blauwe steen.'

[4] See T. C. Izard, *George Whetstone*, New York, 1942, pp. 28–31, 163, 252.

[5] G. Whetstone, *Sir Philip Sidney*, London, 1587.

'mr Watston' with one servant, the billet lost, but at home [24 January 1586] [1]
'mr Wetston' with 2 servants [24 January 1586] [2]

The second, with two servants, could have been his brother Bernard, a friend of Gilpin's [3], who was mustered with three men in The Hague on 10 January [4], again visited Leiden as 'm^r Barnart Wetston' ('two beds') on 10 March, and perhaps was the same 'mr hwatston' (and two servants) who came with Leicester's first entry [5]. In that case the other Whetstone of 24 January must be George Whetstone, who lost his billet but was at home.[6]

This would almost coincide with the sudden English interest of a Dutch poet, Jacob Walraven, who 'had never set foot in England'. Fifteen years before, the writer tells us in a preface, he had learned a little of the language at Antwerp. Then Leicester came, and one of his suite, George Brooke, stayed with him. Brooke, like many others, desired to learn French while travelling in Holland, and so he taught Walraven English in return, Latin serving them as an interpreter.[7] One cannot question this detailed account of the revival of his interest in English. Brooke did indeed visit Leiden, as we know from lists which include:

'mr George brouc' 10 January 1586 [8]
'Mr Jorys brouc' with 3 servants, 3 beds, 12 January 1586 [9]

Officially, however, he was never at Walraven's house or anywhere near. For as to Walraven's guests, we find the following names:

'Sr Arthus bassit' with 2 servants on 2 beds 12 January 1586
'Docter clerc consulier' with 2 servants 16 January 1586
'Januarij den 22 Monsieur thomas' with 2 beds [10]

---

[1] Leiden, Gem. arch., Secr. arch. 7885, '4', f. 5.
[2] Ibid., f. 20^v.
[3] See G. Gilpin to J. Hotman, The Hague, 14 March 1588 (Hotman, 'Correspondance', II, no. 12).
[4] See Tenison, *Elizabethan England*, VI, 1937, p. 46.
[5] Leiden, Gem. arch., Secr. arch. 7885, [3^a], f. 8^v; and id., '3', f. 26,
[6] See Plate 5.
[7] *Honourable reputation*, p. 11. See Appendix II, no. 70.
[8] Leiden, Gem. arch., Secr. arch. 7885, '5', f. 80.
[9] Id., '3', f. 12.
[10] Ibid., f. 7.

nobody [*i.e. 'exemption'?*]
'Mr thomas brouc' with two beds [*erased:* has not yet been there]
  has arrived to day [*i.e. shortly after 24 January*] [1]
'Mr Franchoys fosquij' 10 March 1586
2 young gentlemen 25 July 1586 [2]

The obvious solution must be that 'thomas brouc' was a
lapsus pennae. This at any rate makes George Brooke the guest
of Jacob Walraven. A guest indeed, for Walraven was one
of the few university men to waive the privilege and accept
a soldier's billet. If with Brooke Whitney comes into the
picture even before his academic registration, this would
afford an explanation of the soldier Whitney's introduction
to the Leiden literary world: for they were friends, as one
of Whitney's emblems proves [3].

At that time Thomas Basson began his English school,
probably 'on the Breestraat near the Blue Stone'—like Van
Hout—where his bookshop was situated.[4] There Walraven,
Van Hout, Dousa, and Van Brouchoven learned English.
Apparently there was a general demand for language courses
among Dutchmen and Englishmen alike. Basson was the
local expert, translator of a few pamphlets including Leicester's
Lawes and ordinances. He prepared a now lost textbook entitled
'Coniugatien in Engelsch en Nederduytsch' for which his
dedicatees, the Leiden magistrates, presented him with
a nine guilder gratuity on 8 May of the same year.[5] But
seeing the purely practical necessity of some proficiency in
each other's language, Walraven thought this textbook not
enough and recommended the foundation of schools, the
translation of Sir Thomas Smith's '*De recta & emendata
Anglicae linguae pronunciatione*' [6] which he apparently knew,
and the composition of an English book comparable to
Plantin's 'treasuries' of French and Flemish.[7] As a modest

---

[1] Id., '4', f. [12ᵛ].
[2] Id., [3ᵃ], f. [7]. The 'two young gentlemen' are mentioned on p. 75
  of the *Honourable reputation.*
[3] Whitney, *Emblemes,* p. 69.
[4] See p. 92, note 2; cf. Plate 6; see Plate 5.
[5] See p. 92, note 2.
[6] I.e. T. Smith, *De Recta et Emendata Linguae Anglicae Scriptione Dialogus,*
  Paris, [1567?].
[7] See *Honourable reputation,* p. 12.

73

ENGLISH PRONOVNCIATION:

Or

A SHORTE INTRODVCTION AND
Waye to the Englifh fpeache, very fitte for all
thofe that intende to learne
the fame.

To the diligent Schooler.

Beare loue and labour in your mynde,
Than, what you feeke you fhall it fynde:
For Love vanquifht, and Labour fhall
What firft was fowre, fweete make with all.

ENGELSCHE PRONVNCIATIE:

Ofte

EEN CORTE INLEYDINGHE ENDE
*wech tot de Engelfche fprake, zeer bequaem alle
den ghenen die daer trachten om den
Zelfden te leeren.*

Nu eerft

Niet alleen den Leerlinghen, ter liefden ende profijt: maer
oock mede den Leeraers zelf, tot groot gemack ende gerijf,
in onze tale vertaelt, Door I. WALRAVEN.

Tot den naerftigen Scholier.

In Liefd' end Arbeyt wilt volherden,   VVant Liefd' verwint, en d'Arbeyt doet
Dan, wat ghy zoeft tzal u gewerden: Tgunt eerft zuer fmaeft, haeft werden zoet.

Anno M. D. LXXXVI.

K

Figure 4

The appendix to Whetstone/Walraven, *The honourable reputation of a
souldier/De eerweerdighe achtbaerheyt van een soldener,* Leiden, 1586.

beginning he himself contributed the translating of a small treatise on pronunciation, which served as an appendix to *The honourable reputation* but had a special title page [1]. Their common handbook was probably the 'Grammatica Latina ac Britannica. 8vo.' [2] which the young Dousa had in his library together with copies of 'The honourable reputation of a Souldier, Anglicè ac Belgicè' and 'Emblemata Galfridi Whitnei, cum iconibus, 4to.' [3].

But Walraven's major contribution was a literal translation of Whetstone's book, which he regarded as a profitable and delightful opportunity for exercise, for Dutchmen as much as for Englishmen:

Howe proude and presumptuous many Nations were, in to[o] muche observing theyr naturall tonge, is frendly Reader, not onknowne to those that walke throughe divers Landes. For in what straunge countrey they do not onely haunte, but dwelle also, yea twenty Jeres and more, they care not, but for theyr owne: as if it were a shame, to speake an others speache: desyring notwithstanding, that othermen shall serve and obeye them alwayes, in theyr language. Farre otherwyse with your, and also with our contremen. Which among all, of nature be most solicitous, to be skylled in all tongues. Of ours I am sure: of yours by experience taught, in Spaine, Fraunce, Oostlande, and in other places ... Wherefore I (althoughe a Scholer yet my self, and rude in this exercise) entangled with love of your tonge, was, of a zelous mynde, and favour to the Lovers of our tonge justly moved, to translate this small, but very fyne booke ... [4]

Walraven himself confessed that he was inspired by 'the sweet seduction of enticing Muses, *ante omnia dulces* to me, in my occupations, and to J. Dousa' [5]. Indeed, *De eerweerdighe achtbaerheyt van een soldener* was not a mere schoolbook, but really the first fruit of a pen which had before in vain attempted to translate Theophrastus and Lipsius [6]. A dogged concern with vernacular renderings betrays the disciple of Van Hout.

---

[1] See fig. 4 and cf. A. J. Barnouw, 'How English was taught in Jan van Hout's Leiden', *English Studies*, XVII, 1935, pp. 1–7.
[2] This catalogue entry does not seem to refer to the actual title of Dousa's Latin-English grammar.
[3] *Catalogus librorum* (see above, p. 61, note 1), sig. I iiij.
[4] *Honourable reputation*, p. 10.
[5] Ibid., p. 5. See Appendix II, no. 71.
[6] See ibid., p. 4. Cf. above, pp. 110–111.

As an English teaching manual which was not only in the Dutch language but also contained useful histories, Walraven dedicated the work to the magistrates of Hoorn on 30 August —sixteen days after Leicester had granted Basson the exclusive publishing rights. As far as the translator was concerned, *The honourable reputation* would have to justify his exceptionally long absence from Hoorn.

In this setting the prefatory matter of the Whetstone-Walraven production becomes a small mirror, as it were, of these Anglo-Leiden contacts. Apart from the translator's prefaces [1] it contains six poems: three English, two Dutch, and only one Latin. Their quality varies considerably, from Basson's borrowed lines 'To all freendly readers, uppon the translation of this present Booke' [2] to Whetstone's original 'To the right valiant gentlemen and souldiers, that are, or shalbe Armed under the Ensigne of Sainct George: In recompence of their worthie adventures, Heaven, and ever-lasting honor'. [3] An old-fashioned and anonymous verse

---

[1] To the Magistrates of Hoorn (pp. 3–5); To English Readers (p. 10); To Dutch Readers (p. 11–15); To the Reader, list of foreign phrases (p. 16); To the Magistrates of Hoorn (p. 74); To the Dutch Student (p. 75).

[2] See p. 112, note 3.

[3]   GOD with S. *GEORGE*, Allon, brave Gentlemen,
        Set Speares in rest, renew your auncient fame:
    Rush on the Pikes, the Cannon do not shen,
        Your Ancestors, with passage through the same,
    This Proverbe raisde, among the French, their Foes,
    Vous es si fier, que un Anglois.

    Thou art as fierce, as is an Englishman,
        The French still say, and proofe the same did teach:
    Turne you the french into Castillian,
        It hath a grace in such a loftie speach:
    Your cause is good, and Englishmen you are,
    Your foes be men, even as the french men weare.

    The force of death that raiseth many feares,
        In cravin harts, which courage doe dispise:
    Long lives the man, that dyes in lusty yeares,
        In actions where honour may arise.
    And wherein may you honour more expect,
    Then wronged men, to succour and protect?

    The Lyon prayes, upon the stoutest beast,
        Yet lickes the sheep, the which the wolfe hath wound:
    So worthy mindes, proude lookes, that feareth least,

in Dutch precedes these two poems. Of the remaining three the first came, of course, from the pen of Dousa the Elder, who supported Walraven's defensive dedication in an 'On the time-thriftiness of I.W., now striving after the English also'. This long-forgotten poem is one of his very few surviving Dutch sonnets, and contains a neat argument on the translator's behalf in more or less these terms:

What misapprehensions possesses man's heart! Each finds the day too long, and pastimes seeks, with cards, or dice; backgammon for a third: one only plays at fives, another carouses. Then, when DEAR TIME, by each of them put off, finds nowhere room, is it strange that it should haunt you, WALRAVEN, for comfort and resort? You, who for love nor money Time would praise? Who, unlike those, are no Time-killer but instead Time-keeper: who, tied to your book, find every day too short, yea use the night.
O THRIFTINESS OF TIME, o well-spent hours! Who, all-attempting, also try with zeal and care, for our use, to master ENGLISH. [1]

Young Dousa followed his father in Latin with an eight-line epigram in praise of the art of translating generally, and next

> Doth helpe to raise, the wounded from the ground.
> Like Lyons then, the Armes of *England* shield,
> Pray on your foes, and pittie those that yeld.
>
> I say no more, but God be your good speede,
>   And send you (hap) which I did never taste:
> And if this Booke, you do vouchsafe to reade,
>   You can not thinke, your labour spent in waste,
> Which doth containe, the Morall rules of those,
> That followed *MARS*, in thickest preace of foes.

[1]   OPTE TYT-SPARICHEYT VAN I.W. NU OOCK NA T'ENGELSCH POOGENDE.
SONET
Och met wat misverstant is smenschen hert bestoven!
    Elck valt den dach te langh, en wenscht om tijt verdrijf,
    D'een met de kaert, oft quaert; de derde met de schijf:
    Dees niet dan kaetsen doet, de vijfde niet dan hoven.
Naer dat van yeder dan de DIERBAER TYT verschoven
    Een open nergens vindt, ist vreemt, dat hy zo stijf
    Tot U WALRAVEN neemt, zijn toevlucht, zijn gerijf?
    U, die voor gelt, noch goet, den Tijt zoudt willen loven?
De welcke niet, als deez: een Tijt-verdrijver quaet,
    Maer Tijt-bewaerder zijt: dien steets aen t'boec gebonden,
    Valt elcken dach te cort, ja neemt den nacht te baet.
O SPARICHEYT DES TYTS, ô wel-bestede stonden!
    Diet al te leeren poocht, ja gaet met heeter daet
    En vlijt, ons ten profijt, nu t'ENGELSCH ooc doorgronden.

of Walraven's ability to treat both his own language and the
meaning of his original with equal skill. Last of all came
Whitney, linking the two columns of the book with his
'Uppon the translacion of this present Booke. To the Frendlye
Readers of either of the Languages'. In it he praised

> ... WHETSTONE [1] first, who did the work compile,
> WALRAVEN, next, that turn'd the same for you,
> Whose paines (I knowe) was ioyn'd with care of minde:
> Eche phrase to fitte, and worde for worde to finde.

He ended by inviting the reader to share his admiration,
because

> So shall you, bothe his paines, in parte requite:
> And stirre him up, some greater worke to write.

The conclusion is worth bearing in mind; for it must be
admitted that Walraven's effort, qualitatively, was but a
minor contribution. He admirably reflected his literary
antecedents, and his approach was enterprising enough. But
one feels—with Whitney—that 'some greater worke' was yet
and ought yet to be written.

Walraven's translation was only one symptom of a general
Anglo-Leiden 'integration'. The small University registered
more English students in 1586 than in any of the eleven
years since its foundation. Whitney, Wheteley, Wight, and
Penrudoc were followed in the *Volumen Inscriptionum*, or just
preceded, by various other 'Angli', i.e. men born in England:
Tobias and Jeremias Lul(l)s, Jacobus Courtius, Zebedeus
Damman, Nathanael Richardus, Johannes Marcowinus
(only in the *Album Recensionum*), Joannes Evangelisto ('scotus'),
and also by George Gilpin.

The one-time Marnix-translator, old friend of Rogers,
Dousa, Languet, Melissus, and others who have figured in
our narrative, George Gilpin, former secretary of the Merchant Adventurers at Antwerp, had been appointed as the
Queen's agent in Zeeland and then, on Leicester's arrival
in the Netherlands, as English secretary to the Council of
State. On 29 August 1586 [2] he was entered as 'D. Georgius

---

[1] The text reads 'WETHSTONE'.
[2] The *Album Recensionum* records the same date. On Gilpin and Leiden
in later years, see Bachrach, *Huygens and Britain*, pp. 51–52, 55, 88.

Gilpinus generosus Anglus' in the *Volumen*, having discussed his admission with Saravia—in whose house, incidentally, Benedicti now lived [1]. Gilpin's registration was obviously no ordinary procedure. The magistrates knew, and within less than a fortnight granted him—like every other University member—exemption from the municipal taxation on wine in recognition of his great services 'as secretary to Leicester' [2]. This was done at the request of the Earl himself and of Saravia, but his own initiative is also to be considered. Only when Gilpin himself addressed the local authorities did something of his Leiden interest transpire. Having desired, ever since his honourable appointment, to be near his wife and children, he wrote,

I considered the commodity and opportuneness of various towns where my arrival would be welcome, when my special love and inclination for the liberal arts urged me to think more especially of you. Serious employments of state leave me no time to spend in these studies; but for the benefit of my children (for whom I wish to provide such an education) I have arranged with the *Rector Magnificus* of your University so that I may yet be made a member of it. Meanwhile I have no thought of benefit or gain, except in this, that the occasion will put me in an even better position to offer assistance—for what I am worth—whenever there should be an opportunity to promote the *dignitas* of the Academy. [3]

The letter suggests that Gilpin had played his delicate part in the Leicester-Leiden controversies and had done so to the satisfaction of both parties. One would be tempted to think that Gilpin's removal to Leiden was as much inspired by a desire to live away from the Court as by his 'in literas humaniores amor'. Perhaps the University had reason to thank this one man for its preservation.

Such may well have been the Burgomasters' idea when some weeks after Gilpin's request for full academic membership they recorded in the minutes of the council their resolution

[1] '... apud Saraviam Actum lesten Junij 1586' (*Album Recensionum*, list 1586). In the same house was Thomas de Saravia, 'Anglus stud. phil.', a student since 23 November 1582.

[2] Leiden, Gem. arch., *Gerechtsdagboek*, 11 September 1586.

[3] G. Gilpin to Magistrates of Leiden, Utrecht, 1 October 1586 (Leiden, Univ. Libr., Cur. arch. no. 39, f. 177). See Appendix II, no. 72.

to recognize Gilpin, English gentleman, secretary to his Excellency, as a member of the University, and so to grant him the use of academic privileges and liberties; therefore to order the town secretary [Van Hout] to sign his patent. [1]

Thus one English member of the old faction moved to Leiden, where he rented a house on the Oude Rijn:

This house is occupied by Mr. Gilpin, secretary to his Excellency, with his wife and family. Therefore remember to leave him out when billets are distributed. [2]

In these words another of Van Hout's billeting lists locates the cultured English gentleman who chose to reside near the University, 'for the benefit of his children'.

More serious perhaps than crises from without were the internal commotions that now shook the University when Lipsius threatened to leave.

Officially his reason was bad health. But there is little doubt that non-Calvinistic convictions—a source of frequent criticism from outside—made living in Holland increasingly uncomfortable to so prominent a personality. Since no responsible man could ignore the disastrous consequences if Justus Lipsius should cease to lecture, every attempt had been made to placate him. In May, for instance, he had been given the attractive present of a spacious garden for his own private use and pleasure.[3] But he would not stay, and tendered his resignation. This decision was unacceptable to the University and no one was prepared to let him depart. Finally he had to be content with a few months' sick-leave, and so he prepared to visit the spas.[4]

It has escaped notice that a few days before his intended resignation Lipsius had gone to Utrecht for no other reason than to see Sidney: 'Illustris Domine,' he wrote,

I had come to Utrecht only (in truth) to greet you. That you have escaped me by a few hours before my arrival, I bear although I regret it.

---

[1] Leiden, Gem. arch., *Gerechtsdagboek*, 23 October 1586. See Appendix II, no. 73.

[2] Leiden, Gem. arch., Secr. arch. 7885, '5', f. 53. See Appendix II, no. 74.

[3] Leiden, Gem. arch., *Gerechtsdagboek*, 29 May 1586. Cf. Plate 5.

[4] See *Bronnen*, I, no. 114.

The war now keeps you occupied; but neither learning nor politics must be neglected. I fear—why should I not speak as freely as you have desired me to do in your presence?—I fear I say that some will relish this with too much fondness and affection. The slow minds of such men delight—I know not how— in being led by the slower way. A great number of men have recently been banished from Utrecht, for security's sake. I know, and do not condemn it. But what can I say when it happens haphazardly and one by one? What is the use of one group only? Buys is kept in close custody and not in accordance with his dignity. I declare privately to have been his friend (I am not one of those who change face and heart with fortune), yet I do not excuse him if he has sinned publicly. Have you forgotten my judgement of him? Boldly I then said against him what I deemed beneficial to the country: I may seem to speak in his favour, but to the same end. In zeal for my country or for my honour I yield to none. Time will show it. I declare myself unlike those whose tongue is prompt, vague, and often vain. What I do and feel, I do and feel seriously; nothing outwardly. But concerning Buys: if he was of no use to you, could he not have been removed simply and properly? 'But he is guilty'. Then remember another method, send him out of the country. A dungeon without defence brings disrepute and slander, deservedly or no. Why start new currents when the old ones have not yet come to rest? To you I prophesy (and wish it were to prove untrue) that these rapid torrents are leading us to internal strife. If your rule had complete control, their faults would be less dangerous—obviously they do not see which places may be open in your stronghold. That you will have free and firm use of the reigns of government, that I approve of and do recommend; but only if it is done with moderation and with a certain ease. In so sick a body, will you cure everything in a few months? A diet is required.

I wish I had been able to say this and much more to you by word of mouth: but surely you will see my mind, which is pure and harmless—so help me God. I ask you on the honour of the Realm and your Queen, by the general welfare of us all (which cannot be seen seperately), temper with all that is in you the fervour of those who mistake zeal for love. They seek their own (not your) advantage who force you into these hazards.

Farewell, illustrious Lord who will ever be dear to me. I sincerely wish the Earl and Governor victory and success.

At Utrecht, 30 August 1586.

Your Lordship's devoted *cliens*,

JUSTUS LIPSIUS.

[P.S.] While I have been here, kinsmen and friends of Buys have come to see me; they complain much about the close-

11

ness of his prison. They may not even see him. I pray you to consider and act accordingly. [1]

Lipsius' visit, in other words, served three purposes: to salute
his patron, to admonish him gently, and then to speak out on
behalf of Buys and others of the 'old current'. Lipsius was a
bold critic at the same time as an 'addictissimus cliens'.

Sidney took the Professor's remarks in good part and wrote
from Deventer to 'Clarissimo viro Domino Justo lipsio Amico
me charissimo'—as the endorsement read—to calm the
devoted friend who had unfortunately missed him in Utrecht.
The letter is the only specimen of his correspondence with
Lipsius, and shows (among other things) the affectionate and
respectful nature of the relationship between the two men.
'My dear Lipsius,' Sidney wrote, 'I regret to hear that you
are leaving us'—us indeed, for Lipsius would leave both
Holland and its English leaders, both Leiden and the literary
world, which Sidney had apparently heard after receiving
the letter from Utrecht. 'I am the more sorry,' he continued,

because I fear that of all these things your disgust with the cause
matters as much as your illness itself. If this is what it is (and if
you do not yet despair of our England), I beseech you by our
friendship that you will reconsider your departure to that other
place.

One cannot ignore the fact that Lipsius' proposed 'departure
to that other place' [Louvain?] came immediately after his
unhappy experiences at Utrecht, and one must therefore
assume, with Sidney, that disapproval of Leicester's new
policy, more than anything else, had determined Lipsius'
resolution. After the Saravia episode, this was the second

---

[1] J. Lipsius to P. Sidney, Utrecht, 30 August 1586 (*Epistolae ecclesiasticae
et theologicae*, ed. P. a Limborch, Amsterdam, 1684, no. 2). See Appendix II, no. 75.

Lipsius continued to negotiate on behalf of Buys. On 9 October
he wrote from Amsterdam ('in ipso itinere meo, quod in Germaniam
valetudinis causa parabam'), again as an 'addictissimus cliens', to
Lord Burghley. In it Lipsius refers to Burghley's benevolence towards
'eos, quos fama aliqua commendat eruditionis aut literarum' and
humbly suggests to occupy a place 'extrema linea' among them. His
arguments are roughly the same as in his letter to Sidney, but he adds
an emphatic comment on the pro-English past of Leicester's prisoner
(see W. van Everdingen, *Het leven van Mr. Paulus Buys*, diss., Leiden.
1895, pp. 184–185).

unfortunate Anglo-Leiden occurrence in recent weeks. Sidney's letter is therefore the more remarkable in continuing as follows:

The proposal which I made you some time ago I shall ensure in such a way that it will not prove deficient if I should come to die; I know that you would be very welcome to our Queen and to many others, yea to all others.

Hopefully awaiting his return, he added, he would continue to aid Buys 'quia tu ita vis'. Meanwhile many problems remained, and 'certe tuus Ph. Sidneius' had little time for writing long letters.[1]

If only for its second paragraph, the letter deserves more attention than it has so far received. Obviously, the 'proposal' was an invitation to come to England, where the Queen would have extended a warm welcome to the celebrated Leiden 'refugee' who had, oddly enough, become a victim and critic of her own representatives' policy in the Low Countries. There is no answer to the question whether Lipsius was to be offered a Chair in England, but it seems the most likely 'proposal'. In that case yet another long-established Sidney-Leiden contact led to a remarkable climax in this eventful year.

In 1586 English poets had mixed with Dutch poets: some books had been produced as a result of it; the Leiden milieu had shown its accessibility to English students; finally, the renowned English poet-soldier invited the leading light of Leiden over to England. In this confusing stage of Anglo-Leiden relationships, for all the differences of opinion, literary achievements were evidently judged by other more liberal standards.

The 'proposal' was to be ratified, Sidney promised, to leave Lipsius provided for if his patron 'should come to die'. It is as if Sidney felt a strange foreboding while he was writing this in the camp near Deventer on 14 September 1586.

[1] P. Sidney to J. Lipsius, Deventer, 14 September 1586 (Leiden, Univ. Libr., MS. Lips. 4). A somewhat careless transcription is given in Sidney, *Works*, III, no. 112. See Appendix II, no. 76.

V

LEIDEN AND THE SIDNEY MYTH

ONE week later a skirmish took place outside Zutphen, which many have described as heroic and some as reckless, but all as a waste of noble blood. For Sidney was seriously injured and had to be carried to Arnhem where the most skilful surgeons dressed his wounds while he displayed the equanimity and pious chivalry of which Fulke Greville has left us such a vivid account.

The news was naturally a great shock to Dutchmen and Englishmen alike. Dr. James received a letter saying:

> The rumour about the wound of 'Illustris & generosus Dominus' Sidney has greatly upset us, and from your letter I learn that he is not yet sure to recover: but we pray God that he will restore his Honour to his former health, and long preserve him for us and our churches. [1]

Baudius, Sidney's *cliens*, happened to be at Arnhem as well, carrying letters from Dousa on some unknown commission. One was also to Dr. James, who had just perused it when

> word came that the Earl of Leicester would arrive on that same day; a little later he was already reported to have entered. And thus your [*i.e. Dousa's*] presence would be indeed requisite for the furthering of your affairs with him.
> Sidney was too ill to read your letter. We have told him the whole matter as well as we could. What of it? We have agreed, and one cannot find him more willing to grant. And so he immediately orders that young man [2] to be sent in (whom I remember to have seen with you, very witty and well-educated) and tells him to prepare a letter of personal commendation to the Earl. This he makes, and gladly so because he is most eager to work for your cause. I tell you, he hopes with incredible ardour that you will deem him worthy to be named among your friends. But hearing a little later of the arrival of his Excellency, he judges writing superfluous—as you will readily understand. I shall deal

---

[1] B. Vezekius to J. James, Deventer, 25 September 1586 (Hessels, II, no. 230). See Appendix II, no. 77.

[2] 'That young man': his identity remains a mystery.

with Sidney, that he may mention your business when the Earl comes to visit him officially, and I am certain that he will do as I ask. [1]

Thus, even after receiving his fatal wound, Sidney was in touch with Leiden. He had letters from Dousa, held conference with Baudius, and showed himself open and helpful to the matter they discussed with him. This would not last. For there in Arnhem on 27 October, hardly more than a month after his prophetic lines to Lipsius, Sir Philip Sidney, attended by Dr. James [2], surrounded by kinsmen and friends, passed away piously and peacefully, so setting the world one last example of virtue.

Sidney, while alive, had stirred the pens of numerous greater and lesser poets—foreigners perhaps more than English—as a politician, courtier, poet, patron, and friend. But after his death it was for something more than this that the Muses were inspired to honour him. Wasted youth had made the end romantic, while the cause made it heroic, and religious endurance virtuous. Writers eagerly availed themselves of so 'poetic' an occasion to produce unheard-of quantities of commemorative verse in the conviction that now, by his death precisely, all the classical aspects of a renaissance hero had been united in him. Students have frequently complained that these thousands of lines, though not necessarily insincere, contribute nothing whatsoever to Sidney's biography. But his contemporaries, always tending to translate the particular into the general, presented with a subject so obviously 'universal', would have found a personal epitaph almost absurd.

The sudden awakening of English poets to write commemorative verses results from their seizing the same opportunity. Supported by the official display of pomp and indeed deification which both the Dutch and the English government—

---

[1] D. Baudius to J. Dousa, Arnhem, 26 [September] 1586 (B.M., MS. Burney 371, f. 123); the letter is dated '26 VIIIs', 26 Octobris, which must be a mistake (cf. also p. 155, note 4). See Appendix II, no. 78.

[2] Cf. Sidney's testament: '... to Dr. James, for his Pains taken with me in this my Hurt, the Sum of thirty Pounds.' (Sidney, *Works*, III, p. 374). The great Dr. Johan Wier was on his way, but came too late: see Sidney's last letter, to J. Wier, Arnhem, [26 October 1586] (Sidney, *Works*, III, no. 114).

obviously deliberately—arranged for his transport and funeral, English poets were not slow in helping to build up a Sidney-myth. In representing him as the ideal Christian Knight, the English made him their counterpart to similar foreign myths, such as those of Orange and De Coligny. But as a glorified English hero, Sidney surpassed all alien examples in adding to his courtly virtues, and what might be called glorious death, the special distinction of being a renowned literary patron and himself a great poet.

The universities of England now for the first time imitated the continental practice of composing commemorative volumes. Perhaps it could be said that England was in need of such a hero, and that therefore Sidney would never have become so historic a figure if it had not been for the circumstances of his death. For many years a regular stream of epitaphs and elegies were to pour from the presses of London, Oxford, and Cambridge and among the host of authors we frequently find names that have appeared before in some Anglo-Dutch context. Dousa's friend Alexander Neville edited the *Academiae Cantabrigiensis lacrymae* (to which even King James VI contributed a sonnet); Dyer (or Greville) wrote an epitaph which first appeared in *The Phoenix Nest* and then together with Spenser's 'Astrophel'; Constable composed 'Foure sonnets to Sidneys soule'; and Whetstone, one of the earliest commemorators, published his *Sir Philip Sidney*, the only memorial piece with some biographical—if unreliable—data. And a Dutchman, Theodor de Bry, engraved a vast scroll representing the 'celebritas et pompa funeris'.[1]

In Holland meanwhile, Sidney's death had similar literary effects but without the sense of novelty present in England. After all, no national symbol—such as Orange had been— could be extolled, and Dutch poets simply continued an established literary mode when they wrote verses on Sidney, *in memoriam* this time. Many mournful lines are more remarkable for having escaped attention than for being 'new' in

---

[1] For a list of English poems in commemoration of Sidney, see Siebeck, *Das Bild Sidneys*, pp. 184–187. Theodor de Bry (1527/28–1598) from Liège had only just arrived in England (see A. M. Hind, *Engravings in England in the sixteenth & seventeenth centuries*, Cambridge, 1952, I, pp. 124–137).

any historical sense. Verses could be long, or as brief as Baudius' chronogram:

hIC IaCet eXtInCtVs CrVdeLI gLande phILIppVs sydnaeVs, noMen nosse sat esse potest. [1]

But in tone and manner they all derived directly from earlier poems in his honour. At the same time one can say that there exists a definite body of Dutch (Latin) poetry in memory of the late Governor of Flushing. Whatever their value, curious or literary, in one respect at least they deserve closer inspection, namely that here the original scene of Anglo-Leiden contacts was set up once again as though for a final *tableau*.

The sad news of 27 October 1586 was received with infinite grief, it is well known. Louise de Coligny, writing to Leicester, not inappropriately compared Sir Philip's death to the loss of a brother [2]. Hotman, having confessed to Lipsius his inconsolable condition, added that he expected poetic condolences from him and Dousa whose praises he remembered from Sidney's own lips [3]. Often quoted as an example of Dutch concern is a slim volume of epitaphs printed at Leiden. These three instances already suggest that their regret was a mournful reflection on that happier scene in autumn 1585, only twelve months earlier.

One of Sidney's Dutch *clientes* has left us a more precise indication. It is our Leiden poet Dominicus Baudius, who was present when his patron died. A fortnight later he wrote to Dousa the Younger:

While I was here at Utrecht, my dear Dousa, I happened to run into that woman whom that most noble lady your mother had sent here to find out where your father is. She has asked me to tell you what I know about him.

I left him at Deventer, where he was in good health, on the twenty-third of this month [*i.e. October* [4]]. He had given me

[1] Baudius, *Poemata*, p. 603.
[2] Louise de Coligny to R. Dudley, Flushing, 3 November 1586 (*Correspondance de Louise de Coligny*, ed. P. Marchegay, Paris, 1887, no. 24). Cf. p. 53.
[3] J. Hotman to J. Lipsius, n.p., n.d. (*Hotomanorum epistolae*, no. 95).
[4] The letter has an impossible date: '31 Novembris'. From its contents the proper date may be assumed to be '31 Octobris'. For Baudius' poor dating, cf. p. 153, note 1.

two letters, one directed to Sir Philip Sidney, another to Dr. James. I carried them along; he probably expected an answer, but in vain: for my Master's condition no longer suffered him even to sign his name under a letter, and one day after my arrival in the town of Arnhem that Light of intellect, breeding, and nobility was carried off by death.

Since then I have not heard from your father any more: I am under the impression that he tarries in Deventer hoping for the Earl of Leicester's return; and since he will have been told that the Earl is to go to Utrecht, I hope he will also go, and come here. If he were here, he could complete all his negotiations in as little as one day.

I have nothing else to write, except this: I earnestly desire you to indite some poem on my Master's death, and to exhort George Benedicti on my behalf to do the same. I think I shall be commissioned to write his *universa facta*.

Farewell.[1]

This is how Leiden came to write an 'In Memoriam'. Together, Baudius, Benedicti, and Dousa's son, three young poets of the 1585 embassy, produced 482 lines of verse divided into twenty-seven poems. But such a quantity of occasional composition did not prevent any one of them from gracing his contribution with a very individual approach.

In a curious way this could even be said of Baudius, who dedicated his longest poem—the first of his later *Iamborum funeralium liber* [2]—to Robert Sidney, Philip's brother, in a typical attempt to kill two birds with one stone. After mourning the loss of 'Flos Anglicanae gentis, imo totius flos orbis', he appealed to the other Sidney to adopt his brother's *cliens*:

... of all most unhappy I whom in your death you have left helpless and wanting counsel, in the prime of his youth, while his heart had begun to conceive great hopes. This is all finished— unless there is room for hope in you, Robert Sidney, some promise of rescue.

For this I appeal to you, by the sublime honour of your family, and by your brother's renowned name which fills all regions with admiration: If I have faithfully served him with my honour, if he has held me worthy of his love: then I beg you, leave me not devoid of favour after the great misfortunes that befell me . . .[3]

---

[1] D. Baudius to J. Dousa the Younger, [Utrecht], 31 [October] 1586 (B.M., MS. Burney 371, f. 125). See Appendix II, no. 79.

[2] As for example in Baudius, *Poemata*, 1640, pp. 195–197.

[3] Baudius, *Carmina*, p. 70. See Appendix I, no. 14.

Still more remarkable than this dual-purpose 'Lessus', more interesting also than his chronogram and an 'In obitum fortissimi herois Philippi Sidnaei' [1], is the proposed commission to write Sidney's *universa facta*. Was it to be a Latin prose history, or did it echo the Sidney epic which he had suggested in his poem of 1 January? One would be tempted to ignore his remark and dismiss it as another boastful phrase, had it not repeated that earlier reference; but it seems almost preposterous to think that Robert Sidney would have promised him such a commission. Moreover, not a single line of it was ever published, not a trace survives. But in spite of its doubtful aspects there remains the interesting point that a Leiden poet could seriously discuss the writing of a Complete Life of Sir Philip Sidney—a task which no English contemporary ventured to undertake [2].

From a literary point of view, Dousa the Younger offered more in answer to Baudius' invitation. Two of his poems betray familiarity with the *oeuvre* of his subject, as we shall see, and excel as individual compositions. The other two are short, epigrammatic. One is a comparison between Sidney and Codrus, the last king of Athens, who died for his country: '. . . To fall for one's country is a great Virtue: then how much greater is it, not to shun death in defence of one's Allies?' [3] The second is still more conventional: Phoebus, Pallas, and the Muses weep; '. . . therefore, is it surprising that men should make complaint in verse when the same sad concern affects the great Gods and Goddesses?' [1]

Like Dousa, numerous English poets struggled with the great problem of how to write a proper memorial poem without becoming monotonous. Certain rules of decorum, after all, had to be observed in this kind of composition, and the

---

[1] Ibid., p. 98. See Appendix I, no. 15.
[2] Apart from Moffet's *Nobilis*, there was one other comparable biography, now lost: Sir James Perrot's 'History', perhaps the same as the lost 'booke called the lyfe and death of Sir Phillip Sydney' of 1606 (see Siebeck, *Das Bild Sidneys*, pp. 127, 187). Greville's later *Life* was in some ways laudatory rather than biographical.
[3] Dousa the Younger, *Poemata*, 1607, p. 100. See Appendix I, no. 20.
[4] Ibid., p. 100. See Appendix I, no. 19.

aspects of Sidney's death could not be excluded. Dr. John
Rainolds, the Aristotelian scholar, for example, organized
the writing of an epitaph on Sidney by first—according to
one manuscript copy [1]—drafting its basic contents, then
setting them in order, and finally turning them into verse.
In the case of Sidney, the English writer's task could be
considerably relieved by the fact that his verses could link
up with *Astrophel and Stella* or *Arcadia*, both known in manuscript.

This appears to have been also the younger Dousa's
solution, and he first applied it to the opening lines of the
following elegy:

Like at remendous tempest in a raging sea buries Tiphys as
he steers his course by *the Arcadian star* [2]; thus in a wild turmoil
SIDNEY, who was the anchor of our wreck, is taken from us.
Now it must go like a mother who has lost one of her twins,
unhappy like a man who has lost one eye.

O grief! Fallen is our only hope, the Spaniard's terror, the
choicest glory of his native land, SIDNEY, whose name and excellent virtue is recognized in the East, and recognized in the West:
all Nature could not have contained his fame if Lachesis had
suffered him to run his whole life's course; but sadly he died
before his day, when his years were in full bloom, his youthful
leg pierced by a flying dart, while he kills the savage Spaniards with
a hand of lightning and deserves the wreaths of either Pallas.

Belgia bewails her helmsman, Britannia the child she bred; and
justified is the grief of both for such a violent death: Troy was
thrown in no less disorder when Hector's body was dragged
away, and Hellas wept as much when Ajax was killed. For
whom the end is never certain, life is not unlike fruits falling; some
drop when they are ripe, by the force of a tempest; but others
fall while they are sour, cast down by a hail of stones.

O Sidney, while you pursued our safety in battle, how little
did you mind your own safety! When you first audaciously
attacked the enemy, Spain gained its first honour through you.
Just so did Protesilaus (since he was marked by an adverse fate)
first stain the Trojan soil with blood. What use was your piety
now, and the holy life you had always led, and the nobility of
your father's blood?

You were raised in the two arts of Minerva; one gave you
life, the other a grave: so great a virtue was not unknown to the
Venetians, nor did the BRITISH NYMPH keep your intellect hidden;

---

[1] B.M., MS. Cotton Titus B VIII, f. 291. The poem also occurs in MS.
Cotton Vesp. C XIV, f. 214.

[2] Italics mine.

you were even sent to the EMPEROR as an ambassador, although you had hardly left your fourth Olympias [1] . . .

Needless to say, even Dousa the Younger continued with the 'prescribed series' of complimental complaints, differing from numerous others only in the liveliness of his description, and in that his 'Dutch angle' afforded the common subject some measure of variety. In the conclusion of his elegy Sidney's widow ends her lament and calls for

'. . . the sacred torches to light the pyre of my husband, that it may burn no less fiercely here than my feelings for him now burn within me.'

She would have spoken more, but DUDLEY interrupted her: 'The spirit of so great a man demands no such tears: for from the high heavens he beholds our human cares and pleasures, and enjoys the life of a heavenly being: and we, poor little creatures, what greatness is there that we can give life to? Time is never certain to wait for us. Who knows, great SIDNEY, whether one of us is not close upon your heels?' [2]

More curious still is the last poem, in which he alone among the Dutch poets used the conventions of a pastoral eclogue to convey his grief for the loss of Daphnis, the Bucolic poet, i.e. Sidney, the author of *Arcadia*.

One day, leaning on his rustic staff, Lycidas stood on the bank of the Thames. Many a beech-tree afforded him shade, but, alas, he was disturbed by deep sorrow and mourning: he did not tune his wonted song on the rustic pipe to lament his unhappy loves: nor did he delight in falling asleep amidst the soft rustling of leaves or in leading the tender kids to their sober provender: all this he would ban from his deepest thoughts. But neglecting his herd, his farm, and his poor field, with all his heart 'Daphnis' he sighed, sadly and with great emotion, 'Daphnis, are you dead, alas?

'Echo, who resound in secret valleys, you also lamented, almost forgetting your proper liveliness; and the swans of the river wept in mourning.

'Speak, o Muses, speak of the shepherd's Muse, o speak: for I expect that you have also mixed sighs with songs, and that you have also loudly complained when your dear child was buried.

'Must you lie so, o Daphnis? so miserably, alas?

Must you lie so, Daphnis, killed by cruel death, o Daphnis?

---

[1] I.e. period of four years.
[2] Dousa the Younger, *Rerum Caelestium*, pp. 54–58. See Appendix I, no. 17. The last line strongly suggests that Dousa wrote or altered the poem after Leicester's death in 1588.

'Thus, have you not fulfilled your hopes, nor the hopes of your friends? On the beach that day when your ship left the country, you looked forward (I remember) to your return which would be sweet to you and to your friends—but the good fortune for which you hoped has deceived you. And then you decided on delights—which could never come true—and on times to be marked with a white stone—which were to prove as vain.

'Must you lie so, o Daphnis? so miserably, alas?

Must you lie so, Daphnis, cut off by cruel death, o Daphnis? 'Nor was your wife cheerful when she left you, but she stifled her sorrows deep in her heart; evil omens there were, the owl with its dreadful sound, the crow gruesomely croaking in the hollow oak; ever mindful she was of her cares.

'Must you lie so, o Daphnis? so miserably, alas?

Must you lie so, Daphnis, killed by cruel death, o Daphnis? 'Had it not been better there to have breathed your last breath, there where the mother's milk first comforted your throat and the air first touched you with fleeting tremours, than here to die, far from your native country, a visitor to strange lands, an offering to ruinous Mars?

'Must you lie so, o Daphnis? so miserably, alas?

Must you lie so, Daphnis, cut off by cruel death, o Daphnis? 'On that day, alas, where was Phoebus, or Martial Pallas, when the cruel Parcae broke your vital threads? Why did they not aid you when death approached? But I am wrong: for neither Pallas could have helped nor Phoebus could have strengthened you with infusions of life; but clearly he showed his grief in a purple-black hue as he sank down into the western seas, more sadly than at other time.

'Must you lie so, o Daphnis? so miserably, alas?

Must you lie so, Daphnis, cut off by cruel death, o Daphnis? 'O, you who are loved by the whole country, for you Nymphs weave white lilies with violets and purple amaranthus, and prepare fragrant wreaths for your prison; and now you roam through the blessed light and the blessed field of the Elysian woodland: from there, also, you look down on mortal cares, laughing at mortal delights.

'Must you lie so, o Daphnis? so miserably, alas?

Must you lie so, Daphnis, killed by cruel death, o Daphnis? 'All has changed since your departure, Daphnis: for while you frequented these hills, these dewy meadows, the green hills with their thick woods seemed to smile, the springs and the lush fields smiled. But after relentless fate has carried you away, Daphnis, the trees lose their attraction and the hills are in mourning, the springs dry up, and lush fields fade. And the earth, that once displayed a gay green garb of flowers, is uninviting and now grows thistles.

'Must you lie so, o Daphnis? so miserably, alas?

Must you lie so, Daphnis, cut off by cruel death, o Daphnis?

'Truly, this was the reason why we at your departure said 'farewell, dear friend' and moistened our cheeks with sad tears—by chance, or an evil omen?

'Must you lie so, o Daphnis? so miserably, alas?

Must you lie so, Daphnis, killed by cruel death, o Daphnis?

'O, if next summer you could see the mallows and other herbs blossom again where they have faded: but we, presumptuous little men, are never allowed to return whence we have once departed.

'Must you lie so, o Daphnis? so miserably, alas?

Must you lie so, Daphnis, killed by cruel death, o Daphnis?

'But though your body is dead, Daphnis, oblivion will never extinguish your memory in our hearts. I shall often address you in my verse, and my sorrows will remain day and night. And when I shall thrice call your name in a loud voice, then your sacred image will leave the forests and fields of lush Elysium to address us thus:

' "Shepherd, once the object of our love, now of sorrow and anxiety, my death does not demand these sighs; leave such sighs for them whose impious souls are left to eternal punishment, and for their torturing, to the flames of Phlegethon. But for me, whom God himself has admitted among his Celestial Citizens and enlisted in the Ranks of the Blessed, why should there be so many tears, why such heavy sighs?"

'This, and more, you will say to me; but never can our sorrow be driven away, never our grief be driven away.'

—While Lycidas flung such words at the vacant skies and Titan immersed his sizzling lamp, Thyrsis arrived; Lycidas saw Thyrsis, and said: 'To morrow my pipe will repeat you my wonted song.'

Thus he spoke, and then returned with Thyrsis to his rustic abode. [1]

Of all the Sidney poems produce dat Leiden, this was certainly the most successful. Janus Dousa the Younger, whose Eclogue almost reads like a companion poem to the *Astrophel* collection, made the required three elements blend with great ease and charm. Dutifully bearing in mind what essential points were to be raised, the Dutch Lycidas carefully framed his complaint in the supremely appropriate setting of a Thames-side Arcadia which he enlivened with some subtle touches of private concern and experience. As a poet he proves capable of dealing with this hazardous genre and of

---

[1] Dousa the Younger, *Rerum Caelestium*, pp. 58–61. See Appendix I, no. 18.

bringing his effusion, as the only one among his compatriots, so amazingly close to the new pastoral trend in English poetry.

The volume of *Epitaphia in mortem Philippi Sidneji* [1], published at Leiden in 1587, was not, strictly speaking, a university anthology comparable to those of Oxford and Cambridge as is often assumed; and indeed it was not printed by the *Academiae Typographus* Raphelengius, but by Jan Paedts. Nor were Lipsius and Danaeus responsible for them [2], but Benedicti [3], whose generous compliance with Baudius' request had produced so unusual a publication.

If the verses of Baudius and Dousa the Younger showed the author's characteristics well, so did Benedicti's twenty epitaphs. In their informal triumvirate, he was perhaps the most 'academic poet'. His project of a separately produced collection may have been influenced by Neville's *Lacrymae* from his own *Alma Mater*. At any rate, avoiding both plain suits for patronage and doleful effusions, he produced a strictly academic series of epigrams. Each of them gave a special turn to one aspect of Sidney's death. Thus, for instance, the fifth epigram:

When death approached, Philip is reported to have said: 'Lo, God, Dutch soil is holy to thee. I have received a wound, I do not regret it, the cause is good. To this, if life is given me again, it will again be given.' O voice of Sidney, truly Cygneian: for both holy he once lived, holy he now dies. [4]

Another example may be found in:

If you believe that Philip has died a miserable death, then you are ignorant of what it is to live, and what to die. Life is a short

---

[1] [Benedicti], *Epitaphia in mortem nobilissimi et fortissimi viri D. Philippi Sidneji Equitis ex Illustrissima Warvicensium Familia. Qui incomparabili damno reip. Belgicae vulnere in praelio contrà Hispanos fortiter accepto paucis post diebus interijt*, Leiden, J. Paedts, 1587. No copy is recorded in the Netherlands.

[2] Cf. Poirier, *Sir Philip Sidney*, p. 270; probably misinterpreting Berta Siebeck's statement: 'Es sind zwölf Seiten lateinischer Eulogien, die dem Komandanten von Briel, Th. de Burgh, gewidmet sind. Von den Leydener Gelehrten hatten Lipsius und Danaeus Sidney nahegestanden' (*Das Bild Sidneys*, p. 83).

[3] They all appeared in Benedicti's *Poemata posthuma*, 1601, pp. 21–26.

[4] Benedicti, *Epitaphia*, no. [V]. See Appendix I, no. 25.

death, death is life again: Philip has the latter, had the former: lives he, or has he died? [1]

Put together, Benedicti's twenty 'points of wit' provided a reader—and, who knows, other writers?—with a complete set of applicable conceits.

In Benedicti's approach, especially in his first ten epitaphs, one recognizes, more clearly than in most other writers, a deliberate attempt to find the heroic formulation as referred to above. He actually makes the point that the Sidney myth could not have come into existence without the circumstances of his death:

When Sidney, killed by generous Mars, returned to England, to be buried ceremoniously in native soil, then how much honour to his country, and also how much grief returned!—Both were great, but the latter went surpassed by honour.

Britain saw the wound, and mourned for it: but the glory acquired by that wound was a solace. For more praise flowed from it than blood; and praise made its way to the stars, filling the great orb.

There the Hero joins the celestial throng of Heroes, and in triumphant manner sings of blissful delights.

O happy Hero! At one time you came to Holland as a man worthy of his country, thus you now return from it more worthily. [2]

In these and similar terms Benedicti contributed to the glorification of Sir Philip Sidney—'who went to heaven; and why, do you ask? Because the earth could not contain him.' [3] His *Epitaphia* could be seen as the official tribute of the one foreign university with which Sidney had been most intimately connected: they had a Leiden imprint, and were anonymous, except for a dedicatory verse signed by the author.

Receiver of the dedication was William Cecil's eldest son Thomas, Governor of another cautionary town, The Brill, and therefore Sidney's immediate colleague. Other reasons, too, must have suggested his patronage to Benedicti. There appears to have existed some definite relationship between Leiden and this Englishman whom Benedicti exhorted to imitate Sidney in uniting warfare and letters. Lipsius, in an epistle

[1] Ibid., no. [XVIII]. See Appendix I, no. 38.
[2] Ibid., no. [IX]. See Appendix I, no. 29.
[3] Ibid., no. [XV]. See Appendix I, no. 35.

dated 11 April 1590, was to dedicate his *Epistolarum centuria secunda* to him, and Baudius wrote him a poem in 1587 [1] in which he mentions Dousa, Lipsius, and even Rogers. Perhaps Thomas Cecil was considered eligible and prepared to take over Sidney's Leiden patronage.

With the return of names like Dousa, Lipsius, and Rogers, perspectives widen. The scene opens up with the re-appearance of the 'older generation' in this context, although not a single epitaph by them has survived. It is not unlikely, however, that some were written, particularly after Hotman's earnest request.[2] The same may be said of Leiden's vernacular poets whose verses were almost invariably buried in oblivion. But as it widens, the general picture is, in a sense, also narrowed down.

From what has come down to us, one general conclusion is immediately apparent. In spite of Sidney's fame abroad—of which we have constantly been reminded—no foreign poems on his death are known except those of his Dutch admirers. His loss was a disaster that affected all the Provinces of the Republic: but no commemorative verses are recorded in, for example, Utrecht or Amsterdam or Zeeland. Leiden, therefore, was the only foreign town where a literary circle indited poems in his memory. The reactions to Sidney's death prove his special place in Anglo-Leiden relations.

One exception—invariably recorded in Sidney studies—remains to be discussed, namely the ten-line epitaph which Groslotius composed, supposedly in 1609 [3]. Some have taken it as evidence that France still celebrated Sidney twenty

---

[1]
> Te, vir magne, canent seu genio lyrae
> Sublimi-ve tuba Duzicus impetus,
> Et culti ingenium nobile Lipsij,
> Rogertisque decens venus.
> Felices animae, Musa quibus dedit
> Cedro digna loqui, factaque Principum
> Morti subtrahere, & perpetuum decus,
> Seclis prodere posteris . . .
>
> (Baudius, *Carmina*, p. 38).

[2] See p. 155.

[3] For the reason that it was quoted in Pierre de Lestoile's *Mémoires-Journaux* (October 1609) and introduced by the following sentence: 'M. de Lisle Groslot m'a fait donner ce jour . . . le Tumbeau suivant . . .' (X, p. 42).

8. Sir Philip Sidney, the hero.

From Baudartius, Afbeeldinghe van alle de Veld-slagen, *Amsterdam, 1616, f. 535,*
the engraving showing Prince Maurice and Sidney at the taking of Axel in 1586.

years after his death [1], or, conversely, as 'un témoignage curieux et à peu près unique de la renommée de Sidney en France avant la traduction de *l'Arcadie*' [2]. It is true that our *quadrumvir* wrote it—but at a much earlier date. On 12 December 1586 he sent off a letter to Dousa the Younger in which he declared:

... it is most necessary that you endure this audacity of mine which so impudently troubles you with some of my ungraceful verses on the death of Sir Philip Sidney, which have written themselves by force of bitter grief—much against the will of the very Muses, who deservedly bar such a profane man from their sanctuary, which is unlocked for you only, yea, itself locked up in such sacred hearts.

Of these I send you one copy only, which I should like you to share with Benedicti, because I have no time to write them out for each of you. Besides, this is more than enough for such trifles. I have added a French epitaph, not to please you—who, I think, understand no French—but only for your father who, I know, is familiar with our forms of wit. And although the other things are not much good, yet I shall not forbid you to show them to him, if you like.

You will perhaps praise my good will and endeavour, but not the thing itself: you will not, however, judge it on its own merits, but purely by my affection. Hence, I expect no fame, nor fear infamy. This is what I have desired, and indeed what was due: to perform these last and sad duties of piety for the divine Manes of so great a man and such a friend; I have wanted you to be witnesses of the proper fulfilment of these duties . . . [3]

Then followed the epitaph [4], supported by another, unrecorded, epitaph, the one in which Groslotius specified Sidney's literary accomplishments [5]. A French sonnet concluded the letter, for Dousa only:

EPITAPHE D'ILLUSTRISSIME MESSIRE
PHILIPPE DE SYDNEY CHEVALIER

Passant arreste icy. Icy dans ce tombeau
  Gist l'ame d'Angleterre, et le corps de cette ame.
  Mais l'ame de ce corps, qui ard de vifue flamme,
  Au ciel a reporté ce qu'y est de plus beau.

---

[1] Osborn, *Sir Philip Sidney*, p. 124.   [2] Poirier, *Sir Philip Sidney*, p. 274.
[3] H. Groslotius to J. Dousa the Younger, London, 12 December 1586 (B.M., MS. Burney 370, f. 7). See Appendix II, no. 80.
[4] Ibid., f. 8. See Appendix I, no. 12.
[5] Ibid., ff. 8–9. See Appendix I, no. 13. See p.p. 102–103.

D'un mesme coup la Parque a tranché le fuzeau
    A Mars, Grace, et Pallas, aus neuf Soeurs; a ma trame.
    Non: toutes ces Vertus me serviront de Basme,
    Qui fera que mon Nom vivra tousiours nouveau.
La Vie de mon Nom pour tombe ha tout le Monde.
    J'ay chargé de mes faicts la plume vagabonde
    De la Grand'Renommée: et des Soeurs favori
J'ay gravé mes Lauriers sur l'autel de Memoire.
    Ma jeunesse a passé des vieux l'heur et la gloire.
    Qui meurt en son Printemps, est de Dieu plus cheri! [1]

It was only proper that a French sonnet in the traditional mode should have been written, considering that both Sidney and the Dutchmen to whom it was sent were deeply indebted to the French schools of poetry. It was equally appropriate that it should have been written by one of the 1585 *quadrumviri* for another member of that circle: for this makes it possible to see even the Frenchman's contributions as part of the Anglo-Leiden line of literary exchange in which the late Governor of Flushing had figured for so long.

---

[1] The poem is signed: 'De L'isle'.

VI

THE END OF A PERIOD

As if Sidney's death alone had not been enough to terminate a fruitful development of Anglo-Leiden relations, the general *débâcle* of Leicester's Dutch policy occurred at almost the same time [1]. The Earl's final departure was to be postponed for another year, but losing Sidney did not improve his position. This is how Pieter Cornelisz. Hooft, the Dutch seventeenth-century poet and historiographer, somewhat acidly recalls the events in his renowned *Nederlandsche historien*:

... they paid most dearly for that battle, because twenty-five days later Philip Sidney came to die from a wound in his thigh which he had there received: a gentleman of some thirty years, happy in wit, brave in action, genuine in erudition, polite in speech, sensible and engaging in his manners. He was the offspring of a sister of the Earl of Leicester; found himself notably favoured by the Queen; and was therefore firmly expectant of uncommon preferment.

And some never doubted but (had he lived) his wisdom and modesty (once time and experience had mollified his passions) would have obliged his uncle, whose intelligence could not compare with his, to discontinue his immature enterprises, which were a humiliation to the States. But others judged, that if he should have used his industry, valour, and ability in undermining liberty (which his insistence, from the very first, that Leicester's governorship should embrace unlimited authority, had given them reason to fear), that this would have disagreed with the country even more than the delusions of Leicester, the rash beginnings of whose enterprises caused him to halt half-way. [2]

Hooft's view was no different from other Dutch appreciations of the Leicester episode, whether they included Sidney or not, and the brief English *interregnum* has kept its doubtful reputation ever since. Within a general break-down of Anglo-Dutch relations, cultural relationships, too, could have survived only

---

[1] See J. den Tex, *Johan van Oldenbarnevelt*, I, Haarlem, 1960, ch. 15.
[2] P. C. Hooft, *Nederlandsche historien*, ed. Amsterdam, 1677, pp. 1094-95. See Appendix II, no. 81.

under the most difficult circumstances: especially in Leiden,
where an incredibly naive and immediately frustrated attempt
at a pro-English *coup* in 1587 [1] hastened and decided Leicester's departure from the Low Countries. Throughout the
late 1580s and early nineties, Leiden, where the number
of English undergraduates was seen to drop considerably,
became positively unfriendly. Witness Fynes Moryson's
experiences when he first visited the University in 1592:

> At the faire City of Leyden not wanting many faire Innes, I was
> refused lodging in sixe of them, and hardly got it in the seventh,
> which made me gather they did not willingly entertaine
> Englishmen. [2]

On the other hand, the Republic of Letters had endured
greater trials than these, and some Anglo-Leiden friendships
had already proved capable of maintaining their personal
independence. Regardless of political strife a certain amount
of literary traffic continued. But the old spirit seems to have
vanished when the vision of an Anglo-Dutch alliance of the
kind prophesied by the poets failed to materialize. The 1586
enterprise had proved unfortunate: an Anglo-Leiden literary
activity as originally conceived had lost its purpose—and its
subject-matter.

From the day when Rogers wrote the first foreign epigram
'In Lugdunum novam Batavorum Academiam' to the unhappy hour when Benedicti sent his *Epitaphia in mortem
Sidneji* to the printer's, it would seem that there existed no
small measure of understanding between England and
Leiden. Beginning with incidental friendships, a complex
pattern of personal relationships emerged by 1586, which
resulted in large numbers of poetic and epistolary exercises.
It was natural, considering the humanistic outlook of the
participants, that the literary history of these years should
have begun and ended in a political and academic setting;
and equally natural that its principle milieus in England and
Holland should have produced two literary 'schools', where
themes of wit and beauty and virtue were expressed in the
sonnets, odes, and epigrams which (with a newly acquired

[1] See p. 92, note 2; and p. 127, note 1.
[2] Moryson, *Itinerary*, ed. Glasgow Univ. Press, IV, p. 61.

taste for vernacular composition) became the fashionable forms of literary expression. With them poesy served on the one hand the practical purpose of formulating an opinion, furthering a cause, and celebrating men and events, and on the other hand it gave requisite scope for self-expression. Considering this, these eleven years furnish a vivid illustration of a particular use of poetry. This use of the *bonae literae* was an essential feature of the ideal *Academia* of Leiden as conceived of by its founders; and Leiden must therefore have been particularly congenial to the English poet-scholars with their similar poetic aspirations.

Severed from their former diplomatic setting, Leiden's English interests were to become increasingly academic. It is true, some contacts remained; but no new pattern of exchange was to be established until the beginning of the next century,[1] and when it came it was different from former times. The optimism, energy, hero-worship, and inspired enthusiasm which belonged to that sixteenth-century generation of courtiers and scholars were to give way to a new set of values and a new mode of personalities.

It is therefore possible to regard the eleven years between the foundation of the first Dutch university and the death of Sir Philip Sidney as an identifiable 'period' of Anglo-Leiden relations, a period remarkable for its experiments towards a 'national' poetry in an international system of service to the state and literary performance. In the written remains of these crucial years the two countries have appeared united in letters, in the perhaps never again so intimate world of poets, patrons, and professors.

[1] For this new 'pattern', see Bachrach, *Huygens and Britain*.

APPENDICES

APPENDIX I

Forty Latin poems devoted to Sidney

(1) [1575/1576] Daniel Rogers, Hertford MS., f. 221.

AD PHILIPPUM SYDNÆUM ILLUSTRISSIMAE SPEI
ET INDOLI IUVENEM.

Ergo pererratis Latii regionibus orbis,
   Conspectis Galli gentibus inde soli,
Postque tibi visas Germanis tractibus urbes,
   Et peragrata vago regna Boema pede,
5 Restabat Inverna tibi lustranda Philippe?
   Illa sub occiduos terra reposta sinus?
Crediderim fatis tantos suadentibus aestus,
   Invernae extremas te subiisse plagas.
Non ut in his ageres deses regionibus hospes,
10   Partibus his veluti plurimus hospes agit,
Verum ut quæ regnis didicisses pluribus, isthic
   Exereres, populos erudiendo feros.
Sicque tuo dignum patre Philippe referres,
   Quem Inverna suum prædicat esse patrem:
15 Quis scit, an his terris servent te fata regendis!
   Proregem prorex ut comitere patrem?
Nam Sydnæa domus terræ fatalis Iernæ,
   Digna equidem regnis dicere iura domus.
Quare age, Invernæ iuvenis te assuesce regendæ,
20   Ut pro rege satus, natus ad imperium.

(2) [1577] Paulus Melissus Schedius, *Schediasmata poetica*,
Paris, 1586, I, p. 265.

AD PHILIPPUM SYDNÆUM ELIZABETHÆ REGINÆ
ANGLIÆ AD ROM. IMP. LEGATUM.

Sydnee Musarum inclite cultibus,
Prorex Hybernes cui pater insulæ,
   Rheno secundo navigabis   [p. 266]
   In patrias rediturus oras,

(1) 1 Latii]latii   5 lustranda Philippe? *from* Sydnæe videnda?   11 quae
regnis *from* quae te regnis   12 erudiendo feros *from* expoliendo
rudes   13 referres *from* probares   14 praedicat *from* iactat et
16 ut comitere *from* subssequare   20 ad imperium. *from* ut imperio
(2) 37 Optata:]Optata.

5   Vasti per amplos Oceani sinus.
       Regina vestræ clara Britanniæ
         Resciscere ardet, quid reversus
         Cæsarea referas ab aula
       Legatus. O si me comitem tuis
10   Nereus, & ipsæ Nereïdes viis
         Junctum viderent colloquendo
         Velivola freta longa pinu
       Sulcare: nigros non ego turbines,
       Nec belluarum monstra natantium,
15   Discordiamque Eurum protervis
         Cum Boreæve Notive pennis
       Vector timerem. nam pietas tua
       PHILIPPE salvos incolumesque nos
         Præstaret; & quæ vox tenere
20   Cæsaris ora, tenere linguam
       Serena quivit, hæc eadem maris
       Deos furentes, flabraque tristium
         Fratrum moraretur, sonori
         Turbida per pelagi ruentum.
25   Quamvis remotarum æquor ad Orcadum
       Vis Africi nos sæva propelleret;
         Impune salsos frangeremus
         Remigio superante fluctus,
       Tenta & liceret vela retro dare,
30   Portumque lætis passibus ingredi
         Desideratum. Sed relicta
         Nunc iter est mihi Myrtileto
       Admoliendum dura per Alpium
       Saxa, & tremenda fauce voragines.
35   Utrique nostrum Dij secundent   [p. 267]
         Quæ petimus loca, prosperentque
       Optata: Londinum in patrio sinu
       Te mox receptet, splendidus urbium
         Ocellus: at mi septicollis
40   Vaquerio duce Roma plaudat.

(3) [1577?] Daniel Rogers, Hertford MS., f. 216.
IN EFFIGIEM ILLUSTRISSIMI IUVENIS D. PHILIPPI SYDNÆI.

    Fare age (sic longum molli lanugine cingat
      Illas tuas habitans Dia iuventa genas)
    Quis tibi, quis unus vultum (Sydnæe) venenis
      Pinxit, et hoc roseum sparsit in ora decus?

(3) 10 erat *from* is est   18 mihi, *from* quidem,

5 Quis frontem gestu, radiis animavit ocellos?
Inditus est labris cuius ab arte lepos?
Num rediit superas infernis Zeuxis ad oras?
Ecquid Apellæis ducte nites digitis?
Vana isthæc. nam te quisquis similavit ab arte,
10 Maior erat Zeuxi, maior Apollo fuit.
Vivit enim, enimque hac vivis, Sydnæe, figura,
Quis putet, humanas hanc potuisse manus?
Spectantem argutis sic me respectat ocellis
Aemula naturæ prorsus imago tuæ.
15 Cur tamen heu tacito muta est mage pisce, nec hilum
Eloquitur? mores est imitata tuos.
Nam tu Pythagoræ laudata silentia sectans,
Multa audire mihi, pauca videre loqui.
Caetera conveniunt: hoc sed discrimen in uno est,
20 Quod tu pauca loquens, semper imago tacet.

(4) Ghent, 14 January 1579. Daniel Rogers, Hertford MS.,
f. 42ᵛ.

ELEGIA XIIIa. AD PHILIPPUM SIDNÆUM ILLUSTRISSIMÆ
INDOLIS AC VIRTUTIS IUVENEM.

Te tenet Attalicis Ricemondia compta tapetis,
Septimij Henrici nobile regis opus.
Quam variæ exornant turritæ ex ordine pinnæ,
Quam Thamesis refluæ gurgite radit aquæ.
5 Qua convexa micant auro laquearia sparso,
Undique qua dives atria cultus habet.
Qua modo dum princeps aulam (Sydnaee) celebrat,
Ac natalitiis festa diebus agit:
Æthereæ ducis, (quod laetor), gaudia vitae,

(4) 16 Consulit: *from* Prospicit: 33 At *from* Aut 40 O post . . .deam.
from O post Reginae forma secunda decus *from* Aulæ delicium,
principis atque piae. 42 nobile *from* clara laris. *from* Divis. 44
una *from* ipsa 55 Non tibi corpus enim *from* Non tu corpus habes
60 verba tenore *from* rectius ore 88 apum.]apum 91 suis
from Deæ 104 subire *from* videre 109 adijsti *from* cupijsti stat
112 fultum *from* imbutum 114 rector *from* iudex 120 (Regia
Eliza)](Regia (Eliza) 122 legit acuta viris, *from* legerit ingenijs:
135 Belgas *from* bellum adiret *from* iniret 137 annis]annis,
162 Ambo . . . suæ. *from* Reginæ et patrij fulgida fulcra soli 166
possit abesse *from* absit amice 168 Nil *from* Queis his *from*
haud viris. *from* decus. 174 chara propago *from* pulchra acolumna
189 Musis *from* Parcæ 190 neges *from* potes
Lines 24–25 were later additions.

10   Coelestes cernens, ire, redire, choros.
  Prima vides comitem Divae se ut iungat Elizae
      Relligio, dextrum stipet et alma latus.
  Assidet ad lævam, parili quæ singula lance   [f. 43]
      Dispensat, patrij custos amica soli.
15 Ante stat, et rebus Prudentia vite gerendis
      Consulit: affectus temperat altra vagos.
  Pone sequens, fortis munit Constantia mentem,
      Tendit et invictis laurea serta comis.
  Tum Charites, cernis mixtas certare Camoenis,
20   Ore, manu, buxo, dulce canente melos.
  In medio resident, Divas complexa beatas,
      Nectare et illarum pascit (Eliza) iecur.
  Hic operæ pretium est cantus audire Dearum,
      Attentaque sacros imbibere aure modos.
25 Quid loquar insignes Heroidas ordine stantes,
      Accinctas iussis (Regia Nympha) tuis.
  Quas inter, mater radiat (Sydnææ) sororque,
      Utraque Reginæ maxima cura suæ.
  Queis comes est raro Sussexia culta lepore,
30   Altera pene tibi proximitate parens.
  Nunc etiam iuncta est his Huntinghtonia Nymphis,
      Fida soror matris, mater et altra tibi.
  At quali antistat cunctis Russellia vultu,
      Ingenio, facie, moribus, aequa Deis.
35 Ut sileam reliquas, quae consuetudinis usu
      Sanguinis aut vinclo sunt propiore tuae.
  Innumera quarum ut forsant dote superbum,
      Deterat extimeo nostra Thalia decus.
  Nam quis te merita, Knollesia laude celebret? [f. 43ᵛ]
40   O post sceptriferam forma secunda deam.
  Quisne canat levibus te rite Hovardia Musis,
      Nordovolcæi nobile stemma laris.
  Nemo tuas dotes (Staffordia) dixerit apte,
      Sic Charitum et formæ dotibus una viges —
45 Viveret, has caneret victuro carmine Naso,
      Peligni Naso laurea prima soli.
  Nec tantis formis, Nemesim præferret amicam,
      Albius, Ausoniae nobilitatis eques.
  Nec tibi, vidisses tales si culte Properti,
50   Cinthia perpetuum sola fuisset opus.
  Quas mea sæpe quidem tentavit dicere Musa,
      Sed tenuis nostro manat ab ore sonus.
  Iudice me dignæ, Phoebi celebrentur ut ore,
      Seu (Sydnææ) tuo, sive (Diere) tuo.
55 Non tibi corpus enim sine pectore, nec tibi tantum
      Illustri nasci nobilitate datum est.
  Afflavit mentem, raro tibi Juppiter oestro,
      Erudijt linguam Suada diserta tuam.

Ut seu Romano cuperes sermone profari,
60   Seu malles Gallo verba tenore loqui,
Seu magis Hetrusca depromere sensa loquela,
    Te nullus posset cultius aut melius.
At quando ad nostras sese rapit impetus artes,   [f. 44]
    Ingenii currunt flumina quanta tui?
65 Quis putes? Hæc olim, nato te, Parca canebat,
    Dum neret vitæ stamina prima tuae.
Sit mihi fas brevibus perstringere, quæ fuit olim,
    Ausa loqui cunis Parcias una tuis.
Te fore, praedixit proavis qui illustribus ortus,
70   Anteires genii nobilitate genus.
Quaeque suo excoleret quem munere Diva, foretque
    Virtuti, Musis, qui superisque sacer.
Nascetur varias (inquit) qui tendet in oras
    Qui mores hominum discat et ingenia.
75 Qui pacis bellique potens simul artibus, olim
    Arbitrio regeret numen utrumque suo.
Quo duce, Relligio ritus induta pudicos,
    In templis puro pangeret ore Deum!
Jura patrocinio cuius Themis asseret æqua:
80   Qui Reginarum cura Ducumque foret.
Quem Virtus, Fortuna simul, per foedera iunctæ,
    Eveherent summo constituentque loco.
Dixit: et eventus habitura hæc verba professa,
    Libavit labris basia pura tuis.
85 Evenere rata hæc, nec vana est parca loquuta:
    Sunt sortita suam singula verba fidem.
Vix natum, cunis rapuit glomerata caterva,   [f. 44ᵛ]
    Inque tuis labris mellificavit apum.
Mox Musæ manibus te formavere disertæ:
90   Quæ linguam et mores excoluere tuos.
Certatimque suis te ornarunt dotibus unum,
    Quælibet in cunas officiosa tuas.
Alma Venus formam, Charites tribuere leporem,
    Excoluit sensus, Pallas, et Eloquium.
95 Unde tot insignes, diti sub pectore dotes,
    Ad quas mirantes obstupuere senes.
Inde peregrinas Genius te duxit in oras,
    Et docuit Gallis quæ capienda plagis:
Hic quoque tum fueras, proprium quum Gallia patrem
100   Collinium, infaustæ dedidit atra neci.
Urbs quando in puppos, pueras, matresque senesque
    Sæviret, partus Parrhisiana suos.
At te, subductum tantis (Sydnæe) periclis,
    Teutona iusserunt regna subire Dei.
105 Qua sacer audisti quas Sturmius explicat artes
    Sturmius Aonij Duxque paterque gregis.
Queis satur, Ausonios cupijsti visere tractus,

Discere et hic quicquid regna latina docent.
Qum quoque Pannonias adijsti fervidus oras,
110   Lustrastique oculis regna Boema vagis.
Queis tibi Languetum iunxti regionibus: illum,   [f. 45]
Humani fultum cognitione fori.
Ille per historias regnorum duxit et ortus,
Iudicium rector finxit et ille tuum.
115   Credo etiam Antipodos subijsset cura videndi,
In patriam Princeps ni revocasset humum.
Singula quæ prima lanugine visa, beato
Subtiles sensus asseruere tibi:
Acceptumque magis fecere potentibus aulis,
120   Ac gratum placitis (Regia Eliza) tuis.
Quid loquar, ut viridis princeps te in flore iuventæ,
Ex multis unum legit acuta viris,
Legaret magni quem ad Cæsaris ora disertum,
Cuique arcana animi crederet ima sui.
125   Nec minus ipsa tuas stupuit Germania dotes,
Quam mirata bono patria iure fuit.
Non mage te poterit Lecestrius ipsus amare,
Ille Palatinus quam Casimirus amet.
Qui pia florentes ducturus in arma phalanges
130   Te sortis comitem quæsijt esse suæ.
Nam tibi non pigro torpet sub pectore sanguis,
Ad belli, ad pacis munia dexter ades.
Scimus ubi classem Regina armaret in hostem,   [f. 45ᵛ]
Queis animis, una miles iturus eras.
135   Scimus et ut Belgas Princeps Casimirus adiret,
Quo sumptu accinctum fervor in arma tulit —
Nempe tibi teneris animus constantior annis
Surgit, et est pulchro qui fluit ore lepos —
Quid dicam, ut reduci Romani Cæsaris aula,
140   Init in amplexum Regia tota tuos.
Quæ tibi pene domus facta est modo patria, dum te
Regina assiduum mandat adesse sibi —
Sive igitur dubio stringit viridaria gressu,
Contigna aula sibi quæ Ricemonda videt,
145   Sive per apricos spatiatur leviter hortos
Principis ad nutus fidus et aptus ades.
Si iuvat in lætos excurrere celitem campos,
Conscenso Dominam mox comitaris equo.
Quod si legatus peregrinis venit ab oris,
150   Commendat curæ protinus huncce tuæ.
Denique quicquid agis, Dominæ sis præsto necesse est,
Seria seu tractet, ludere sive iuvet.
Fortunate nimis, qui dum famularis Elizæ,
Mixtus Sydereis usque deabus ades.
155   Quid? quod sæpe hilari tecum sermone fritinnit
Ac spargit faciles Regia Nympha sales.

In tua cum monstrat proclivi vota favore,   [f. 46]
   Obsequijs quantum sit capienda tuis.
Adde, quod hic geminus tibi sternit avunculus instans
160   Ad summi verum culmen honoris iter:
Warvicius Martis, Jovis at Lecestrius ardor,
   Ambo patres patriæ, fulcraque certa suæ.
Qui duo præradiant, ceu Sydera bina, nepoti,
   Lucentes puppi seu Cynosura tuæ.
165 Quin et adest genitor Invernæ rector ab orbe,
   Ne quicquam votis possit abesse tuis.
At quales quantique viri bellove togave?
   Nil tribus his maius conspicit aula viris.
Nec desunt fidi, iucunda caterva sodales,
170   Queis pius adstricta compede sudat amor.
Ex quibus antistat dia virtute Dierus
   Iudicii condus, promus, et ingenij.
Dein prætextatis Fulco tibi notus ab annis,
   Fulco Grevillææ chara propago domus.
175 Cum quibus aut summo de iure, Deove, bonove
   Disseris, his studijs dum vacas hora pijs.
Ornamenta omnes aulæ vos propter ocellos,
   Regia (scit Nemesis) gratior aula mihi est.
Quos inter si te nobis permittis amari,
180   Est satis: hæc voti summa suprema mei.
Sed quo vester amor tenero me carmine raptat? [f. 46ᵛ]
   Musa sile: herois hæc recinenda modis.
Scilicet in Morinis dum regia iussa capesso,
   Languetoque tuo iungor, itemque meo.
185 Sermones de te serimus Sydnæe frequentes,
   Quos tibi, quos de te scribere iussit amor.
Fallor? an et sentis spatijs divisus id ipsum,
   Dexteroque hinc auris tinnijt icto tibi.
At facio finem, commendo et cætera Musis
190   Ne me posse neges gaudia ferre mea.

               Gandavi. 14. Januarij 1579.

(5) [1585?] Janus Dousa, *Odarum Britannicarum liber*, Leiden,
1586, p. 21.

DOUSIANI VOTI SOLUTIO. AD ILLUSTREM VIRUM DN.
PHILIPPUM SIDNEIUM HENRICI PRO-REGIS HIBERNIÆ F.
CUM EIDEM PETRONIUM ARBITRUM MUNERI MITTERET.

   ARBITRUM en tandem tibi. Nam quis iste
   ARBITER? dices. Tuus, O PHILIPPE:
   Quippe desertor domini prioris
      Perfugium ad te

5 Certus EX VOTO facere; hercle vero
Serio, at sero. fateor: neque ire
Quippiam hinc possum inficias, prehensus
     Crimine in ipso.
Caussa sed cuius tamen haud videtur
10 Aspra defensu: quia nec tui unquam
Immemor, pactæ aut fidei, meave
     Parcus opella:
Sed quod EXEMPLORUM ope destitutus
Illa ab extremi petere usque RHENI
15 Faucibus; cognati, habui necesse,
     Trans vada ponti.
Cui malo accessit remeligo & illa
Insuper, quod, vento operam negante,   [p. 22]
Littore a nostro dare vela nantes
20   Aura vetavit.
Proinde (QUOD FELIX tibi, mique, & ipsi
ARBITRO) ACCEPTUM FACE REDDITUMque
Quicquid id VOTI est: neque DOUSIANOS
     Despice lusus.
25 Hoc sat: AUCTOREM nec enim indigere
Voce præconis reor; haud imagis, quam
CAECUBUM appensis hederis, quod annus
     Coxit OPIMII.
Iamque quid restat, nisi ut ARBITRI ipse
30 ARBITER fias? neque me EDITOREM   i. inspector
Dedecet MUNUS, neque te instituti ab   antique.
     CONSULE LUDI.

(6) [1585?] Paulus Melissus, *Schediasmata*, 1586, p. 161.
AD PHILIPPUM ET ROBERTUM SYDNEIOS,
          VIROS ILLUSTRES.

          PHILIPPE Musarum nitor
               Phoebique, & orti Pleiade;
          Honos ROBERTE Palladis,
               Flos Gratiarum germinans;
5   Anglicæ decora aulæ:
          Ambo Deabus omnibus
               Cari Deisque singulis;
          Ambo Dionæ suavibus
               Digni reperti basiis,
10   Amplexuque Dianæ:
          Lenem favoris halitum
               Meis Camenis obsecro,
          Vestræque mollem gratiæ
               Adflate mi Favonium,

15   Dignus sim modo, & illæ.
        Natæ verecundo genas
            Pudore suffusæ, timent
            Vulgi sub ora publica
            Prodire nondum puberes,
20   Necdum amoribus aptæ.
        Pater veretur, ut satis
            Cultæ politulæve sint.
            At purpurisso, polline,
            Fuco, œsipove succido,
25   Aut Archæide creta,
        Unctæve cerussæ litis   [p. 162]
            Adulterari pharmacis
            Vultus puellares negant,
            Pigmenta cuncta respuunt,
30   Adscitosque colores.
        Ac proinde nativæ magis
            Amabitis formæ decus;
            Magis figuras has sine
            Colore comprobabitis,
35   Sincerasque probasque.
        Natura naturæ æmula
            Quæque est suæ. Si filiæ
            Sui Minervam simplicem
            Parentis exprimant, sat est;
40   Sat est, si nihil adsit.

(7) [1585/1586] Janus Dousa the Younger, *Britannicorum
carminum silva* (in Janus Dousa, *Odarum Britannicarum
liber*), Leiden, 1586, p. 54.

ILLUSTRISSIMO PRINCIPI PHILIPPO SIDNÆIO, HENRICI
HIBERNIÆ PROREGIS FILIO, GUBERNATORI VALACHRIÆ.

O Sidnaeie, suas Pallas cui tradidit artes,
Eloquiumque Hermes, animos Mars, Carminis artem
Cynthius, & privam largita est Suada medullam,
Plutus opes, formam Cypris, Charitesque leporem,
5 Unde tuas laudes exordiar, ingeniumne
Præclarum, & Graiæ Latiæque peritia linguæ
Carmine maiori laudabitur, an speciosas
Corporis eximij dotes, generisne vetusti
Stemmata, maiorumque extollam facta tuorum,
10 Virtutis quod fama tuæ longe anteit omnes:
An referam quas tu gentes, quæque oppida & urbes
Lustraris, magnis missus de rebus ad ipsum
INDUPERATOREM Legatus ab ELISABETHA   [p. 55]
Utque Antenorea sis mox receptus in Urbe.

13

15 Vestra autem virtus præcone haud indiget ullo
Clara satis per se, nec ego SIDNAEÏE tantas
Tantillæ possum laudes intexere chartæ,
Quæ nec comprendi maiore volumine possint,
Non si aliam novus Iliadem contexat Homerus,
20 Umbraque ab Elysiis redeat rediviva Maronis,
Teque hic ÆNEÆ præponat, & alter ULYSSI,
Atque Seni PYLIO, qui sæcula terna peregit,
Consilio, rerumque usu, eloquioque suavi,
Doctrina, generisque vetusti nobilitate.
25 His etenim cunctis & ULYSSEM & NESTORA vincis,
Ætate atque annis tantum superaris, at ipse
Omnibus in rebus superabis utrosque, si eorum
Virtutem ut superas, sic & superaveris annos.

(8) [1585/1586] Dominicus Baudius, *Carmina*, Leiden, 1587,
p. 28.

AD ILLUSTRISSIMUM HEROëM PHILIPPUM SIDNEIUM.

Non quod vetusta nobilis ab domo
Fulges, & amplis mactus adoreis
  Princeps Iuventutis Britannæ,
    Te veneror, generose Sidnei.
5 Haud ima laus est illa quidem, bonis
Prognasci, & inter splendida nomina
  Parere celsius prophani
    Ingenijs, geniisque vulgi.
Verum ista laudis quantula pars tuæ est
10 Præut ter alti pectoris abditas
  Dotes, & illibata dicam
    Eloquij, Sophiæque dona?
Mentem cupido suscitat arduus
Laudum supremis tollere te modis
15   In astra victorem procacis   [p. 29]
    Invidiæ, dominique fati.
Sed spes avaras, cœptaque turgida
Sors Dædalei territat Icari,
  Vetatque ne maiora coner
20   Viribus ingenijque captu.
Quod si mea olim candidior dies
Optata lætos ducet ad exitus,
  Si me unquam amica sors honestis
    Inseret ordinibus tuorum.
25 Favore mente, erectus eimodi,
Ter maxime Heros, differar in tuas
  Laudes, & ingentem Lecestrum
    Non humili referam cothurno.
Vos concinam, o par nobile Principum,

30   Afflicta quod iam Belgica vindices
            Suspirat, optatamque tali
                Sperat ab auspicio salutem.
        Sperat, spei nec decipitur suæ,
        Si quid piorum sollicitæ preces
35   Possunt, & utcunque antecedens
                Culpa trahit Nemesin sequacem.
        Nil Anglicæ non efficient manus
        Quas & faventis magna Dei manus
            Defensat, & virilis ardor
                Omnibus expediet periclis.

(9) [1585/1586] Georgius Benedicti, *De Rebus gestis Illustriss.*
Principis Guilielmi, Comitis Nassovij, &c. *Lib. II.*, Leiden,
1586, p. 47.

ILLUSTRO VIRO D PHILIPPO SIDNEO.

    Si tibi Sidneæ non essent nomina gentis,
        Doctrina posses nobilis esse tua.
    Nunc inter sese certant doctrina, genusque,
        Hoc plus adjiciat laudis, an illa, tibi.
5 Tu virtute tua dirimis, quia (judice fama)
        Majus utrique addis, quam tibi utrumque decus.

(10) [1585/1586] Georgius Benedicti, *De Rebus gestis,* p. 54.

ILLUSTRI VIRO D. PHILIPPO SIDNEO.

    Ingenium, doctrina, genus, prudentia, virtus,
        Hæc data sunt paucis singula, cuncta tibi.

(11) [January 1586] Dominicus Baudius, *Carmina,* p. 66.

AD ILLUSTRISSIMUM DOMINUM MEUM

PHILIPPUM SIDNEIUM.

    Ecce iterum Iani auspicijs redit annus in orbem
    Solemnes relegens sua vestigia cursus.
    Quæ tibi quæ prisco dabimus munuscula ritu
    Magne heros, triplici quem nobilitate potentem
5 Condecorat Virtutis honos & avita propago   [p. 67]
    Ingeniumque bonas excultum rite per artes?
    Cuncta tibi superant, quibus aut Natura beare
    Mortales aut Cura solet: quid dotibus istis
    Adijciam, talique viro quæ dona rependam?
10 Sanguis hebet, torpetque gravi ceu tacta veterno
    Mens animi, nullæque meo stant pectore vires.
        Officium-ne igitur cessabit, inersque voluntas
    Proferet haud ullum grati testamen amoris?
    Non ita, namque etsi cunctarum munera rerum

15 In te contulerit manibus bona copia plenis;
　 Attamen illa tuas illustrat adorea laudes
　 Quod Phœbum colis, & Phœbi socia agmina Musas,
　 Musas qui cibus est suavissimus ingeniorum.
　 Hac spe nostra tuos accedere Musa penates
20 Sustinet, ingenuo quanquam suffusa rubore
　 Virgineam faciem, dum se considerat ipsa,
　 Virtutesque tuas merito veneratur honore.
　 Sed quantum absterret pudor & reverentia, tantum
　 Invitat tua me bonitas, & certa faventis
25 Signa animi, tumidosque exosa modestia fastus.
　 Sume igitur placido vultu clarissime Sidnej
　 Quæ tibi donamus prisco munuscula ritu,
　 Parva quidem, pretio si rem metiris & usu,
　 Maxima, si immensum spectas donantis amorem.
30 Est animus mihi magna volens, magna omnia volvens,
　 Liber ab ingenio quantumlibet usque paratus   [p. 68]
　 Imperijs servire tuis, mentemque regendam
　 Virtutis normæ, & rigido permittere honesto.
　 Quod tua si nostris subscribet gratia votis,
35 Si tenuem bone Mæcenas dignaris alumnum
　 Tollere humo, vitæque procul subducere inerti,
　 Gratus ut indultas divino a numine dotes
　 Protrahere in medium, patriæque impendere possim:
　 Non ego tunc versu, nec munere fungar inani
40 Pro tali merito (quamvis quoque ludere versu
　 Fas sit & austeram Musis condire Minervam)
　 Sed res historijs accingar dicere gestas,
　 Dudlaeumque heroa canam, teque optime Sidnej
　 Dudlæo comitem, & consanguinitate propinquum
45 Lætus in astra feram fusos memorare iuvabit
　 Te duce Bætigenas, longique incendia belli
　 Sopita, atque urbes Parmensie ex hoste receptas.
　 Sic eat, o longum vivat Regina, regatque
　 Belgasque Albionasque pari moderamine utrosque,
50 Concordes pietate, animis, ac fœdere gentes.

(12) 12 December 1586. Hieronymus Groslotius, B.M. MS.
Burney 370, f. 8.

TUMULUS V. C. M. PHILIPPI SYDNÆI EQUITIS
ILLUSTRISSIMI, AC DOCTRINA ET VIRTUTE
INCOMPARABILIS.

Ecce arto terrae in tumulo, exiquique sepulchri
Visceribus, sanctae exuviae Sydnaei immensi;
Olim Divi animi domus inculpata: sed illum
Coelum habet, et gaudet tanto hospite. Gaudet et orbis

5 Vivente effigie in nata, et praegnatis amatae
Coniugis in casto gremio. Viget alite Fama
Quod Marte et Musis nomen sibi condidit: illud
Namque olli nequijt rapere aut Mars invidus, aut Mors
Tam iuveni. Victus Fatis visit quoque Fatum.
10 Sic vixit vivitque Deum genus, et mixtus Dijs!

(13) 12 December 1586. Hieronymus Groslotius, ibid.
EPITAPHIUM EIUSDEM.

Siste, heus Viator, et parumper hic adsta.
Te Divus orat Genius hospitis Divi,
Ut has bibente lumine haurias voces.

Sydnaeus ille vixi. et, anne vis plura?
5 Posuisse sat sit nomen. haut capit nomen
Immensus orbis: mente tu intima capta,
Memorique conde. mente cepi ego totum
Domuique mundum vivida ingenii luce,
Ovans superbus orbe disciplinarum,
10 Quae nobiles tam nobilem virum illustrant.
Nulli secundus artibus Camoenarum;   [f. 8ᵛ]
Testis Brittana Musa, Tusca, Romana,
Galla, et Pelasga: tantae imaginem tantam
Laurus inumbrant, tot mihi faces vitae;
15 Quae propter illas, o vigebit aeternum!
In castra Musas sum sequtus, et Martem;
Nulli secundus Marte; consilii felix,
Manuque promtus; Imperator eccelens,
Nimiumque miles strenuus. sed invidit
20 Mavors meae virtutis inclytum fulmen,
Tremuitque dextram, quam nec aggredi e . . . us
Aut cominus palamve; sed dolo incau . . .
Morti dedit malignus eminus vibr . . .
Ignitum, aheneum in meam necem telum.
25 Sic me enecat Mors, Marsque. Mars reus Mortis
Tantae, tam acerbae, mi paravit et Vitam
Superstitem post fata mortuae Vitae,
Onerans me opimis saepius favens praedis,
Adoreisque, et laureis sacris frontem;
30 Quae mi virebunt, dum vigebit et Fama
Contermina orbi, saeculis coaequalis.
Ab aemulo sic Marte mi decus Vitae,
Tum Mortis umbra, quae mihi dedit sanctio
Sanctae videre lumen et frui Vitae.

(13) 9 orbe disciplinarum *from* artibus Camoenarum   12–13 *originally after* 9   21–23 *margin damaged.*
The poem is signed: Hier. Groslotius Lislaeus Flens Moerens Posui.

35 Namque ille ocellus, ille amor, voluptasque,
Sydusque mundi nuper; en poli nunc sum
Amor, voluptas, flosculusque, ocellusque,
Sydusque princeps, et reluceo in summi
Sinu Iovis; cui Morte redditus iam sum.
40 Mea inde terra est rite reddita huic terrae
Pietas ubique te, Viator, offendat   [f. 9]
Aeque pium, quam erga pios meos Manes,
Qui gratias tibi ob piam moram reddunt.
Nunc, si voles, abi, et Valeto. nam Dixi.

(14) [1586/1587] Dominicus Baudius, *Carmina*, 1587, p. 70.
AD NOBILISSIMUM EQUITEM ROBERTUM SIDNEIUM.

O Sidneianæ columen unicum domus,
Lumenque, postquam lumen illud desijt
Lucere terris, patrioque nunc polo
Refulget inter astra sydus aureum,
5 Philippus ille frater, heu! quondam tuus,
Flos Anglicanæ gentis, immo totius
Flos orbis, audiente dicam Fascino.
Quid o super nunc relliquum est misero mihi
Præter perenne flere, solamen gravis
10 Inane luctus? huc perennes lacrymæ,
Huc eiulatus, næniæque lugubres,
Ut evaporem qui meis inæstuat
Dolor medullis, o mihi sanctum caput
Philippe, magni nomen instar numinis,
15 Quot corde curas obseris moriens meo.
Tecum meæ spes atque opes sitæ iacent,
Tecum iocus lepos & omnis occidit,
Tum si quid olim e parte læva pectoris
Musis amicum exsculpsit improbus labor,
20 Vel efficaci amore laudis incitus
Profudit ardor, omnium harum nunc mihi   [p. 71]
Finis voluptatum atque vastitas venit.
Vix jam pedestrem languidus Musam traho,
Vix tertiatis hiscere audeo sonis,

(14) Major variants in Baudius, *Poemata*, 1640:
22 Finis . . . venit]Distractioque vastitasque rerum ades   26 fert
. . . loquor:]reapse sentio, loquor,   36 fovet]beat   52 adquirit
ve proprius]aut industrius parit   53 Hoc]Id   publicæ]
temporum   62 Trahenda]Ducenda   63-66 corda . . . mihi]
præsidi orbum, consili omnis impotem / In hoc juventæ flore, cum
spes arduas / Mens inchoabat, morte destituis tua. / Actum est,
nisi in te specula restat locus,   78 civem polo]coelo decus

25 Vix ulla signa in me ipse conspicor mei.
  Parum præut fert veritas rei loquor:
  Tecum ipsa cessit vita ab isto pectore,
  Nam viva mors & vita mortua est mihi,
  Te Sidnei adempto, mortuus me interficis.

30 Nec restat alio hic fine spiritus, nisi ut
  Fato superstes usque suppetam meo,
  Lentisque me perire sentiam modis
  Hei si tyrannos, helluones funerum,
  Portenta terræ, generis humani luem.

35 Sacerrimasque hirudinum propagines
  Tam longa vitæ pausa fælicis fovet:
  Cur o severa, o sæva Parca sic manu
  Tagace carpis, & diurnare invides
  Ut quidque vita est dignius diu frui?

40 Sed fallor atque more vulgi rem puto,
  Rerum æstimator improbus cælestium,
  Rerumque curvus morio terrestrium,
  Verboque ut uno cuncta comprehendam, homo.
  Non tu querelis, mollibusque lacrymis

45 Urgendus heros, mortui fleant suos
  Virtute cassos, ipsa te cœlo beans
  Vetat mori mors & nova vita induit   [p. 72]
  Mortalitatis exsolutum nexibus.
  Humana quod si nos iuvant solatia,

50 Vixti beatus, omnium rerum satur
  Quas aut benignæ sortis indulgentia
  Largitur, adquirit ve proprius labos.
  Hoc deerat unum faustitati publicæ,
  Mundique votis, interesse uti diu

55 Posses caduco cœtui mortalium
  Sed nec suo carere deposito amplius
  Iam sustinebat cœlitum fulgens domus,
  Nec terra tanti muneris capax erat.
  Ergo oppetisti morte præclara cadens.

60 Fælix ter o quaterque: nos miseri quibus
  Tui carendo morte quavis tristior
  Trahenda vita est: ast ego in primis miser
  Quem corda luctu sauciatum, & omnium
  Rerum indigentem morte destituis tua:

65 Nisi si quid usquam speculæ monstras mihi
  Roberte Sidnej, quæ salutem spondeat.
  Quo obsecro te perque stemmatis decus
  Sublime vestri, perque fratris inclytum
  Nomen quod omnes implet uno se plagas,

70 Si ego illum honore prosequutus sum meo,
  Si me ille amore censuit dignum suo,
  Ne quæso ne me compotem tantis malis
  Tuo insuper favore frustrari sinas.   [p. 73]

Sic te usque amica Numinis benignitas
75   Conservet orbi sospitem & superstitem,
Tandemque fratri fata te tuo, tibi
Fratrem redonent, & novum civem polo.

(15) [1586/1587] Dominicus Baudius, ibid., p. 98.
IN OBITUM FORTISSIMI HEROIS PHILIPPI SIDNEII.

Viderat hostili grassantem cæde Philippum
Marspiter, & clari fortia facta ducis.
Tum livore malo stimulisque agitatus amaris:
Bella mihi Pallas, bella minatur, ait.
5   Agnosco horrificos turbatæ virginis artus,
Agnosco armisonæ vimque manumque Deæ.
Non alius tali se turbine mittit in hostem
Præcipitesque virum demetit ense globos.
Qua ruit, una salus fugisse, fugacibus instat
10   Segnior, adversos sternere solus amor.
Quid moror? an-ne novo violet dum vulnere Martem?
Simque trimphalis gloria victus ego?
Non ita, surge animo, & vindictam perfice dulcem
Qua datur, ac meritas exigat ira vices.
15   Dixit, & in Iuvenem, quo sol nil clarius usquam
Adspicit (heu pietas! heu veneranda fides!)
Dirigit ille manum trepidam latitantis Iberi,   [p. 99]
Quo nunc ille iacet vulnere flos hominum.
Impie Mars tantum potuisti extinguere lumen,
20   Nec tibi tunc animi, nec cecidere manus?
Hei mihi quo lustro poterit scelus hocce piari?
Quis reparet deinceps talia damna dies?
Quantam spem patriæ mors aspera circumvenit?
Quale tibi periit Belgica præsidium!
25   Parva tamen magni superant solatia luctus,
Parva quidem, forti sed tamen apta viro.
Victor enim vera Sidnei virtute triumphas,
Indice morte ipsa, indice Marte fero.

(16) [1586/1587?] Dominicus Baudius, *Poematum nova editio*,
Leiden, 1607, p. 603.
PHILIPPI SYDNEI,
M D LXXXVI

hIC IaCet eXtInCtVs CrVdeLI gLande phILIppVs
sydnæVs, noMen nosse sat esse potest.

(15) Major   variants   in   Baudius,   *Poemata*,   1640:   10 solus]fervet
28 Indice . . . fero]Vincere quem timuit Mars nisi fraude mala

(17) [1586/1587?] Janus Dousa the Younger, *Rerum cælestium liber*, Leiden, 1591, p. 54.

D.M. ILLUSTR. HEROIS PHILIPPI SIDNÆI.

Qualiter Arcadio Typhin dum pendet ab astro
    Obruit insano vasta procella mari;
Turbine sic rapido nobis SIDNÆUS ademptus,
    Anchora quassatæ qui fuerat tabulæ:
5 Quæ nunc, ex geminis amisso ut pignore mater;
    Altero uti, infelix, lumine captus, agit.
Pro dolor, occubuit nostrum spes unica, Iberum
    Terror, natalis gloria prima soli
SIDNÆIUS, cuius, iam nomen & inclyta virtus
10   Cognita & Eois, cognita & Hesperiis:
Et famæ vix tota capax Natura fuisset,
    Si Lachesis fusos currere passa suos;
Sed miser ante diem florentibus excidit annis,
    Percussus volucri crus iuvenile pila,
15 Fulminea sævos dextra dum mactat Iberos,
    Ex utraque sibi Pallade serta parans.
Rectorem amissum flet Belga, Britannia alumnum;
    Et necis est tantæ iustus utrique dolor:
Haud aliter tracto confusa est Hectore Troia,
20   Hellas & exstincto flevit in Æacide.
Scilicet haud dispar pomis est vita caducis,
    Certa cui nullo tempore finis adest;
Hæc matura cadunt, vi tempestatis: at illa
    Deiecta, aut lapidum grandine, acerba ruunt.
25 O SIDNEI, dum nostra salus tibi propugnata est,
    Quam fuit heu ipsi non tua cara salus!
Primus & adversos audax dum tendis in hostes, [p. 55]
    Primam etiam de te gloriam adeptus Iber.
Troada sic primus, fato signatus iniquo,
30   Sanguine fœdavit Protesilaus humum.
Quid te nunc iuvit pietas, sancteque peractum
    Omne ævum, & patrij nobilitas generis?
Artibus instructus fueras utriusque Minervæ,
    Quæque dedit vitam, quæque dedit tumulum:
35 Nec Venetis obscura fuit sic inclyta virtus,
    Nec latuit mentem, NYMPHA BRITANNA, tuam;
INDUPERATOREM missus Legatus ad ipsum,
    Vixdum etiam quartam ingressus Olympiadem.
Ingenio major dubium, an prudentior esses:
40   Inculpata tibi vita fidesque fuit.
Atque utinam ætati, quam candidus ipse fuisti,
    Dii concessissent candida fila tuæ!

(17) 124 haud]baud

Quid memorem formam? quid opes? quid cætera?
   Vicisti ingenii nobilitate, genus?   [quid quod
45 Omnia quæ poterant, Lachesis, te flectere, staret
   Ni solido fultum cor adamante tibi.
Vana queror demens. Lachesis nihil infera peccat.
   Præscripta evolvens a Iove fata sibi.
Te penes est tantæ crimen, Mars improbe, cædis;
50   Hanc tuus iste rigor sustinet invidiam:
Tu juvenem tentantem acris certamina belli
   Fulminea furam traiicis ipse pila:
Vicenis octo vix annumeraverat annos,
   Prima suæ referens tempora militiæ.
55 Dic mihi, qua culpa tantum tua numina læsit,
   Exstingui sola posset ut ira nece?
Scilicet hic prenso tibi vincula cæca paravit?
   Hic geminos mergi iussit in amne tuos?
Scilicet hæc iterum propter te, Cypride læsa,   [p. 56]
60   Dextera divino est sanguine facta nocens?
Scilicet, usque tuis fumum pariturus ocellis,
   A Venere obductus æmulus iste tibi est?
Atqui non ullo Divos hic læserat unquam
   Crimine, ni crimen belligerare vocas,
65 Quid tamen hæc prosunt? etiam hunc cita fata tulerunt,
   Ah semper nostris invida fata bonis.
Exspectant reducem affines, socrusque sororque
   Et præsumta animo gaudia vana fovent.
Fida sed huc conjunx, fluctus emensa Britannos,
70   Ferre viri nequiens flebile dissidium,
Venit, & optatum præsens complexa maritum;
   Lætitia heu miseræ quam brevis illa fuit?
Nam sua vix iterum repararat cornua Phœbe;
   Confusa est subito tota domus gemitu;
75 Vulnere cum, Sidneie, gravi percusse iaceres,
   Et tecum regio saucia tota fuit.
Singula captabant medici momenta cubantis,
   Prætermissa tuis cura nec ulla tui:
Sed fata immoto cum stant adamante notata,
80   Nescit opi Lachesis cedere Pœoniæ.
Occidit ille, cui Lauros iam læta parabas
   Anglia, Cupressi nunc preme fronde comam:
Ad vos jam funus transfertur, mortuus illam,
   Quam nequiit vivus, ut repetat Patriam.
85 Ille quidem repetit natalem corpore terram,
   Sed rediit veram spiritus in Patriam.
Et iam tempus adest toti lachrymabile genti;
   Itur ad exequias, magne Philippe, tuas.
Flent pueri, flent & iuvenes, flet serior ætas;
90   Præcipue, proprior sanguine si quis erat.
Inter quos uxor, penito percussa dolore,   [p. 57]
   Sic tandem fractis flebilis orsa sonis:

Istane sustineo tua, speratissime coniunx,
Imposita arsuro membra videre rogo?
95 Hisve ego tam propere feralia munera solvam?
His poterit flammas subdere nostra manus?
Me miseram, quantum fax hæc face distat ab illa,
Læta meos quondam quæ subiit thalamos?
Mansisset utinam diuturnior illa, vel a te
100 Hæc esset nostro subdita flamma rogo.
Nunc prior ipse iaces violenta morte peremtus,
(Vix ah, vix tanti Belgia tota fuit)
Isala spumifero radit qua flumine terras,
Nomine iam factus notior ille tuo.
105 Aut animam in patria licuisset ponere terra, aut
Illic fata minus passus acerba fores.
Hic mihi, væ miseræ, torquet præcordia luctus:
Hic dolor est ipsis tristior exequiis.
Scilicet idcirco, nimium male cognita Iberis
110 Regna, procul nostro regna remota solo,
Volventem, atque animo iam trans maria alta volantem
Et Patris & nostræ detinuere preces,
Externo ut caderes miserabilis hostia Marti,
Deque tuo lætus funere ovaret Iber?
115 At tu, hominum sancto qui corda astringis amore,
Sancte puer, sanctas, quod facis, adde faces,
Coniugis hic isto rogus ut flammescat ab igne
Haud aliter, flagrant quam mea corda mihi:
Plura locuturam DUDLÆÏUS interrupit:
120 Non tanti has lachrymas exigit umbra viri:
Ille quidem humanas curas ac gaudia ab alto
Despicit, & vita cœlicolum fruitur:
At nos quid magnum miseri spiramus homulli? [p. 58]
Quos hora haud ullo tempore certa manet.
125 Fallimur? an, SIDNEIE, tibi fortissime, calcem
Ex nobis aliquis jam tibi calce premet?

(18) [1586/1587?] Janus Dousa the Younger, ibid., p. 58.
IN EIUSDEM OBITUM DAPHNIS ECLOGA.

Forte pedo stabat Lycidas innixus agresti
Ad Thamesis ripas, quem plurima fagus obumbrat,
Heu nimio mœrore & luctibus externatus:
Non solitum agresti modulatus arundine carmen
5 Difficiles dominæ lamentabatur amores;
Non leni somnum gaudebat inire susurro,
Cogere non teneras ad pabula vesca capellas:

(18) 86-88 ciebo . . . umbra.]vocaro; / Elysii tunc forte lubens viridaria
linquet, / Et nos magna tua sic compellabit imago: *Poemata*, 1704.

Omnia quæ tota penitus de mente fugarat:
Sed neque tum pecoris, neque villæ aut pauperis agri
10 Ille vicem curans, toto te pectore, Daphni,
Toto animo extinctum, Daphni, heu grave suspirabat.
Tu quoque secretis resonans in vallibus Echo
Lugebas una, proprij haud memor amplius ignis,
Flumineique suo flebant cum funere olores.
15 Dicite Pierides, pastoris dicite Musam,
Dicite; nam vos & gemitus iunxisse canenti
Crediderim, & cari planxisse in funere alumni.
    Siccine Daphni iaces? sic o miserabilis, eheu,
    Daphni iaces, crudeli extinctus funere Daphni?
20 Sic fallis spes ipse tuas, spes ipse tuorum?
At (memini) lætos reditus tibi, Daphni, tuisque [p. 59]
Jam præsumebas, sed te sperata fefellit
Sors rerum, & frustra ventura heu gaudia, frustra
Tempora fingebas niveo signanda lapillo,
25 Solveret a patrio tunc quum tua littore puppis.
    Siccine, Daphni, iaces? sic o miserabilis eheu
    Daphni iaces, crudeli absumtus funere Daphni?
At non te conjunx lætanti mente relinquens
Tristia multa suo sub pectore condensabat,
30 Jam præsaga mali, infausto seu carmine bubo,
Seu lugubre cava cantaret ab ilice cornix,
Semper & in proprios erat ingeniosa dolores.
    Siccine Daphni, iaces? sic o miserabilis eheu
    Daphni iaces, crudeli extinctus funere Daphni?
35 Non satius fuit hic animam exhalere supremam,
Guttura ubi primum tua lacteus imbuit humor,
Et pulsata tibi tremulis vagitibus aura;
Quam procul a patria peregrinis hospes in oris
Oppetere infesto miserabilis hostia Marti?
40   Siccine Daphni iaces? sic o miserabilis eheu
    Daphni iaces, crudeli absumptus funere Daphni?
Heu, ubi tunc Phœbus fuit aut Mavortia Pallas,
Cum tua crudeles ruperunt stamina Parcæ?
Cur non auxilium suprema in morte tulerunt?
45 Sed fallor, nam & Pallas opem tibi ferre nequivit,
Nec potuit Phœbus succos adhibere salubres:
Sed satis ostendit nigra ferrugine luctum,
Tristior occiduas solito dum trahit ad undas.
    Siccine Daphni iaces? sic o miserabilis eheu
50   Daphni iaces, crudeli absumtus funere Daphni?
O Patriæ communis amor, tibi candida Nymphæ
Lilia cum violis & purpureis amaranthis
Intexunt, tumuloque parant fragrantia serta: [p. 60]
At tu jam spreto mortalis carcere vitæ
55 Felices lucos, felicia rura pererras
Elysii nemoris, & nos quoque respicis istinc,

Mortales curas, mortalia gaudia ridens.
    Siccine Daphni iaces? sic o miserabilis eheu
    Daphni iaces, crudeli extinctus funere Daphni.
60 Discessu heu mutata tuo sint omnia Daphni:
Nam dum tu hos colles, dum roscida prata colebas,
Ridebant denso viridantes robore colles,
Ridebant fontes, ridebant frondea rura.
At postquam te, Daphni, immitia fata tulerunt,
65 Iam lugent tristes inamœno robore colles,
Arescunt fontes, & pallent frondea rura,
Quæque prius læto florum vernabat amictu,
Num tantum lappas tellus ingrata reponit.
    Siccine Daphni iaces? sic o miserabilis eheu
70   Daphni iaces, crudeli absumptus funere Daphni?
Nempe erat hoc, quod vix abeunti diximus ore
Invito: dilecte vale, & tristi maduerunt
Imbre genæ, sive id casu sive omine factum.
    Siccine Daphni iaces? sic o miserabilis eheu
75   Daphni iaces, crudeli extinctus funere Daphni?
Hei mihi, quod malvas, ubi defecere, sequenti
Cum reliquis herbis videas æstate renatas:
At nobis. qui iam magnum spiramus, homullis,
Cum semel exiijmus, nunquam datur inde reverti.
80   Siccine Daphni iaces, sic o miserabilis eheu
    Daphni iaces, crudeli extinctus funere Daphni?
At quanquam extinctus sis corpore, Daphni, tamen te
Extinctura animo non ulla oblivio nostro est:
Quin ego sæpe meo te carmine compellabo,
85 Nec mihi decendent aut luce aut nocte dolores; [p. 61]
Cumque tuum nomen magna ter voce ciebo
Tunc tua sacra libens linquet lucosque locosque
Divitis Elysij, & nos sic affabitur umbra.
    Noster amor quondam, nunc luctus & anxia cura,
90 O Pastor, non hos gemitus mea funera poscunt,
Verum illorum, anima æternis quorum impia poenis,
Et Phlegetontæis crucianda est tradita flammis:
At mihi, quem Deus ipse poli censere Quirites
Inter, & ordinibus parat ascripsisse beatis,
95 Quorsum tot lachrymæ? quorsum suspiria tanta?
Hæc, & plura mihi dices: sed nulla dolores,
Nulla dies poterit nostros extinguere luctus.
    Talia dum Lycidas vacuas jactaret ad auras,
Et iam stridentem mersaret lampada Titan,
100 Accurrit Thyrsis; Lycidas ut Thyrsida vidit,
Dixit: Cras solitum repetet mea tibia carmen;
Dixit, & agrestem repetit cum Thyrside villam.

(19) [1586/1587] Janus Dousa the Younger, *Poemata*, Leiden, 1607, p. 100.

D.M. ILLUSTR. HEROIS PHILIPPI SIDNÆI.*

Quod Sidnæe, tuum decorent tot carmina funus,
     Nec riguis quisquam temperet a lachrymis,
Ne mirere, sacros Pindi liquere recessus
     Omnis cum Phœbo grex Heliconiadum,
5 Hæc lugubre levi modulatur arundine carmen,
     Ad citharam mœstos præcinit illa modos,
Ista smaragdifluos manibus disrumpit amictus,
     Impetus huic flavam vellere cæsariem,
Altera cum lachrymis cineri iacit oscula muto,
10   Nec, sua quæ manibus pectora tundat, abest;
Ipsa etiam Pallas te lamentatur, & omnes
     Expulit e tot pectore lætitias.
Quid mirum ergo, homines faciant quod carmine lessum,
     Quum tanget magnas hæc quoque cura Deas?

* Scripsit puer.

(20) [1586/1587?] Janus Dousa the Younger, ibid., p. 100.

CODRI ATHENARUM REGIS, ET PHILIPPI SIDNÆI
COMPARATIO.

Ob Patriam Codrus mentito occisus amictu est,
     Instinctu Sortis motus Apollineæ;
At tu pro Belgis propriam, Sidnæe, salutem
     Dum spernis, tibi mors intulit atra manus.
5 Pro Patria, Virtus magna est, occumbere; quanto
     Maior, pro Sociis non renuisse mori?

(21) [1586/1587] Georgius Benedicti, *Epitaphia in mortem Sidneji*, Leiden, 1587, [I].

AD HOSPITEM.

Sidneii vitam & mortem vis scire viator?
     Doctus, amans æqui, relligiosus erat.
Sic coluit Musas, Astræam, ante omnia Numen:
     Mitto genus. fama nobilis ipse sua est.
5 Omnia non dixi: quis enim queat? ultima dicam
     Facta, quibus vitam perdidit, & meruit.
Dum ruit Hispanum pro Belgis acer in hostem,
     Accepit telo vulnus, & interijt.
Mors bona felicem reddit, sed & hunc bona vita:
10   Felix, qui vixit tam bene & occubuit.

(22) [1586/1587] Id., [II].

AD EUNDEM.

Ades viator, & volens audi & dolens,
Quod te docere mortui Manes volunt.
Nomen vide. Philippus est, Eques domus,
Virtutis, ingeniique fama nobilis.
5   Nimis sed heu Philippus. Hoc nomen fuit
Omen sinistrum Belgicæ & Britanniæ.
Nam dum tuetur utriusque gloriam
Turmas fugaces hostium insequens equo,
Letale vulnus accipit. nunc hic jacet:
10   Luctum sui reliquit omnibus bonis.
I nunc viator incliti Ducis memor,
Tuosque oculos hujus tumuli spectaculo
Puta beatos esse, te miserum puta.

(23) [1586/1587] Id., [III].

Dum pugnat medios acer Sidnejus in hostes,
    Et celeri illorum terga fatigat equo.
Obstupuit Mavors, fulgentiaque arma Philippi
    Aspiciens, victrixne hoc duce Pallas? ait,
5 Dixerat: ille ducem letali vulnere figit
    Eminus, & vincit, dum fugit ipse, Deam.
At non Sidnejum: nam robur pectoris ingens
    Immotum extremum mansit adusque diem.
Quid loquor? accessit major quoque fama cadenti:
10   Ordine Eques vixit, vulnere eques moritur.
Sic decus Ordo fuit vivo, nunc mortuus illi est.
    Pro fluxo æternum sed dedit: hoc superat.

(24) [1586/1587] Id., [IV].

Occidit Hesperiam contra Sidnejus in armis.
    Omen in occasu sed latet: ortus ibi est.

(25) [1586/1587] Id., [V].

Vicinus leto fertur dixisse Philippus,
    En Deus, en sacrum Belgica terra tibi.
Accepi vulnus, non pœnitet, optima causa est:
    Huic iterum dabitur, si mihi vita datur.
5   O vox Sidneji vere Cygnëia: utrique
    Ante sacer vixit, nunc sacer emoritur.

(26) [1586/1587] Id., [VI].

> Magnanimus vitam Belgisque Deoque Philippus
> Vovit & impendit, unus utrique sacer.
> Roma tace Decium: vicit voto ille Latinos,
> Hic votum: utrique est fama, sed illa minor.

(27) [1586/1587] Id., [VII].

> Sidnejum juvenem rapuit Mors invida: vivo
> Dixisses olim Belgica, Et hic pater est.

(28) [1586/1587] Id., [VIII].

> Quid Musis cum Marte? nihil: Sidnejus, utrumque
> Qui prius in sese junxerat, occubuit.
> Nunc lugent Musæ, luget Mars tristis, & ille
> Qua perijt, vellent se perijsse nece.
> 5 Scilicet hoc illis tantum commune remansit,
> Quod simul hunc doleant, quo viguere simul.

(29) [1586/1587] Id., [IX].

> Dum redit exanimis generoso Marte Britannis
> Sidnejus patria rite ferendus humo,
> Quantus honor patriæ, quantus redijt dolor idem!
> Magnus uterque: sed hic victus honore fuit.
> 5 Aspexit vulnus, luxitque Britannia: verum
> Gloria solamen vulnere parta fuit.
> Nam plus laudis ab hoc fluxit, quam sanguinis: illa
> Orbe redundanti facit in astra viam.
> Mixtus ubi Heroüm turbis cælestibus Heros
> 10   Læta triumphali gaudia more canit.
> O felix Heros! patria nam dignus ut olim
> Veneris ad Belgas, dignior inde redis.

(30) [1586/1587] Id., [X].

> Anglia quod sibi me, quod Belgica terra reposcit,
> Indicium vitæ est, indiciumque necis.
> Vita accepta fuit, mea mors gravis omnibus una est:
> Causa meos cineres hæc facit esse leves.

(31) [1586/1587] Id., [XI].

IN MORTEM.

O Mors, quid dira petijsti glande Philippum?
    Credideras tantum posse perire virum?
Non potuit: quippe æternum virtute superstes
    Vivit, & est fama mors tibi, vita sibi.
5 I nunc, & fracta speres cervice triumphum,
    Nimirum hunc jaculo quo petis, ipsa peris.

(32) [1586/1587] Id., [XII].

AD HOSPITEM.

Non hic Sidneji tumulus, ne crede viator,
    Non est: sed geminæ Palladis, & Charitum.
Vivebant olim, in terris dum viveret ille,
    Scandentem cælos non potuere sequi,
5 Non potuit fluxum quoque corpus: at ille lepores
    Secum, & Palladium vexit in astra decus.
Arma reservavit Pallas sibi nuda: sed illæ
    Nomen inane, &, quos urna tegit, cineres.
His se junxerunt: Pallas tumulo arma dicavit,
10   Fletum aliæ: doleas, hospes, & adde tuum.

(33) [1586/1587] Id., [XIII].

Et Pietas, & sancta fides hac mole jacerent,
    Si possent illæ, posset & ipse mori.
Sed neque mors illis nocet invidiosa, nec ipsi:
    Vivus hic utraque est, utraque viva Deo.
5 Vivite felices, felices vivite Manes,
    Vobis mors non mors, sed nova vita fuit.

(34) [1586/1587] Id., [XIV].

Vixit Sidnejus. quam durum est dicere! vixit:
    Sed Patriæ & Belgis: nam sibi vivit adhuc.
Belgica tu luge, populosa Britannia luge,
    Quod dedit huic Mavors vulnus, utrique dedit.

(35) [1586/1587] Id., [XV].

Sidnejus petijt polos.
Causam quæritis hospites?
Terra non potuit capi.

(31) *Nos. 31–40 headed*: Ph. Sidnejum adhuc vivere.

14

(36) [1586/1587] Id., [XVI].

> Cur fles Sidnejum? quia vulnere mortuus? erras.
> Hoc ipso incepit vivere, quod moritur.
> Mortalis fuerat, mortalis desijt esse,
> Ut nunquam posset, debuit ille mori.

(37) [1586/1587] Id., [XVII].

> Et vivit pariter Sidnejus, & hac jacet urna
> Parte sui cælo, parte solo genitus.
> Cælo animam, mortale solo sed corpus habebat:
> Quam juste moritur! reddit utrique suum.

(38) [1586/1587] Id., [XVIII].

> Qui credis misera sublatum morte Philippum,
> Ignoras, quid sit vivere, quidve mori.
> Vita brevis mors est, mors rursum vita: Philippus
> Hanc habet, illam habuit. vivit, an interijt?

(39) [1586/1587] Id., [XIX].

> Mors quia sejunxit divinum a corpore pectus,
> Sidnejum luges, & parijsse putas.
> Falso: mutata Sidnejus sede remansit:
> Cælum habitat, cælo traxerat ante genus.
> 5 Sic orbem liquit, quem plenum motibus horres,
> Sic, quem tu speras, incolit ille polum.
> Confer utrumque genus vitæ: nisi desipis, hospes,
> Dices, hic vivit, vivus ego emorior.

(40) [1586/1587] Id., [XX].

> Quæris, quo cessit Sidnejus? mens in Olympo est,
> Sanguis apud Belgas, Anglia corpus habet.
> Sic nihil amissum est Sidneji: viva supersunt
> Omnia, & ille omni parte superstes adhuc.
> 5 Discrimen tamen est: terras tantum ante colebat,
> Nunc colit has terras, nunc colit ille polum.

APPENDIX II

Original reading of texts quoted

(1) Hubert Languet to August Duke of Saxony, Prague, 1 March 1575.

> ... Tanta est iam confidentia in Geusiis, ut cogitent de Schola publica seu Academia instituenda in oppido Hollandiae Leiden, quod Hispani ante non multos menses obsiderunt. Ob eam rem nuper venit Heidelbergam Philippus Mornixius Aldegondus, ...

(2) Guillaume Feugueray, 'Accuratissimæ simul et expeditissimæ institutionis formæ in Lugdunensi Batavorum Academia posthac usurpandæ Hypotyposis.'

> Divinus ille Plato, quem Tullius philosophorum deum appellat, tanta sapientiae opinione floruit, ut Thebani ac Phocenses urbem a se conditam legibus ei informandam suo arbitratu permiserint; is inter cetera, aureo politeumate, omnes artes et animi et corporis, ante vigesimum aetatis annum percipiendas definiebat, reliquam vitam in publicis belli pacisque temporibus constituebat. . .

(3a) Janus Dousa, 'Carmen ... in gratiam novæ ... Academiæ conscriptum.'

> ... / Nobis non licet esse tam solutis, / Præcinctisve male, aut manuleatis, / Qui Musas colimus politiores: / Sentimusque seorsum ab his & illis, / Queis nos vix homines videmur esse, / Quotquot integrior tenet Minerva, / Sinceræ fidei nutrix Minerva: / In manum cui de manu Themistim, / Scripturæ & Genium Sacræ & Medendi / Artem tradidit ipse Dux profundi, / Et dixit, Tibi cura sit Lycæum, / Quod volens tibi iure cedo ...
> ... / Cedat Lovanium ergo Lugoduno, / Et cum Lovanio suo Duacum: / Et quantum est Academiarum in orbe. / Ecce nescio quid modo hac in urbe / Pisa, Parrisijs, Dolaque, & ipsis / Maius nascitur Atticis Athenis. / ...
> ... / Huc ab auspicijs boni profecti / Omnes confluite undecunque Ephebi / Artis Palladiæ futuri alumni, / Non non Lanificæ illius vetustæ, / Aut Sellariolæ ullius, sed huius / Nostræ, quam Sophiam vocare Græci, /

Romani Sapientiam fuërunt: / Usu ac Mnemosine pa-
rente natam. / Merces ipsa sibi futura quæsit, / Cum
virtute suos beare sueta. / Ergo confluite undecunque
Ephebi, / Quo Phoebus vocat, & novem Sorores: / Et
quæ præsidet huic, & his Minerva, / Batavis simul,
exterisque ab oris: . . .

(3b) Bonaventura Vulcanius, 'Orationes'. 1592.

. . . utque ita Batavia sua non tantum viris qui bellica
fortitudine patriam tuerentur, sed qui consilio etiam a
prudentia stabilirent, abundaret . . .

(3c) Id. 1591.

. . . in quo nova soboles Batavica optimarum artium ac
scientiarum studijs exculta ad Reip. Ecclesiæque usum
succresceret. . .

(3d) Id. 1592.

. . . cum in alijs Academijs una aliqua ars vel scientia
præcipue floreat, reliqæ neglectæ incultæque iaceant: in
hac omne genus artium ac disciplinarum ita viget, ut
singulæ inter se de principatu contendere videantur . . .

(4) Daniel Rogers, 'In Lugdunum novam Batavorum Academiam'.

 Seu tibi Lugduni nomen sub nomine priscis
  Extitit, hoc Legio seu tibi Leida dedit.
 Sive alia sub voce vago tua constitit orbi
  Fama, recens vicit prisca trophæa fides.
5 Nam quis murorum fuerit latet ambitus olim,
  Nunc compage valent moenia fulta nova.
 Derivatus aquas præbet tibi Rhenus, & altas
  Navigat is fossas, quas tremit hostis Iber.
 Templa augusta micant, vicos interfluit amnis:
10 Sed quid ego his parvis cætera magna premo?
 Qualis adest urbi genius? constantia morum

(4) *Variants, alterations, and additions in Hertford MS., f. 166:*
 Title Ad Leidam, urbem Batavicam. 3 vago *into* olim 10 Sunt
fora, mundities quæ colit, utque domos. / Læta penu, glebaque soli,
coeloque revidens: *added between 9 and 10* 13 cura]corda
16 Fœdaruntque . . . fames *from* Cum populum premeret pestis et
atra fames 17 Sed . . . merente]Nixa Deo fregit sed spes adversa,
merente 19 duce . . . profundi *from* Nerei quod munerem salvam
21 quo . . . Leida *from* tibi, Leida, salvatas 22 Et . . . Musas,
from Vindice quo musas *dated* Leidæ. 26. Aprilis. 1575.

Quanta? quis hic puræ Relligionis amor.
Proque focis arisque simul quæ cura tuendis
   Civibus, Hispano bella fremente fero?
15 Ille quidem cinxit Leidam obsidione superbus,
   Fœdaruntque urbem pestis & atra fames.
Sed spes nixa Deo vicit mala cuncta, merente
   Cive decus rarum, dedecus hostis habet.
At quantum est urbem, duce quod Rectore profundi.
20   Musarum intrarit Marte furente chorus.
Quis non tale probet bellum, quo vindice Leida
   Et pariter Musas, & sacra pura colis?

(5) Daniel Rogers, ['De frequentia omnium gentium in Ianimedio, vulgo die Burse'].

> ... / Nam notat undecimam cum gnomon temporis horam, / Sextaque labentem cum trahit hora diem, / Omnigenas denso videas huc currere gentes / Agmine, quas claro Phœbus ab axe videt. / Huc venit Anglorum genialis turba, locumque / Hunc subit, hæc medium gens tenet una locum, / Italus a dextris & ei coniunctus Iberus / Ambiguo stringunt atria prima pede. / Ambulat a læva quod gignit Gallia parte, / Hac etiam Belgas cernere parte licet. / Ante sed aspicies antiquo Tuiscone natos; / Et quoscunque dedit Rhenus & Ister habes. / Atergo Burgundus adest, fortisque Batavus, / Et quos Arctoïs conspicit Ursa plagis. / Dissonus auditur rumor, locus ipse repletur / Et variis linguis, vestibus & variis. / O decus eximium, visu & mirabile cunctis! / Orbis in exiguo maximus orbe viget.

(6) Daniel Rogers, 'De Scaldi glacie constricto initio anni. 1565. ad [E. Demetrium]'.

> ... / Caupo meri dotes per strictum frigore flumen, / Vendidit, et libros bibliopola suos. / Ipse ego dulce bibi vinum, librosque coëmi, / Qua medio Scaldis tramite frictus erat. / ...

(7) Janus Dousa, 'Ad Rogerium'.

> ... / Tunc mihi dicebas te non modo versibus ad me / Verum etiam totis ire voluminibus. / ... / Sed quid nulla queror demens mihi verba dedisse, / Quem mihi nil præter verba dedisse liquet? / ...

(8) 'Hadrianus Junius'.

> ... vitam cum morte commutavit, anno Christi M D LXXV. ætatis LXIII. mensis cognominis die XVI.

Sub mortis tempus Academiæ nascenti inter primos
Professores destinatus. Sed inter ipsa initia morte abrep-
tus inchoare munus non potuit . . .

(9) Janus Dousa to Daniel Rogers, Leiden, 1575.

. . . Neque enim inficiaberis spero, me totum illud tempus, quo primum in patriam ex Gallijs reverso liberorum
quærundorum gratia uxor credo obiecta est mihi, usque
ad annum LXXII quo felici meo magis, quam publico
fato, in Britannia vestra legatiunculam communi
nomine obivi, ne tenuissimam quidem de te, aut de rebus
tuis auditionem opera tua accepisse, nedum scedulam,
aut literam, unde ego cum nescio quam de benevolentia
nostra diminutionem factam nullo cum merito tuo
levissime suspicatus essem, memini me tum temporis,
atque adeo dum memini a lachrymis vix tempero,
ætatis fervore impulsum scribere, verba mihi a Rogerio
meo data fuisse. cui ego orationi nunc hercule lumbos,
si liceat, defractos velim. O terra, o cœlum, o maria
Neptuni. Douzane huiusmodi de Rogerio? cuius egregia
fides re cognita iampridem antea, & quidem Gifannianis
temporibus, omnem ipsi de immutata porro voluntate
dubitationem in posterum adimere poterat: cui si non
ob illius eruditionem, prudentiam, probitatem, at saltem
hoc nomine bene velle debebat, quod Valenti, Bucha-
nano, Aurato, Baifio, Florenti, Altario, Thorio (at quibus
viris?) etiam esset carissimus . . . [cont. no. 12]

(10) Janus Dousa, 'D. Elisabethæ Britanniarum reginæ, Principi opt. max.'

Regina magnis edita regibus, / Ipsa erudita o Pieridum
manu, / O Gratijs secunda nulli: / . . .
. . . / Exempla cur vero ista peto foris, / Praesertim apud
te? tam modo nun tuo / Periculo edoctam, . . .
. . . / Sic o Deus, sic ditis & insulæ / Regina faxis, unius
ut Dei / Ductu, tuoque restitutam / Rem patriae videa-
mus olim. / Tunc digniori te citharæ sono, / Ventura
nec quem secla redarguant, / Canemus: . . .

(11) Janus Dousa, 'Ad Danielem Rogerium Albimontanum'.

. . . / At quis o bone cogitasset illud / Fore unquam,
medijs ut in Britannis, / Londinique Lutetiam inve-
nirem? / . . .

(12) Janus Dousa to Daniel Rogers, Leiden, 1575.

. . . deinde oblitum me putas comitatis eius, qua mecum
non modo tum primum typis excusos, publicique iuris

factos, verum etiam manu descriptos, scrinioque signatos
& tuos & aliorum doctissimorum familiarium, eorum
inquam quos fere in Gallijs communes habuimus,
labores atque egregia ingenij facinora benigne commu-
nicasti, mihique exscribenda dedisti. Atque inter cætera
magni illius Buchanani de Sphera opusculum, cuius
exemplum Migrodio me acceptum referre par est, qui
illud mei honoris gratia tuo permissu, manu sua accura-
tissime excepit ... Ut hæc tamen omittam, quibus apud
animum meum nihil carius habeo, literæ illæ quas ali-
quanto post discessum meum, Ronsardi Franciadi, &
Bellaquæi Bucolicis libellis comites dedisti, quantam
habent declarationem amoris tui? ...
... Proinde te para, cum homine Batavo tibi res est, &
qui iam aliquid sapiat ad genium huius adolescentioris
Academiæ. nosti tamen quam morosi, plenique fastidij
sint, qui poëtica malacia laborant. dediscendæ tibi sunt
Musæ istæ severiores, serieque omnes de Repub. cogita-
tiones in aliud tempus reijciendæ ...

(13) Janus Dousa, 'Ad Gulielmum Niveldium.'

... cui ut est nil, sic nihil unquam / Aut fuit, aut alia
posthac aetate futurum est / Doctrina, eloquio, forma, &
pietate secundum. / ...

(14) Hubert Languet to Robert Beale, Vienna, 7 September
1573.

... Est hic nobiscum Philippus Sydneus eximius adolescens, quem ego summopere diligo propter morum sua-
vitatem, acre ingenium, et verum peritiam fere maiorem
quam eius ætas ferat. Ut uno verbo dicam, mihi videtur
plenis velis ad virtutem contendere, et indico fælices pa-
rentes qui tam præstantis indolis filium genuerunt ...

(15) Daniel Rogers to Hadrianus Junius, Antwerp, 4 February 1575.

... Tui nominis iam a multis annis studiosissimus fui, ac
quis sim ex Clarissimis viris Carolo Boisotto, ac Douza
tuo, simul meo, abunde cognosces ...

(16) Hadrianus Junius to Daniel Rogers, Middelburg, 23
January [1575].

Vetus est, ex ungue leonis molem metiri, Rogeri doctiss.
at ego ex uno, atque altero carmine, cujus legendi co-
piam mihi potestatemque fecit clariss. Janus Douza,
ingenium tuum in numerato positum, ita perspexi, ut ad

tui cognitionem prorsus fuerim inflammatus, eamque
ambitu quodam, & quasi precario expetendam duxerim
. . .

(17) Daniel Rogers, 'Ad Ianum Douzam epigramma'.

> Orta fuit superis de te lis, Douza, vocante
>   Marte suum, Phoebo teque vocante suum:
> Phoebus ait, Nobis cunis vigilavit ab ipsis,
>   Castra sequens nobis, Mars ait, æra mæret.
> 5 Dissidium veritus Divorum triste duorum
>   Iuppiter, Ah rixas ponat uterque, refert.
> Pace colet Phoebum, belli sed turbine Martem.
>   Douza tuus, Mars, est, sic &, Apollo, tuus.
> Dicta Iovis rata, Douza, facis, qui tempore belli
> 10   Et Martem, & pariter Numina docta colis.
> Nam tibi Mars dulcis, dulces ante omnia Musæ,
>   Una manus gladium tractat, at illa librum.
> Unde tui genij miratus uterque vigorem,
>   Dat tibi Mars ensem, dat tibi Apollo lyram.

(18) Janus Dousa, 'Guill. Erlæo Britanno'.

> . . . non ego ille quem putas, / Non ille Apollo, quem
> tuus / Poëta nuper iste mentitus est. / . . .
> [*In margine*:] Daniel Rogerius Albimontanus.

(19) Georgius Benedicti, 'De Ianis Dousa & Hauteno'.

> Dousiadem Hautenum duos tulit unica Vates
>   Leyda, illum Latii Carminis, hunc Batavi.
> Ianus uterque: quibus si Janus tertius adsit,
>   Ingeniis pandent omnia clausa suis.
> 5 Quod cum viderit hic; te dicet utroque beatam
>   Optabit Claves & sibi Leyda tuas.
> Romaque, quem coluit, Ianum pertaesa relinquet
>   Optabit Ianos & sibi Leyda tuos.

(20) Justus Lipsius, 'Ad I. Hautenum, Non esse aptum se
Belgicæ Musæ'.

> Hautene Vates, vatis interpres sacri
> Idemque iure Belgicae Princeps lyrae,
> Quo me remotos abripis tecum in locos?
> Quae memora quod lustrare me iubes iugum?
> 5 Qua nulla Vatum trita semita est solo.
> O parce, parce non profano vertici
> Debetur ista laurus hanc olim tibi
> Parnassi ab ipso detulit Phoebus iugo.
> Qui primus ausus fila Belgicae chelys

10   Movere plectro. & a bicorni vertice
Novem citare ad stagna Thetyos, Deas.
Quod invidebunt haec & illa saecula.
Tua o tua istaec laus: ego quid nisi iocum
Risumque nautis debeam & cauponibus?
15   Fallace ut olim cecidit ales Icarus
Penna levatus: frustra sic famam novi
Et carmen omnes aemulemur Pindari.

(21) Justus Lipsius, 'Ad I. Hautenum. De versione eius Plauti'.

> ... / Vis verum tibi dici amice? dicam, / Te vivo pariter sales Batavi / Vivent, & pereunte te peribunt.

(22) Daniel Rogers to George Buchanan, London, 30 August 1576.

> ... Crebro etenim ex *Zelandia* & *Batavia* Literas ad te per populares tuos isthinc in Patriam redeuntes dedi. Habes autem in illis Regionibus plurimos, duos imprimis tui Nominis studiosissimos, *Janum Douzam*, & *Philippum Marnixium*, Ingenio, Genio, et Genere nobilissimos, quorum alterum cum *Lutetiæ* commorareris ad te deduxi, cujus ad te Poemata nuper illa edita ex Authoris Scientia et Voluntate transmitto; alterum nosti Parisijs, qui Principi *mehercle* optimo, Merito suo vel gratissimus. Is cum nuper à Principe redirem, Literas his adjunctas ad te scripsit ...

(23) Janus Dousa to Daniel Rogers, Leiden, 1576.

> ... de festiva illa selectissimorum librorum copia loquor, quos ad me usque ex penitissimis Gallijs recens advectos, Londino porro in Bataviam transportandos ...

(24) Daniel Rogers to George Buchanan, London, 30 August 1576.

> ... Literis enim non facile expressero, quanto Studio laboraverim, ut Causa quam christianissimus Princeps constantissime tuetur, *Reginæ* etiam Patrocinio confirmaretur ...

(25) Daniel Rogers to George Buchanan, Westminster, 28 February 157[7].

> ... Philippus Sydnæus ... nuper ad Imperatorem Rudolphum a serenissima Regina legatus est, qui Casimirum Ducem, fratremque Electorem in itinere conveniet, de mediis quibus foedus Anglis cum Protestantibus Germanis coire possit ad religionis salutem tuendam ...

(26) Hubert Languet to August Duke of Saxony, Prague, 1 March 1575.

> ... Imperator his diebus eum ad se accersivit & valde clementer accepit. ...

(27) Daniel Rogers to Abraham Ortelius, Norwich, 19 August 1578.

> ... hic autem Wilsonus secretarius Reginae Serenissimae illud detinet, ut symbolum suum curet adpingj:. ...

(28) Hubert Languet to Joachim Camerarius the Younger, Frankfort, 17 June 1577.

> ... Profectus est Colonia Antverpiam, & inde Bruxellas, ubi audio redditas fuisse ei literas a Regina, quibus jubebatur ire ad Principem Orangium, & nomine Reginæ fidejuberet in baptismo filiæ ipsi Principi recens natæ. ...

(29) Philip Sidney to Hubert Languet, The Court, 10 October 1577.

> ... Amo enim Principem illum, et forsan aliquo modo magis ei inservivi, quam ipse noverit. Ita sane nostri animi hoc tempore inclinantur, ut (si bella ex Belgio continuentur) in aliquam spem adducar, vaticinium illud tuum, quod mihi de ipso aliquando Viennæ dixisti, felicem eventum habiturum. ...

(30) Hubert Languet to Philip Sidney, Frankfort, 12 August 15[7]7.

> ... Verum bono tuo fato, huc sub noctem appulit Dominus Daniel Rogerius, qui cum dixerit, se habere a te literas ad me, ardorem illum & impetum animi mei fregit: ...

(31) Hubert Languet to Philip Sidney, Frankfort, 22 October 15[7]7.

> ... Ejus suavi consuetudine interea fruimur, & tui mentionem sæpe facimus, ...

(32) Hubert Languet to Philip Sidney, Vienna, 11 June 1574.

> ... Pulchre quidem epressa sunt pleraque tua lineamenta, sed est longe magis juvenilis, quam deceat. Puto te fuisse non absimilem quum duodecimum, aut decimum tertium ætatis annum ageres. ...

(33) Hubert Languet to Philip Sidney, n.p., 6 June 1575.

... Pictor expressit te subtristem & cogitabundum.
Mallem fuisses vultu magis ad hilaritatem composito,
cum pingendum te præbuisti...

(34) Daniel Rogers to Janus Dousa, Antwerp, 16 January
1578.

E mensis plurimis itineri difficultatibus, Optatissime
Duza, tandem ex Germania in Belgium sum reversus ad
illustrissimum principem Aurasinum, quem hac hora
optime valentem, magno animi gaudio conveni. Quod
si tu affuisses, nihil foelicitati privatae defuisset. Miror,
autem cum Francofurtum te venturum ad nundinas
mihi promiseras, te nec apparuisse isthic, nec literas,
mutati consilii mi indices ad me misisse. pluribus tuo
nomine cum Wechele egi sed exspectabaris indies.
Nunc ex Sylvio intelligo, se cum Typographia ad nos
migraturum. Quare quod antea ad Academiae ampli-
ficationem et gloriam deerat, illius beneficio recipietis,
quo modo privatim tibi consultum erit: sed vereor ne
Catomanae theologiae supercilium, Basia tua omnia
apro(pro)bare recuset: quamvis nostro nomini sint
inscripta: Hibernia mea exspectant promissam Oden,
addo etiam Epigramma, sine quibus Typis Wecheli
non ausus fui eam committere: Nam (ut usurpem
Buchanani illud) quod ab ingenio Domini sperare
nequibit, Debebit genio forsitan illa tuo. Hic paucis
tantum diebus commorari mihi in presenti licebit: cras,
Principem Bruxellas sequor: unde in Angliam pegaseo
advolatu cogito contendere. Villerius qui nuper ad Principem venit mecumque hodie est pransus, narravit mihi,
Tragediam Johannis Buchananicam Londini impressam:
unde eam brevi exspectabis: cum verbosiori Epistolio:
haec enim mihi excidunt occasione oblata ad te mittendi,
per Elegantissimum Modium: qui aetatis vere, insignitor
Verronianum illud comprobat, Ingenio non annis nos
discere: qui si solus advenisset, beasset quidem me, sed
cum Carrionem una deduceret, dici non potest, quanto
beneficio me affecerit: Una hora fruebar duobus quos
unice desiderabam videre. Gratulor illi ad te iter dignus
siquidem tuo est amore. Utinam una ad te liceret mihi
cum eo proficisci: Ego illi me adiunxissem, si Serenissima
Regina reditum meum non exspectaret indies, quae
unice scire gestit ...... illis meae cu .... tecum
.... aggeres Alcmarianes .... communica ......

(34) *The verso of this letter is badly damaged.*

nare haec . . . . . . consule, qui spatiis excludor unguis,
quo minus plura ad te nunc exarem:
Deus opt. max. te cum coniuge atque adeo fami[lia]
integra servet incolumem, tuosque conatus prosperet et
fortunet.

(35) Philip Sidney to Hubert Languet, The Court, 10 March
1578.

> [*P.S.*] . . . Meum D. Rogerium oro ut in meam gratiam
> adhuc magis ames.

(36) Paulus Melissus to Janus Dousa, Nuremberg, 25 March
1578.

> . . . De Rogerio liberando, quæ spes, mi Duza? Si
> caris me, si de illius incolumitate vel unum saltem
> ad me verbulum. Honestissime illi cupio; ut qui a me
> mirum in modum ametur. . .

(37) Hubert Languet to Philip Sidney, Antwerp, 22 October
1580.

> . . . Communis noster amicus Dn. Daniel Rogerius
> missus a Serenissima vestra Regina in Germaniam, captus
> est a prædonibus prope Cliviam oppidum, & abductus in
> arcem Blimbeck, quæ ad Martinum Schenck pertinet.
> Vestrum est procurare ipsi libertatem: nam Princeps
> Auriacus nihil in ea re potest: sunt enim ejus hostes
> infensissimi ii, a quibus est captus. . .

(38) William Camden to Abraham Ortelius, Westminster, 22
November 1580.

> . . . De D. Rogerio valde sumus hic solliciti: quo tu
> ingenii nervos intendis, scire aveo. . .

(39) Hubert Languet to Robert Beale, Delft, 15 February
1581.

> . . . sunt infesta latrocinijs itinera quibus hinc itur in
> Germaniam, ut nemo se ijs audeat committere. Id
> suo magno malo expertus est infœlix noster Rogersius
> cuius ego vicem valde doleo. Fefellerat nuper appositos
> sibi custodes, eo opera cuiusdam mulierculo effugerat,
> sed est ex fuga retractus, & ut audio, iam arctiore
> custodia quam antea, detinetur. . .

(40) Hubert Languet to George Buchanan, Delft, 20 February 1581.

> ... hinc abest trium horarum Itinere *Leida*, seu *Lugdunum Batavorum*, ut isti jam loquuntur; ubi vivunt *Justus Lipsius, Jannus Douza* Poeta, & *Donellus* ... Viri docti, & clari. ... *Daniel Rogersius*, communis noster Amicus, qui te unice colit, ante quatuor Menses captus est à *Germanis* ...

(41) Paulus Melissus, '... liber tertius. Ad Elisabetham ...'

> ... / Testes meorum sint volo carminum / Uterque SYDNEIUS, ROGERSque; / ...

(42) Paulus Melissus, 'Ad Ianum Dousam Nordovicem, et Iustum Lipsium Iscanium.'

> ... / Ferreas capti manicas ROGERSII / Duraque vincla / Cogor invita procul abdicatus / Aure inaudire, & tacitas per auras / Surda Pegnessi vada lacrimoso / Frangere questu. / ... / O quis, & quando, mihi nunciabit / Esse laxatas hilaris ROGERSII / Compedes, tendemque frui redemptum / Aëre aperto? / ...

(43) Joannes Sturmius to [Francis Walsingham], 29 January 1585 [*n.s.*].

> Ecce vidi ante te Rogersium vestrum et meum: de quo non semel scripsi ad vos... Gratum mihi fuit et jucundum: Dominum Rogersium mihi confessum esse de tua erga se benevolentia et studio et patrocinio. quam id mihi gratum sit: non dico fuerit: perpetuo enim gratum erit: potes tu per te ipsum satis æstimare. Primum igitur gratias ago Deo: quod liberatus sit ex diuturna et magna molestia. Deinde quod prius ad me venerit: quam ad vos sit reversus: credens atque confidens vobis: quo maioribus propter vos molestijs et angoribus cruciatus fuit: eo vos magis elaboraturos. ut ista tristitia diuturna maiore lætitia compensetur: atque utinam brevi abs te habeam literas non fatales atque lethiferas: sed tamen lætas atque lætiferas... [*P.S.*] Recreate Rogersium nostrum: coniuge bona, antequam cani augeantur.

(44) Justus Lipsius to Janus Dousa, Leiden, 1 September 1585.

> ... De itinere eo Anglicano: di boni quam voluissem, quam nunc vellem... Rogersius noster qui valet? in-

video illi te, tibi illum. fabulamini, muginamini cottidie,
cum libet, quamdiu libet: o beatum par, et quod
utinam per me impar! Nobilissimis Dominis Burgleo,
Sidnaeo, Diero, quaeso cultum omnem a me nuncia et
amorem... felix hac quoque dote Anglia, quod nobilitas
in ea vere nobilis, culta studiis virtutis et doctrinae.
... [*P.S.*] Plantinus noster abiit sed ... brevi rediturus.
...

(45) Janus J. Boissardus, 'Paulus Melissus'.

> ... Post Vindemiam anni 1582. navigavit ex portu
> Dipensi in Angliam, offerens Richemonti Elisabethæ
> Anglorum Reginæ sua Poemata, ibique per hyemem in
> aula mansit... Sed postquam comite itineris Hieronymo
> Groslotio Lislæo nobili Gallo, cuius maiores ex Francia
> Germaniæ oriundi erant, qui cum adolescentulo Iacobo
> VI. Scotiæ Rege sub Georgio Buchanano educatus
> fuerat, Academias Oxoniensem & Cantabrigiensem,
> Bibliothecasque libris veteribus refertissimas perlustrasset,
> a Regina humanissima, quæ aliquoties ipsum antea
> sponte sua compellaverat, veniam abeunti impetravit ...
> Præter linguam vernaculam, quæ est Teutonica superior,
> & eas, quæ in scholis Academiisque addiscuntur, maxime
> illi cordi fuerunt Italica, Gallica, Hispanica, item
> Belgica & Anglica...

(46) Hieronymus Groslotius to Janus Dousa, London, 28
March 1586.

> ... nunc vero primum scribo occasione iuvenis amicissi-
> mi Georgij Benedicti, qui vocatu patronorum abit a
> nobis sane quam invitis... Cum haec scriberem, nuntia-
> tum est mihi excessisse nuper Petrum Ronsardum Prin-
> cipem nostrum vatem, in uno Bartasio minor. obijt autem
> quod notes novissima die anni superioris. Aurati Poemata
> multa iunctim excusa sunt primulum Lutetiæ inscio
> auctore...

(47) 'Vita Dominici Baudii'.

> ... Sub finem ejus mensis accessit numero comitum
> splendidissimæ Legationis, quæ tunc ab Illustrissimis
> Ordinibus missa est ad reginam Elizabetham. illic
> innotuit multis a fama vel dignitate claris viris, sed uni
> instar omnium maxime charus fuit Philippo Sidneo; ...

(48) 'Amicis suis Dom. Baudius æger S.D.'.

> ... / Tris præter omnes nobili fama viros / Cultu Philip-
> pos prosecutus sum meo: / Te coelitis, Mornæe, felicem

stili; / Te, clare Sidnei, quem diurnare haud tulit /
Virtus in orbe, fas ubi versum ac nefas, / Terrisque ademit
debitum coelo decus; / Te magne Marnix, providens
vir & graves / Perpesse curas patriæ rebus super: / ...

(49) Justus Lipsius to [Janus Dousa], Leiden, 23 August 1584.

> ... Nobiliss. VV. Philippum Sidnæum, & Dierum, si
> vides, saluta à me quæso: & ijs iudica, per te stetisse
> quod eos non viderim tecum...

(50) Janus Dousa, 'Ad Hieronymum Groslotium Lislaeum'.

> ... / Quot risus simul in ioco atque vino / Risissemus,
> ego, HOTTOMANNUS, ac tu, / Coniuncti SCHEDIO: ...

(51) Jean Hotman to Scipio [Gentili], Basle, 12 February
1593.

> ... mihi vero magnus etiam Poëta, si tu is es, ut profecto
> es, quem tota olim Anglia admirata est...

(52) Jean Hotman to Scipio [Gentili], Basle, 10 December
1592.

> ... Venit mihi in mentem Carminum tuorum, quae
> Sidneio nostro mire placebant...

(53) Dominicus Baudius to Justus Lipsius, [Flushing, No-
vember/December 1585].

> Scitum est, ubi amici ibi opes. Ego id verum esse com-
> perior cottidie. Nam sive id foelici quodam fato meo
> fit, quo modo mihi persuadeo, sive merito meo quod
> quidem mihi non arrogo, libere possum gloriari permul-
> tos mihi amicos contigisse nec eos e multis quorum
> opera et comitas summo mihi et ornamento et adiumento
> semper fuit. Taceo reliquos, unum illud nobile par
> loquar, D. Dousam, inquio, et D. Rogerum per quos
> interpretes factum est ut, quo nihil mihi optabilius
> accidisse potuit, in familiam illustrissimi equitis D. Phi-
> lippi Sidnei reciperer. Quid tibi eius doctrinam, quid
> humanitatem, quid cæteras dotes commemorem?
>   Non nostri ingenii est oras evolvere laudum
>   Tantarum, meritisque virum celebrare Camoenis.
> Verum tamen nescio quomodo prorsus hic sum quod
> aiunt κῶφον πρόσωπον non quidem voluntate mea, non
> etiam opinor ullo meo vitio nisi forte pudore subrustico.
> Nunc illud quanta possum animi contentione serio a te
> peto, mi Lipsi, naturæ meæ verecundiam subleves, et

primo quoque tempore literas ad eum mittas indices
amoris erga me tui, indices eorum qua et tu de me pol-
liceri salva veritate poteris, ego affirmationem tuam
bona fide præstiturus confido. Narro tibi, nullus te
vivit impetrabilior, ita eum tui admiratio inflammavit.
Id igitur si feceris, non hoc quidem consequeris ut te
ardentius amem (non enim ullam partem augere meus
in te amor potest) sed ut plura tibi debeam, et magis
solvendo esse possim. Vale.

Tuus ex animo D. Baudius.

[*P.S.*] Iterum resecro, mi Lipsi, quod dudum obsecra-
veram de literis illis huc mittendis. Ego hic Vlissinghae
sum apud Pensionarium van der Becke. Velim potius
mittas plures eodem exemplo diversis temporibus, unas
tantum ei tradam et si plures perferantur, alias servabo.
Salutabis a me D. Donellum, itemque familiam Hauteni.
Vale meum decus.

(54) Paulus Melissus, dedication, Augsburg, 31 July 1582.

... Accepisti quidem iampridem Schediasmata mea
Poëtica, sed hæc recentiora nondum ad manus pervenere
tuas: ...

(55) Paulus Melissus, 'Georgio Gilpino'.

... Tu precor interim / GILPINE, quid Regina mandet, /
Quid jubeat mihi adordiendum, / Felice nutu signifi-
caveris. / Me, quantus hic sum, devoves illius / Famæ
celebrandæ, Britannum / Omnis ad obsequium paratus.

(56) Paulus Melissus, 'Ad Auroram'.

... / AURORA salve. Te meis venustam / Quoties ocellis
lætus adspexi, palam / Videre ELISAM sum ratus, / Britanniæ illam doctam et eruditam / Reginam, in illiusque
viva imagine / Meam ROSINAM, tot libris / Tot luculentis
carminum involucris / Claram; poëtarumque mille versibus / Pridem celebratam, in mei / Tantum favorem,
gratiamque Nymphæ. / ...

(57) Paulus Melissus, 'Ad Janum Dousam'.

... / Tecum est filius una, / Vivax ingenio puer, / Quem
dignata suo Melpomene sinu / Artes Pieridum condocuit
bonas, / Romanoque disertum / Vatem carmine reddi-
dit. / ... / HAGANAE teneris aurea virgines / DUDLÆO
manibus dona parant duci, / ... / LUGDUNUM unanimi
te simul omine / Expectat reducem, non minus in tuam /
Quam LEICESTRIDA laudem / Æternum meditans epos. /
At tu ne propera tam cito, NORDOVIX: / ...

(58) Paulus Melissus to Janus Dousa, London, [December? 1585].

Ego et Lislæus te invisemus ante abitum, ut heri promisimus. Itaque fac, mi suavissime Dousa, qua hora sis conveniendus, sciamus: ne scilicet & tibi & tempori simus detrimento. Si prandium exspectas, a prandio vobis erimus præsto, navim votis mutuis prosequuturi. Fortassis carmen te & filium postmodo subsequetur. Angustia temporis prævenior. ... Si diutius heic commoror, linguæ Anglicæ operam dabo. Philippum Sydneium, mihi ante multos annos notissimum, fac quæso et me officiose salutes. Vale. Londini. Tuus ex animo. Melissus.

(59) Paulus Melissus, 'Ad Nerea Pro Jano Dousa'.

... / Stantes in aucti margine fluminis / Fidi sodales, ipse, ROGERSIUS, / Unaque LISLÆUS, Poëtam / Prosequimur satagente voto. / ...
Londini. Die VII Decemb. Anno M D LXXXV.

(60) Paulus Melissus to Jean Hotman, London, 12 February 1586.

Munus meum Philippo Sidneio placuisse libenter ex Epistola tua intellexi, mi Hotomane, utinam mihi illum hic videre contigisset; citius sane negotia mea in Aula, expeditiusque confecta fuissent, illo praesente. Nunc discedere quamprimum cogito, ne plus temporis sumptuumque perdam. Recta Caletas Deo favente petam, inde Parisios. Tibi gratias ago interim de labore, quam sumpsisti in perferendo Libro. Resaluto Lipsium, Dousam, amicos ceteros. Pace in Gallis facta, fortassis iterum conveniemus ...

(61) Paulus Melissus to Francis Walsingham, London, 19 February 1586.

Quod ad te scribo, Walsinghame vir præstantissime, eo fit, ut te certiorem faciam de discessu meo in Galliam. Constitui ire equis celeribus. Quod si aut Reginæ serenissimæ aut tuo nomine quidquam mihi credere volueris litterarum, offero meam operam atque studium promptissimum. Nihil me amplius heic remoratur, præter litteras salvi conductus, in portu necessarias: quas Nicasium secretarium jam scribi [*inserted*: & Reginæ manu signari] curavisse spero. Si quid fortuitu ad me litterarum ab ill. viro Philippo Sidneo, amico meo vetere, perlatum esset, eas mihi transmitti cuperem. Cras Deo volente in aulam advolabo. Bene vale.

15

(62) Daniel Rogers, 'Jano Antonio Baifio'.

> ... / Nuper quum peterem tuos Baifi / Penates, legeres mihi tuæ quum / Musæ delicias venustiores. / ... / Illum [*i.e.* *Ronsard*] dum video audio tuasque / Cantantem lepido sono camoenas / ...

(63) Anon., 'In Zoilum'.

> Douza, quis hunc stringet verrucæ crimine vatem, Dissimulans monstri tubera magna sui?

(64) Janus Gruterus to Janus Dousa, Rostock, 27 April 1586.

> ... totus tamen in otio sine negotio. et despondi prorsus mentem animi, posse me quondam nomen aliquod inter literatos tenere. Imo et Sonnettorum illa vorsuta concinnatio totaliter dissoluta est; quique nuper in hæc verba prorumpere ausus: (...) nunc paratus sum cedere, & jam nunc cedo, omnium mortalium minimo. Sed jam satis garrivi. Da jam si placet alijs operam. Salutem filio, cui misissem carmen, sed nondum accessit ultima stropha.

(65) Jacob Walraven, dedication, Leiden, 30 August 1586.

> ... Dwelc ic na een pooze hervattende in I. Lipsii (niet buyten zijn zelfs raet) *de Constantia*, noch versch uyten druck, was voortvarende, met drie streken van een veel veerdigher voorby gezeylt. ...

(66) Burgomasters of Leiden to Robert Dudley, Leiden, 18 January 1586.

> ... Wy zyn ten hoochsten verblyt geweest verstaen hebbende by uwe F. G. Resolutie genomen te zyn ooc voor een wyl zyn hof binnen dezer stede te willen houden, daermede deze stede grote eere zal werden angedaen. Ende zoo wy billicken derhalven bezorcht zyn over Uwer Exc. F.G. ende zyn hofgevolch ten besten te doen logeren ende accommoderen ende alle ongeregeltheyden tot noch toe daerinne gepleecht te doen voorcomen ... ende te verzorgen dat niemandt boven zyn vermogen en worde bezwaert, hadden wy uyten onzen aen uwer F.G. afgevaerdicht (ende) onsen medebroeder. ...

(67) Franciscus Dusseldorpius, [Anno 1586].

> ... Dum Leidae esset universitatem illam famosam videre et Justum Lipsium, magni nominis literatorem, ibidem Taciti Agricolam publice explicantem, audire voluit,

comitatus filio Antonij pseudoregis Portugalliae aliis-
que proceribus. A lectione Lipsium prensat et secum ad
prandium ducit; hospitium namque haud procul inde
habebat in monasterio monialium sanctae Barbarae
sacro et jam ab Auraico olim occupato, ubi ipsum cum
dicto filio Antonij et pseudoepiscopo Coloniensi sacris
quadragesimae diebus epulantem videre erat, mensa
carnibus instructissima. . .

(68) Justus Lipsius to Henricus Ranzovius, Leiden, 5 April
1586.

> . . . Comitem ipsum ac Sidneium apud nos habuimus;
> egregium sane Principem illum, benignum, Heroicum: &
> hunc ejus cognatum, ex sorore filium, insigni prudentia
> & doctrina. . .

(69) Justus Lipsius, dedication, Leiden, 17 March 1586.

> Quaeris a me serio, Vir illustris Philippe Sidneie, de
> Pronunciatu Latinae linguae quid sentiam? germanum-
> ne & verum hunc, quo nunc utimur: an alium fuisse anti-
> quitus, qui ut multa alia, exoleverit tenebris ignoran-
> tiae obrutus & longi aevi. Tenuis subtilisque inquisi-
> tio: . . .
> Quis ergo finis? tibi o Sidneie parere. quia durus, sive
> improbus, si illi quidquam negem, *cui dij ipsi* (usurpabo
> Laberianum illud de Caesare) *nihil negaverunt.* Corporis
> tui bona intueor? ad robur pariter factus es, & ad
> decorem. Animi? cultissimus ille: & uberrimae in te
> ingenij iudicijque dotes. Externa? stirpe nobilissimus es,
> opibus splendidissimus. nec quidquam facile tibi deest,
> quod Naturae aut Fortunae adest. Macte his dotibus!
> eo magis, quod non ad ambitionem, ut pleraque ista
> nobilitas, aut ad pompam abuteris: sed confers eas, qua
> potes, ad tuam & publicam salutem. Idque domi &
> foris, toga & sago: cum vegeta illa animi vis ad omnia
> sufficiat: & Marti ita lites, ut sacrum numquam deseras
> Sophiae & Musarum. Quod Archilogus ille de se
> gloriatus olim; tu magis iure:
> * Sum quidem ego famulus　　* Εἰμὶ δ'ἐγὼ θεράπων μὲν
> 　cultorque Dei armipotentis:　ἐνυαλίοιο ἄνακτος,
> 　Sed tamen & Musarum　　Καὶ μουσέων ἐρατὸν
> 　incluta dona habeo.　　δῶρον ἐπιστάμενος.
> Sed libo hoc laudum tuarum limen, non penetro. quia ut
> sacratum silentio potius, quam plausu spectamus: sic tuas
> ego virtutes. quas veneror, non exsequor; adoro paene
> dixerim, non adorno. Tu tantum, o Britanniae tuae
> clarum sidus, (cui certatim lucem affundunt Virtus,

Musa, Gratia, Fortuna) tenuem obscurumque hunc
laborem a me libens accipe, & paullisper instar doni
pendere patere in Famae templo. None nim ut verum
legitimumque donum: sed ut illius obsidem, & velut
sponsoriam tabellam. Alia sunt te & me digna. quae
dabo, dedicabo, si vivam: atque ita vivam.
Salve a Lipsio, qui scripsi haec Lugduni in Batavis. . .

(70) Jacob Walraven, 'Duydelick onderwijs, hoe, en waerom
de Engelsche tale te leeren.'

... Vraechdy van waer ict hebbe, hebbende Engelandt
noyt betreen? ende ooc zulcke Scholen hier noch onbe-
kent zijn? . . . Zijnde alhier gearriveert zijn Excellentie
gheviel my ten deele van zijnen gesinde, een treftich
Edelman, *G. Broock*, een fijn, oprecht ende Godvruchtich
Heere: wiens welsprekentheyt my (t'was Engelsch, ver-
stont een weynich, over vijfthien Iaer tot Antwerpen
geleert, maer nu niets weert, als zijnde meest al gevlogen)
gantsch verlustichde: ende hy begeerich na t'Françoys,
geriefden wy malcanderen, by onderstant vant Latijn,
onzen tolc. . .

(71) Jacob Walraven, dedication, Leiden, 30 August 1586.

... tot noch toe belet, door t'noch lieflick lieflocken
vande aentreckende *Musis*, my (immers in mijn bedrijf)
met I. DOUZA *ante omnia dulces*; . . .

(72) George Gilpin to the Magistrates of Leiden, Utrecht,
1 October 1586.

... Cogitantem vero de commoditate et opportunitate
multarum urbium, quibus adventus meus satis gratus
fuisset, ut V.A. tectis potissimum considerem, singularis
in literas humaniores amor meus et propensio impellebat.
Et quamvis Reip. graviora negotia non permittant ut
hisce studiis plane vacare possim, tamen liberorum
meorum caussa, quos ad ea accurate educandos curo;
egi cum Magnifico D. Rectore Academiæ Vestræ, ut in
eandem tanquam membrum aliquod asciscerer. non ha-
bita ullius interea commodi aut utilitatis meæ ratione:
hoc solum fine, ut promptiorem me hæc redderet occasio,
ad ea, pro virium mearum modulo, conanda quæ ad
dignitatem Academiæ augendam profectura aliquando
incidere possent. . .

(73) 'D. Gilpin' [23 October 1586].

Es by Burgemeesteren geresolveert Gilpin Engelsch edelman en Secretaris van zyn Ex. als lithmaet vande univer-

siteyt te erkennen ende zulx te laten gebruycken de
privilegien ende vryheyden vande universiteyt hebbende
zulx de secretarys dezer stede belast zyn belet van
vrydomme te onderteyckenen.

(74) 'Ouden Rijn Dirc van Kessel.'

[1586] ... Dit huys wert geoccupeert by mr gilpin
secretarys van zyn Excellencie met zyn huysvroue ende
familie. Deromme tgedencen opt forieringe hem
verby te gaen.

(75) Justus Lipsius to Philip Sidney, Utrecht, 30 August
1586.

... Ultrajectam veneram, & id tantum, vere dico, tui sa-
lutandi causa. Elapsus mihi es paucis ante adventum
meum horis; quod fero, etsi deleo. Res bellica vos nunc tenet; sed nec togata ista & politica negligenda est: in
qua vereor, (cur non utar libertate quam apud te mihi
esse voluisti?) vereor inquam, ut quidam calide nimis
& cum affectu versentur. Lenta istorum hominum inge-
nia, nescio quomodo tractari gaudent via lentiore.
Emissi Ultrajecto nuper magnus numerus, securitatis
causa: scio, nec damno. Sed quid si carptim & per partes?
Uno agmine quid opus fuit? Busius arcte, nec ex digni-
tate, detinetur; cui privatim amicum me fuisse fateor (nec
enim ex iis sum qui vultum & animum mutant cum fortuna) publice tamen si quid peccavit, non excuso. An excidit tibi judicium de illo meum? Libere tunc, & quod pro
patria censebam, in illum dixi: dicam quod pro illo videatur, sed eodem fine. Studio patriæ, aut honoris vestri nulli
mortalium cedo. Res docebit. Parem me non fateor tamen
illis, quibus lingua prompta, vaga, saepe vana. Quod
ago, sentio, serio ago, sentio; nihil in frontem. Sed de
Busio: si non usui ille vobis, nonne ordine moveri satis
erat? At nocuisset. Ecce telum alterum, patria & finibus
emitte. Carcer, nec causae dictio, invidiam habet &
sermones, etiamsi meruerit. Quid novos fluctus movent,
ubi veteres nondum quievere? Ego tibi vaticinor (utinam
vane) ad dissidia interna nos ducent rapidi & torrentes
isti; quod si imperium vestrum ubique firmum, minore
periculo peccarent; nunc scilicet quae loca praesidiis
careant, non vident. Asseri habenas vobis plene &
firmiter probo, suadeo; tempestive modo id fiat & cum
quodam tractu: in corpore tam aegro, omnia paucis
mensibus curatis? opus est diaeta. Haec & plura utinam
in sermone potuissem: sed mentem meam tu certe vides,
quam puram & innoxiam esse Deus mihi testis. Ego te

rogo per Regni & Reginae vestrae honorem, per commu-
nem omnium nostrum salutem (nec enim disjungi
potest) tempera, quod in te est, fervorem illorum qui zeli
specie & amoris fallunt. Se, non vos, auctum eunt, qui
in praecipitia ista vos trudunt. Vale vir illustris &
aeternum mihi care. Illustriss. Comiti & Gubernatori,
victoriam & successum precor ex affectu.
Ultrajecti in diversorio. xxx. Augusti, M D LXXXVI.
Illust. D.T. addictissimus Cliens
                                                    JUSTUS LIPSIUS.
[*P.S.*] Dum hic sum, convenerunt me affines & amici
Busii, qui valde queruntur de carcere strictiore. Imo
nec accessum iis patere. Ego precor, sed ita ut tu quid
in rem sit, videas, facias.

(76) Philip Sidney to Justus Lipsius, Deventer, 14 September
1586.

Mi Lipsi. Doleo quod a nobis discedas, et eo magis
doleo, quod verear ne istarum rerum tedium tam sit
in causa quam ipsa valetudo. si ita sit, (et nisi etiam
de nostra anglia desperes) obtestor te per nostram
amicitiam ut velis de te eo transferendo cogitare. con-
ditionem quam tibi aliquando obtuli ita ratam faciam,
ut me moriente non deficere potuerit. novi te gratissimum
fore nostræ Reginæ et multis alliis imo omnibus aliis.
. . . nos cum multis difficultatibus luctamus, credo deum
ita velle in suis rem mitigare, ut non sint nobis nec
currus nec catenæ. Diutius tecum nec calamus potest
morari. Tu me ama et vale. . .

(77) Bernardus Vezekius to John James, Deventer, 25 September 1586 (o.s.).

. . . rumor de vulnere Illustris et Generosi Domini Sid-
næii nos plurimum consternavit, neque carere atiam
periculo ex tuis intelligo: Oramus autem Deum, ut eius
Generositatem pristinæ sanitati restituat, nobisque et
Ecclesijs nostris diu incolumem servet. . .

(78) Dominicus Baudius to Janus Dousa, Arnhem, 26 [Sept-
ember] 1586.

. . . Sed ecce tibi vix literas tuas Doctor James per-
legerat & se caussa tua velle significaverat cum rumor
adfertur Comitem Leicestriæ eopse die affuturum ac
paulo post iam adesse nuntiatur. Itaque præsentia tua
scilicet maxime esse opus ad expeditionem tui negotij.
D. Sidneji invaletudo non tulit ut epistolam tuam

legeret. Nos pro captu nostro rem omnem ei narravimus.
quid multa? rem pactam habemus, nihil eo dici potest
impetrabilius. Itaque statim accessiri iubet Juvenem
illum cuius apud te memini, singularis ingenij & doctrinæ non tralatitiæ, dat ei in mandatis ut ad Illustrissimum Comitem literas paret non perfunctoriæ commen-
dationis. Paret ille ac lubens. id enim unice expetit
aliquid facere quod e re tua sit. Serio dico, ardet cupi-
ditate incredibili nomen ut suum in numero tuorum
habere digneris. Cæterum de adventu Excellentiæ mox
certior factus (quod facile intelligis) operam scribendi
supervacaneam existimat. Agam cum D. Sidnejo ut cum
officij caussa eum Comes inviset, mentionem tui negotij
faciat, quod certo scio eum facturum...

(79) Dominicus Baudius to Janus Dousa the Younger,
[Utrecht], 31 [October] 1586.

Cum hic Ultraiecti essem, mi Duza, forte incidi in eam
mulierem quam huc matrona nobilissima Mater tua
miserat sciscitandi caussa ubinam locorum pater tuus
esset. Ea petijt ut quæ scirem super illo, tibi impartirer.
Daventriæ ipsum reliqui salvum & incolumem 23 die
mensis præteriti [alter.: huius]. Literas mihi binas tradi-
derat quarum unæ ad Illustrissimum Sidneium alteræ
ad Doctorem Jacobum dirigebantur. Eas ego pertuli,
responsum forte expectavit sed frustra: non enim Domini
mei Valetudo patiebutur ut vel nomen Epistolæ suum
subscriberet, postero siquidem die post meum adventum
in Urbem Arnhemium lumen illud ingenij, Doctrinæ,
Nobilitatis morte extinctum est. Ab eo tempore nihil
rescire de patre tuo: labor ut suspicer eum Daventriæ
commorari spe reditus Comitis Leicestriæ, ac proinde
ubi certior factus fuerit Dominum Comitem hic Ultraiecti
futurum spero fore ut in viam se det, & huc se conferat.
Si hic esset vel uno die totum eius negotium expediri
posset. Aliud quod scribam nihil habeo, nisi hoc unum
serio a te peto ut aliquid Musæum pangas super obitu
domini mei, & Georgium Benedicti meis verbis obnixe
horteris ut idem faciat. Puto mihi datum iri negotium
conscribendi universa eius facta. 31 Novembris 1586.
stylo novo. Vale.

(80) Hieronymus Groslotius to Janus Dousa the Younger,
London, 12 December 1586.

... qua nimium opus est ut subvenias quoque huic meae
audaciae, quae tibi impudenter obtrudit tam insulsos
versus aliquot meos in obitum V. C. M. Sydnaei, qui

editi mihi prae acerbi doloris nisu invitis sane ipsis Musis, quae me profanum merito arcent a suis adytis, quae reclusa vobis solis, imo vero inclusa ipsa pectoribus tam sacris. eorum unicum exemplar mitto, quod cupio commune tibi et Benedictio nam cuique vestrum suum describere occupato mihi nunc non licet. deinde etiam sic satis superque nugarum. addidi etiam Epitaphium Gallicum, non vestra, quos puto non intellegere, verum unius patris tui caussa, quem scio capere quoque lepores nostrates; cuique etsi non sunt illa tanti, non impedio, quin ostendatis, modo vobis videatur. laudabitis voluntatem et conatum meum fortasse nequaquam rem ipsam. quamvis illam æstimabitis quoque non a se, sed a solo affectu meo. istinc nec famam spero, nec timeo infamiam. tantum volui, ut debui certe, defungi novissimo hoc et lugubri pietatis officio erga Divos illos Manes tam magni viri, tam amici; cuius rite soluti volui quoque vos habere testes. . .

(81) Pieter Cornelisz. Hooft.

. . . Echter stond het gevecht hun dierst; alzoo Philips Sidney, aan een'wonde daar gekreegen in zyn'dye, ten vyventwintighsten daaghe quam t'ooverlyden: een heer van ontrent dertigh jaaren, heughlyk vernuft, dapper beleidt, fraaye geleertheit, aardighe taal, zinlyke en minlyke zeeden. Hy was gebooren uit een' zuster des Graaven van Leicester; zagh, by de Kooningin, zich in blaakende jonste; en in vaste hoope, der halven, van ongemeine verheffing. En zommighen sloegen'er geen twyfel aan, oft hy zoude, in geval van langer leven, naa't meuken van den moedt door tydt en ervaarenis, zynen oom, wiens verstandt by't zyne niet haalen moght, in't voortvaaren met zyn'onrype aanslaaghen tot verneedring der Staaten, door zyne wysheit en bescheidenheit geschorst hebben. Maar andren oordeelden, dat zyne nyverheit, wakkerheyt, en behendigheit, indien hy ze aan't ondergraaven der vryheit hadde willen besteeden (gelyk zyn dringen op onbepaalt gezagh voor den Graave, toen men dien de Landtvooghdy eerst aanbood, te erduchten gaf) den Lande quaalyker zouden bekoomen weezen, dan de lossigheit van Leicester, die, met het onbesuist aangaan in zynen toeleg, ten halven weeghe steecken bleef. . .

INDEX OF PROPER NAMES

PRINTED IN THE NETHERLANDS

BY J. J. GROEN & SON

LEIDEN